CUBA
INFORMATION MANUAL

THE DEFINITIVE GUIDE TO
LEGAL AND ILLEGAL TRAVEL TO CUBA

MICHAEL BELLOWS

KP

KETTLE

PUBLISHING

D1557141

Cuba Information Manual
The Definitive Guide to Legal and Illegal Travel to Cuba

Published by: **Kettle Publishing**
P.O. Box 4510
Key West, FL 33041-4510
www.cubatravelpro.com

Printed by: **Falcon Books**
2010 Crow Canyon Place, Suite 100
San Ramon, CA 94583
www.falcon-books.com

Library of Congress Cataloging-in-Publication Data

Bellows, Michael
  Cuba Information Manual
  The Definitive Guide to Legal and Illegal Travel to Cuba/by Michael
  Bellows— 1st edition.

      p.   cm.
    ISBN 978-0-615-26691-6

    LCCN 2008943219

10 9 8 7 6 5 4 3 2 1

CONTENTS

NOTE TO READER

It is not the intent of this travel manual to encourage people to violate any law associated with the U.S. trade embargoes against Cuba.

At the same time, the author empathizes with those who object to certain clauses of the embargo laws because of the suffering and duress it inflicts on innocent people and because of the way the laws infringe on a number of basic rights and liberties promised in the U.S. Constitution and international accords.

In the spirit of healthy rebellion and civil disobedience, the author respects the efforts of any U.S. traveler to Cuba to defy the questionable restrictions of the trade embargo laws and minimize the consequences of noncompliance. Questioning our government's actions and policies imposed on its citizens and others around the world is another right guaranteed by the Constitution, a right that has shaped the conscience of a nation and molded the United States and her people into the great land of freedom and justice that it is.

As the legal eagles at the Center for Constitutional Rights cautioned in their booklet, *Know Before You Go: Restrictions on Travel to Cuba*, this manual is not a complete discussion of all the applicable laws and regulations of the embargoes. It does not cover all possible questions, concerns, and contingencies. Since laws, regulations, and their interpretations often change, the information in this manual may be outdated by the time you read it. The author and publisher do not guarantee the accuracy of the information in this manual as of any point in time.

For those wishing to consider all their options and the possible consequences of their actions, the author strongly recommends that they seek the advice of a licensed attorney who specializes in Cuba travel and embargo law.

The author and publisher accept no responsibility for citizens or residents of the United States nor for citizens or residents of any other country who act in contravention of any U.S. laws restricting trade with or travel to Cuba.

INTRODUCTION

When people I meet find out that I've been to Cuba, their reaction is often the same; their eyelids snap open, they straighten their backs, and they rapid-fire questions plump with disbelief. "Isn't that illegal? Didn't you get in trouble? They let you in? How did you get there?"

These questions lead to lengthy discussions about Cuba that veer into a myriad of avenues and tangents covering politics, communism, democracy, human rights, Fidel Castro, economic conditions, culture, and social mood. Once, a Cuban émigré fishing with his wife in the Dry Tortugas threatened to throw me overboard because he didn't like the fact that my tourist dollars were helping to support the communist government in Cuba—the same logic the U.S. Congress used when it enacted the crippling trade embargoes.

Invariably, after one of my lengthy talks with someone who is a little more tolerant, if not fascinated with the idea of traveling to Cuba, I'll get a telephone call a day or two later from this person seeking more information. How can I get a permit to visit Cuba? Who do I contact? Is there a way to go to Cuba without a permit without getting into too much trouble? Do planes fly into Cuba from the U.S.?

This travel manual is written for people like those who call me back seeking more information. When the idea of writing a guide about travel to Cuba first came to me, I said to my good friend, Ron Heck, who owns Harpoon Harry's (a popular diner and gathering place) in Key West, "When people can't believe I've been to Cuba and pepper me with a thousand questions about how to get there, I want to be able to hand them a book and say, 'Here, take this. It has all the information you need to make your own decision about whether to go or not, and all the information you need if you do decide to go.'"

I never had the benefit of such a book. I had to run all over the Keys and track down sailors who'd been to Cuba themselves. I bought beers and sweet-talked friends of friends who'd found flights to Cuba from other countries. I made costly and often dead-end international phone calls to Canada, Spain, Mexico, Cuba, and the Bahamas. And I spent hours upon hours sifting through hundreds of websites—many of which offered conflicting information. Oh yeah—and I endured the threat of getting thrown off a fishing boat while I was on one of my many fact-finding missions.

Which is why I think $11.95 for this manual is pretty cheap.

SECTION 1

DECIPHERING THE U.S. TRADE EMBARGOES AGAINST CUBA

1. I'm confused about the current U.S. laws that forbid or restrict travel to Cuba. What's the scoop? Are U.S. citizens allowed to travel to Cuba or not?
The embargo laws do not forbid U.S. citizens from traveling to Cuba. They do, however, forbid U.S. citizens from spending money there without the proper permits[1], which essentially amounts to the same thing—unless you plan on begging your way around the country (from Cubans who don't have much themselves) and sleeping on cardboard in the parks. Even if you brought your own food, you'd still violate the law by paying the twenty-five dollars to the immigration guy for your tourist card. You even have to pay to get out: twenty-five bucks for a "departure tax."

The penalty for violating the embargo law is stiff: Up to ten years jail time, $250,000 in criminal fines, and $55,000 in civil fines for each violation[2]. So that *café con leche* you drank at the *Hotel Inglaterra* in Havana could end up costing you a bundle if a U.S. customs officer finds the receipt in your pocket.

The U.S. restrictions on spending money in Cuba apply to all citizens and residents of the United States—no matter what country you travel to Cuba from and even if you have dual citizenship. The restrictions also apply to non-U.S. citizens physically in the U.S[3].

2. How can I get a permit to spend money in Cuba?
You need to write a letter to the U.S. Department of the Treasury[4] requesting a 'Specific License.' Only those requesting permission to travel to Cuba for certain professional, humanitarian, or educational purposes will be considered[5]. In the letter, you must provide convincing details outlining the purpose of your trip, including category of travel, description of your research, and documentation of your qualifications. A format of the letter—gleaned from the Treasury Department's own guidelines—is provided on page 169 in the appendix at the end of this manual. If you are approved, you will not be allowed to spend more than $185.00 per day in Cuba for

land costs[6] (i.e., hotel, dining out, and taxis), $500.00 in transportation costs to and from (not within) Cuba, and you will not be able to bring back any goods or merchandise purchased or otherwise acquired in Cuba[7]. For a period of five years after your trip ends, you must keep a record of all your travel documents and expenditures, and you must furnish these records to OFAC[8] or other law enforcement officials upon demand. A word of warning: The licensing department that receives the applications has a very small staff that receives thousands of requests for permits weekly. It may take months before you get a reply, so give yourself plenty of lead time.

NO APPLICATION FOR A LICENSE TO TRAVEL TO CUBA IS NECESSARY if you can demonstrate that a) you are a full-time journalist on assignment[9], b) you are a full-time professional conducting research in Cuba, c) you are an official of a U.S. or foreign government traveling on official business, or d) you are attending an international professional conference or meeting taking place in Cuba[10]. Anyone traveling to Cuba under these categories is granted an unwritten "General License" by OFAC that does not require any pre-approval before you leave. But upon your return from Cuba, you will likely receive a letter in the mail from OFAC requesting proof and documentation demonstrating that you indeed fall within the qualifications and guidelines for travel to Cuba under a General License.

If you were born in Cuba, regardless of your current citizenship, or if you have any immediate family members in Cuba, the rules change a bit. For example, it will be easier for you to obtain a Specific License from OFAC to visit family members, but you can only travel under this category once every three years. And anyone who left Cuba permanently after December 31, 1970, must have a valid Cuban passport or special papers that can be obtained from the Cuban Interests Section in Washington, D.C.

3. Are there any OFAC-authorized travel agencies in the U.S. that can help me with the permit and application process and travel arrangements to Cuba?
You can get assistance in your quest to visit Cuba legally by contacting one of the many special interest groups or **travel service providers** (TSPs) in the U.S. that are licensed by OFAC to make travel arrangements for those who have obtained a Specific License or who are traveling under the General License provisions. These companies will help you with all your travel needs, including flights, accommodations, and ground transportation. Marazul Charters, Inc. in Weehawken, NJ (201-319-3900/www.marazultours.com) is one travel agency you can contact; their agents have an excellent reputation, are very helpful, and know their stuff. Tico Travel (949-646-1299/www.destinationcuba.com) is another company with a

good track record. When you contact a TSP, remember to tell them you want to visit Cuba for educational or research purposes. They will not help you if you tell them you want to go to Cuba for a vacation or for pleasure. A few TSPs and their phone numbers are listed in Appendix 3 on page 174. You can get a complete list of OFAC-licensed travel service providers and carriers by visiting the U.S. Department of the Treasury website at www.treas.gov/OFAC. Click on "sanctions," "Cuba sanctions," then "Authorized Travel, Carrier, and Remittance Forwarding Service Providers[11]."

A list of OFAC-licensed, **special interest tour operators** that organize cultural, educational, and humanitarian-themed trips to Cuba from the U.S. is provided in Appendix 4 (page 180). It's likely you can find a lesser-known, small nonprofit organization in your own area that holds a license by OFAC to carry out charitable and humanitarian services in Cuba. For instance, in Lyndonville, Vermont, there is a nonprofit organization called Caribbean Medical Transport that donates medical equipment and supplies to hospitals and disaster victims in Cuba. Reef Relief in Key West, Florida fosters technical and educational support for Cuban marine scientists who endeavor in reef conservation, and the Key West Symphony arranges cultural and humanitarian trips to Cuba through the Bringing Hope Foundation, an OFAC-licensed humanitarian group. If a similar organization in your area can convince OFAC that you are needed for an upcoming Cuba project or trip, your chances of qualifying for a Specific or General license are good.

4. I am unhappy that I have to endure a lengthy application process with a department of the U.S. government in order to exercise my fundamental right to travel to another country. I'll be even more angry if I'm denied. Isn't there any way to by-pass this process without getting into serious trouble?

There are no sure-fire ways you can travel to Cuba and back in contravention of the embargo laws without some risk of getting nabbed—but there are ways you can reduce the risk. The information in Section 1 and 2 of this manual offers invaluable tips used by veteran blockade runners and also unveils the best tactics to fight the civil penalties sometimes—not always—levied on those caught violating the embargo laws.

Most blockade runners slip into Cuba by air via a third country. As a rule, the immigration officers in Cuba will not stamp your passport on arrival because they know you can get into trouble with the U.S. authorities when you return home[12]. When you fill out the customs declaration card[13] that you are required to present to the U.S. immigration officer back in the States, do not list Cuba under "countries visited on this trip prior to U.S. arrival," and under no circumstances admit to an officer that you were in Cuba, even if you are asked[14]. Discard all evidence related to your stay in Cuba, including all receipts, airline tickets, telephone numbers and addresses, travel documents, Cuban money, baggage tags, or products purchased in Cuba. Without any physical or testimonial evidence of your Cuba visit, the U.S. authorities have next to nothing they can use against you should your case ever be brought to court.

Questions 2-7 in Section 2 of this manual explains in more detail how to get through U.S. customs and immigration checkpoints on the departure and return legs of an illegal visit to Cuba while keeping your risks of getting busted to an absolute minimum.

You can also slip into Cuba and back by boat from the U.S. or via a third country. Currently, there are no commercial passenger boats from any country that call on Cuban ports (except for an occasional cruise ship), but private yachts from all over the world (including the U.S.) pull into Cuban marinas every day. Until recent years, crossing the Gulf Stream without clearing in or out with U.S. customs was a small gamble. But because of the 9/11 fallout and the ongoing problem of drug and human smuggling by go-fast boats, the Department of Homeland Security is maintaining a much stricter surveillance of the Florida Straits than in the past.

5. What will happen if a U.S. immigration or customs officer determines I visited Cuba illegally?
Depending on the mood and/or political sympathies of the officer you may simply be scolded before being waved on through or you may be subjected to a long and uncomfortable search and interrogation. But you will never be denied re-entry into the U.S., nor will you be arrested. You may be asked to fill out an OFAC form requesting details of your trip and expenditures. EXERCISE YOUR FIFTH AMENDMENT RIGHTS that protect you from self-incrimination. This may lead to further harassment, intimidation and threats in an attempt to get you to 'fess up and provide them with more evidence against you. But in the end, they will let you go. You may or may not receive in the mail from OFAC either a "Requirement to Furnish Information" letter or a "Pre-penalty Notice" assessing a civil fine (in the thousands). If you receive a "Requirement to Furnish Information" letter, write OFAC back telling them that you decline to provide the requested information because it violates several of your basic human and constitutional rights such as your right to travel, your right to seek information through foreign travel, your First Amendment rights protecting you from political and national origin discrimination, and your Fifth Amendment right that protects you from self-incrimination. You can use the form letter (provided by the National Lawyers Guild) in Appendix 6 on page 182 or you can download the letter at www.ccr-ny.org. If you receive a "Pre-penalty Notice," write back and request an official agency hearing. (Form letter in Appendix 7 on page 183.) FEW

HEARINGS ARE EVER HELD, and more than likely your case will be shelved indefinitely. OFAC may send you a follow-up letter offering to settle your case for a reduced fine (usually in the $1,500—$2,500 range). Reply to this offer with the same arguments you used in your previous letters to them. The Center for Constitutional Rights in New York has an excellent booklet that offers tips on how to protect yourself and your rights if you travel to Cuba. The booklet also presents a number of possible scenarios of the legal consequences of your illicit journey. You can download the booklet at www.ccrjustice.org. Although the CCR no longer accepts Cuba travel clients for direct representation, the Center can help you find an individual attorney if you feel the need for an ally to assist you through the legal proceedings[15].

6. There are reports in the U.S. media that President Barack Obama is keen on lifting the travel restrictions, opening the dialogue between the two countries, and softening the U.S. stance on the trade embargo. Do you foresee a lifting of the travel restrictions anytime soon?
Most of the reports in the news about any immediate changes in U.S.-Cuba policy refer to the lifting of travel restrictions (and caps on remittances) for Cuban Americans who have family members in Cuba, not for U.S. citizens. Anything more than that, president Obama's Latin America foreign policy advisor, Frank Sanchez, has said, "will have to wait[16]." Obama actually supports the trade embargo—he demonstrated this during his tenure as Senator and said so throughout his '08 campaign for the presidency—but he has also said that he is open to establishing a dialogue between the two countries in order to improve relations. For a formal dialogue to take place, however, Obama insists that the Cuban government make some changes, such as freeing political prisoners.

   The Cuban government, which includes current president Raul Castro, has also expressed an interest in improving relations between the two countries. But Castro and his government remain defiant and steadfast in continuing the policies and traditions of the socialist Revolution. In a January 2009 speech commemorating the 50-year anniversary of the Revolution's triumph, Raul Castro said, "Let us commemorate this half a century of victory by reflecting toward the next fifty years." He also leveled some angry words at the United States government and accused it of decades "vengeful hate" against his country.

   This forebodes more of the usual polarizing stubbornness that threatens to prolong the fifty-year standoff. My take is that the relationship between the U.S. and Cuba will improve during the Obama administration, and I think the restrictions on spending money in Cuba will eventually be lifted or modified. The lifting of the restrictions, however, is not going to take place immediately. It is going to require some give-and-take, a few concessions on both sides, and some small, pride-saving steps at a time. I wouldn't rule out a revolt if the Castro brothers die within a relatively short time of one another and a renegade army officer leads the charge.

7. Will I encounter any problems with the Cuban immigration and customs authorities when I arrive in Cuba?

Absolutely none—if you behave yourself and don't try to smuggle in any drugs or weapons. The Cuban immigration and customs authorities are the most courteous and pleasant I have met anywhere in the world. Like all tourism-oriented destinations around the world, the Cuban people know that tourists bring money and are a crucial cog in their economy. In addition, I have found that American visitors, in particular, seem to be especially appreciated for a number of reasons. For one thing, given the embargo climate that has endured for the last forty-five years, an American visitor is a rarity and comes across as a valiant blockade runner defying the unjust laws that have tried to keep him out. For the Cuban youth, America is a hip super-power that boasts everything they don't have; for the old, America is something dear that they lost. An intimate and complex relationship existed between the two countries prior to the communist-inspired Revolution.

There are other, more ingrained reasons why the Cuban people, for the most part, are the friendliest and most sociable anywhere. The emphasis of their values seems to be firmly placed on family, neighbors and people rather than on money and things. In the streets and in the neighborhoods it is easy to detect an endearing sense of community, trust and respect that the Cuban people have for each other and for human life in general. During the day, doors are left open and children play in the street. Men sit around tables on the sidewalks and play dominoes, while women sit on the stoops and peel yucca or cull rice for the evening's meal. At night, one can stroll any part of any city without being afraid of getting mugged or shot. Strangers are called 'Uncle,' elderly ladies 'Grandma.' I'm not sure if this is a result of their Spanish heritage, forty-five years of socialist indoctrination, or the basic nature of humans pulling together in difficult times. Probably a combination of all of these things, plus many more that gives Cuba and her people a reputation for passion, sensuality and *joie de vivre*.

SECTION 2

GETTING TO CUBA: BY PLANE, BOAT, AND KAYAK

1. If I manage to get a permit from the Licensing Division of the Office of Foreign Assets Control to spend money in Cuba, where can I find a flight or boat to the island?
U.S. citizens who are traveling to Cuba under the General License provisions or who are granted Specific Licenses by the Licensing Division of the Office of Foreign Assets Control to spend money in Cuba can catch a charter flight to Havana from Miami, New York, or Los Angeles. To get on one of these planes, you must make arrangements with an OFAC-licensed travel service provider (TSP) or a special interest group that is licensed by OFAC to make such travel arrangements. As mentioned in Section 1, the Appendix on page 174 lists a few of these companies. The TSP will ask you to fill out an application and sign an affidavit stating that you have secured a Specific License from OFAC or that you qualify to travel to Cuba under the General License category. Many of the TSPs are charter companies that buy blocks of seats on OFAC-licensed air carriers (which include American Airlines, Continental Airlines, Delta, and United Airlines, believe it or not) and even if they sell out, they can find you a seat by booking through another OFAC-licensed charter company. Flights depart from Miami International Airport daily. You will need a visa from the Cuban consulate before you can reserve a seat; the TSPs can help you get one (for a fee—fifty dollars or more). Visa processing differs for anyone born in Cuba, regardless of one's current citizenship; ask the TSP about this or contact the Cuban Interest Section in Washington, D.C.[17] If you don't make your accommodation arrangements with the TSP that arranges your flight, the TSP—in order to get your visa—will require you to provide them with an address where you will be staying in Cuba. If you have obtained a Specific License from OFAC or are traveling to Cuba under the General License provisions, you don't HAVE to board a flight from the U.S. You can fly, swim or kayak to Cuba from anywhere you prefer. For information on flights to Cuba from other countries, see the table on page 21.

Currently there are no commercial boats to Cuba that depart directly from the U.S., even if you have a permit to go. Before Fidel Castro's takeover of Cuba in 1959, a five-hundred-passenger, 125-car luxury steamship sailed three times per week between Key West, Florida and Havana, Cuba.   It boasted air-conditioned passenger lounges, private cabins, six continuous hours of music, and was one of only two steamships in the world with an escalator. The ferry's owners, however, ended the crossings because of a sharp decline in the number of travelers to Cuba—a direct result of the rapidly deteriorating relationship between the U.S. and Castro's brazen new government. Also, the steamship's owners feared that Castro might seize the ship as he had all other U.S. businesses in Cuba. The last ferry to Cuba from a U.S. port left on Thursday, November 3, 1960—but there were no passengers aboard the ship. The journey was made to drop off the ship's crew in Cuba, after which it was piloted to Jacksonville, Florida by a relief crew. Hope for resumption of any kind of ferry service between the U.S. and Cuba was dashed when President Kennedy banned U.S. citizens from traveling to Cuba in January of 1961.

If you are interested in sailing to Cuba from the U.S. on a private boat, check the community bulletin boards at local gathering spots and talk to live-aboards at marinas and anchorages in Marathon, Key West, Miami, Fort Lauderdale, Fort Myers, Naples, and other cities on the southwest coast of Florida. Question number six below explains the proper procedures for getting through Cuban and U.S. immigration and customs checkpoints when you travel to Cuba by private boat.

2.   I want to travel to Cuba via a third country without the proper permit from the Licensing Division of the Office of Foreign Assets Control. What third countries offer commercial flights there?
Many countries offer commercial flights to Cuba. Mexico, Canada and the islands of the Bahamas are the most convenient jump-off points for those living in the United States. See the table on page 21 for a list of countries and their airlines flying into Cuba.

3.   How can I purchase a ticket from an airline or travel agency in one of these countries?
You will have to contact the airline or travel agency located outside the United States. Even if the foreign airline or travel agency has a U.S. office, the embargo laws forbid their U.S. branches from booking flights to Cuba. In some cities, such as Nassau, Bahamas, you can buy your ticket at the airline ticket counter on the same day that you are traveling with little risk that the flight might be sold out. Havana Turs Bahamas (1-242-393-5281, www.havanaturbahamas .com), will even hold a seat for you without any prepayment or

LIST OF COUNTRIES WITH FLIGHTS TO CUBA

Antilles
ALM Antillean Airlines

Argentina
Aerolineas Argentinas
Cubana

Aruba
Aeropostal

Australia/
New Zealand
Aerolineas Argentinas
Air New Zealand

Bahamas
Bahamas Air
Cubana

Belgium
Cubana

Brazil
Cubana

Cape Verde Islands
Taag

Canada
Canadian Airlines
Cubana
Royal Airlines
Skyservice
Transat

Chile
Aeroflot
Ladeco Airlines

Colombia
Cubana
Ladeco
SAM

Costa Rica
Cubana
Ladeco Airlines
Lacsa

Cayman Islands
Cubana

Dominican Republic
Aerocaribbean
Lacsa
Ladesco Airlines
Cubana

Ecuador
Cubana

France
AOM French Airlines
Cubana

Germany
Cubana
LTU Int Airways

Great Britain
Cubana

Holland
KLM
Martinair Holland

Jamaica
Cubana

Ireland
Aeroflot

Italy
Italia

Luxembourg
Aeroflot

Mexico
Cubana
Mexicana de Aviacion

Nicaragua
Aerocaribbean
Aeroflot

Panama
Cubana

Peru
Aeroflot
Aeroperu
Cubana

Russia
Aeroflot
Cubana

Spain
Cubana
Iberia

Venezuela
Aeropostal
Cubana
Viasa

deposits necessary. If you plan to purchase the ticket on the spot, keep in mind that the Cubana ticket counter in Nassau will only take euros or U.S. dollars. Credit cards are not accepted at the Cubana ticket counter in Nassau, and, anyway, you wouldn't want to use one as that would leave a nasty paper trail. If you make a reservation through a third country travel agency it is best if you wire the money (i.e., via Western Union). A list of travel agencies outside the U.S. that can help you book a flight and make other arrangements for you can be found in the appendix on page 185.

4. Please explain in detail how to best get through customs and immigration checkpoints on the departure and return legs of my trip if I fly into Cuba via a third country without the proper permit from the Office of Foreign Assets Control.

When you arrive in the third (springboard) country, you are better off not informing the immigration officer of your plans to carry on to Cuba, even if you are just passing through. Sometimes, the Bahamian immigration officials will stamp your passport "transit," or "admitted for one day only" and the Jamaican authorities have been known to stamp "Departure for Cuba" in your passport. Have on-hand the address of a hotel or some kind of accommodation in the springboard country because the immigration officer will ask you where you will be staying and for how long. Actual proof of a reservation in your springboard country is usually not demanded. When re-entering the Bahamas from Cuba en route to the U.S., sometimes you can persuade the Bahamian immigration officers to only stamp your immigration arrival card and not your passport. This will prevent a red flag that might arise if the U.S. immigration officer you will meet later notices that you have two Bahamas "admitted" stamps in your passport within a short span of time—and no other intervening stamps from another country. (How can you be admitted to the Bahamas twice in a week if you never left?) But don't sweat it too much if the Bahamian officer won't oblige. First of all, the U.S. immigration officers themselves frequently do not stamp your passport when you return to the U.S.—they only stamp the customs and declaration card, so the officers won't flinch much if they see two Bahamas "admitted" stamps in your passport and no intervening stamps showing that you left. (Of course, any information not in your passport will pop up on their computer screen.) As mentioned in Section 1, do not list "Cuba" under the "countries visited on this trip prior to U.S. arrival" when you fill out the customs declaration card. If you are uncomfortable lying to an immigration officer, you have good reason: Perjury may be added to the charges if you are busted. Perjury is easier to prosecute and carries stiffer penalties. If you don't want to lie on the customs declaration card or to the officer, you will have to chance being questioned further and sent a Pre-penalty Notice by OFAC.

In the past, U.S. citizens did not need a passport to travel by air to Mexico, Canada, and other Caribbean countries. All they needed was a copy of their birth certificate and their driver's license or some other government-issued photo ID. This was the best loop-

Mexico—Cancun in particular—seems to be the best springboard country that offers the least risk of detection for the following reasons:

1. U.S. citizens returning to the U.S. from Mexico do not pre-clear at a U.S. customs and immigration checkpoint located at the Mexican airport (unlike airports in Canada and the Bahamas). This reduces the chances of encountering a U.S. customs and immigration agent looking for U.S. citizens getting off planes from Cuba. (Note: There are reports that the Dominican Republic and Jamaica immigration and customs officers cooperate with U.S. undercover agents.)

2. Since Cancun is one of the most popular tourist destinations for U.S. citizens, there is no reason U.S. customs and immigration authorities would suspect you have been anywhere but Cancun.

3. Mexican immigration officers are less apt to stamp your passport on your return from Cuba, if you ask them nicely. Pull out a twenty-dollar bill and inquire if you can pay a small "fee" for this "service" if the immigration officer acts hesitant when you first ask.

4. Mexico has a much better trade relationship with Cuba than the U.S., and Mexican tolerance for U.S. government meddling in its affairs with Cuba appears to be waning. Mexican customs and immigration officers are likely to disagree with the U.S. trade embargo against Cuba and, therefore, more likely to sympathize with U.S. citizens who travel to Cuba illegally.

hole of all for illegal U.S. travelers to Cuba because it denied U.S. customs and immigration authorities at airports the opportunity to peruse a passport for inconsistencies or red flags. Unfortunately, this loophole is now closed because in 2007, the U. S. government began requiring passports for U.S. citizens re-entering the United States by air from all countries, including Mexico and Canada.

However, in July of 2008, the U.S. State Department inaugurated production and delivery of U.S. passport cards that can be used in lieu of your passport book for U.S. *land and sea ports-of-entry* when arriving from Canada, Mexico, the Caribbean, and Bermuda. The passport card looks just like a driver's license and is meant to expedite passage and document processing for U.S. citizens who exit and re-enter U.S. land borders and seaports on a regular basis. If you like the idea of using a passport card to re-enter the U.S. by land or sea instead of your passport, your main task will then be to find a way to a U.S. land border checkpoint or sea port-of-entry after you get off your flight from Cuba. A ferry from the Bahamas to Florida might appeal to you (see Appendix 9 on page 187), or you could journey north through Mexico by air, bus, or car. Obviously, crossing into the U.S. by land or sea port is going to take more time than flying, so be prepared to spend more on motel rooms, ground or sea transportation, and meals. For details about how to apply for a passport card, turn to Appendix 10 on page 188. An excellent web site for getting around Mexico by air and bus is www.larpman.com.

Another good tactic that will lessen your chances of being stopped by U.S. customs and immigration authorities looking for U.S. citizens returning from Cuba via third countries is to book a three-leg flight via a second domestic airport in the third country. For example, fly from the U.S. to Canada, and then catch a domestic flight to another Canadian city where you will board your plane to Havana. The Canada—Cuba—Canada flights are purchased as separate tickets. This way, you never run the risk of exposing yourself to U.S. agents looking for U.S. citizens transferring from Cuba flights to U.S.-bound flights within one airport.

Turn to the appendix on page 189 for a step-by-step checklist for getting through the immigration and customs checkpoints of all legs of your trip.

5. If I travel to Cuba on my own by plane—via a third country and without the license from the Office of Foreign Assets Control—what papers do I need to have in order?
You will need a passport (good for at least six months), proof of a paid return ticket that will get you out of Cuba, and a tourist card that you can obtain at the airline ticket counter or from the foreign travel agency that sells you the plane ticket or from the Cuban immigration officer when you arrive in Cuba. You also need to provide the immigration officer with an address where you will be staying in Cuba. (Don't list a private home that is not licensed to rent to

foreigners.)   If you don't provide the immigration officer with an address, they will make you book a hotel room.

Visas are required of business travelers and journalists on assignment and they can be obtained from a Cuban consulate.[18]   If you are traveling to Cuba with a visa, you will need to apply for an exit permit at an immigration office[19] in Cuba shortly after you arrive. As mentioned earlier, visa processing differs for anyone born in Cuba, regardless of the current citizenship; ask any OFAC-licensed travel service provider about this or contact the Cuban Interest Section in Washington, D.C.[20]

If you fly to Cuba from Mexico, make sure you obtain TWO Mexican tourist cards: One for your arrival in Mexico from the U.S. and one for your arrival in Mexico from Cuba. Without these tourist cards, the Cuban authorities might not let you in.   The airline or travel agency that sold you the tickets can tell you how to obtain these Mexican tourist cards. Regardless which country you travel through to get to Cuba, always ask the airline, consulate, or travel agency in that country what papers the Cuban authorities require. This includes vaccination papers (none required if you are departing from Mexico, the Bahamas, or Canada) as well as visas and tourist cards.

The illustration on page 66b shows what your Cuban tourist card (*tarjeta de turista*) looks like. The fee for the tourist card (fifteen to twenty-five dollars, depending on who issues it) is usually added to the bill when you pay for your plane ticket. Don't lose your tourist card or you will have to buy another one before you depart Cuba. As a general rule, the tourist card allows you a stay of up to thirty days and can be renewed a maximum of two times (at a cost of twenty-five dollars each time) with relative ease for additional thirty-day stays.

WARNING—if you are planning on sticking to a close budget while you are in Cuba, put fifty dollars of cash aside for the taxi ride to the airport (twenty dollars from anywhere in Havana) and a twenty-five-dollar departure tax that was not included in the total when you paid for your plane ticket.

6. What are the procedures for clearing in and out by private boat to Cuba?

U.S. citizens sailing to Cuba by boat from the U.S. do not need to show the Cuban authorities a clearance document. U.S. citizens entering Cuba from any other country must have clearance papers that list Cuba as the destination.

Everybody, regardless of whether they have permission or not from OFAC to travel to Cuba, must get clearance from the United States Coast Guard before they enter (by boat) Cuban Territorial waters from Florida. Clearance from the Coast Guard is not an authorization to enter Cuban Territorial waters but rather an authorization to DEPART a U.S. "Maritime Security Zone During a National Emergency" that exists in the Straits between the United States and Cuba. Even if you are breaking the embargo, do not sail to Cuba without this Coast Guard clearance. Enforcement of this maritime clearance law is far more aggressive than enforcement of the trade embargo laws, the prosecution of violators is more vigorous, and the penalties are more severe (vessel forfeiture, up to $250,000 in fines and ten years in jail). Getting clearance from the Coast Guard used to be fairly routine—boat captains sent in their requests by fax and an approval (if the captain didn't have any blemishes on file) was usually granted the next day. But ever since the Department of Homeland Security was created and given the responsibility for overseeing all U.S. law enforcement agencies, all boat captains requesting Coast Guard clearance must now furnish a copy of their Specifc license from OFAC (or a letter explaining in detail why you qualify for the General license). On top of that, the Coast Guard requires proof of an export license or a temporary sojourn license from the U.S. Department of Commerce that gives boat captains permission to "export" the vessel to Cuba. These licenses are only granted if the vessel is solely registered to transport goods and is engaged in the regular transport of bulk commodities. As you can see, the obstacles to private boats getting permission to sail to Cuba legally are quite formidable. There's a chance that the Department of Commerce might issue sojourn licenses for the transport of humanitarian goods or religious articles, but boat captains will have to present a good reason why it is necessary to transport the goods by boat rather than by OFAC-licensed air charter companies or third country commercial carriers.

Contact information for requesting vessel clearance from the Coast Guard is provided in Appendix 13 on page 193.

Should U.S. Customs officers ever determine that you did go to Cuba illegally (through your own admission or evidence obtained during a customs boarding while at sea), the embargo laws allow U.S. authorities to confiscate your boat and everything on it.[21]

Whether you are sailing to Cuba legally or illegally, follow these procedures for clearing in at the Cuban port-of-call:

Somewhere inside the twelve-mile boundary that marks Cuban Territorial waters, raise your Cuban courtesy flag and fly the yellow quarantine flag below it. Try to contact the Cuban marina harbor master by radio (Marina Hemingway harbor master in Havana monitors VHF channel 72, and the Marina Acua harbor master in Varadero monitors VHF channel 68) and inform them of your estimated time of arrival. If you don't get a reply when you first call, wait another mile or so and try again. The VHF reception may not work very well until you get closer. In any event, your yellow quarantine flag is a visual request for clearance, so that will calm any Cuban patrol boats if they decide to come out to meet you.

When you finally establish radio contact with the marina, be prepared to give them answers to the basic questions: Departure country, number of people aboard, name of boat, size, etc. Also, they will ask if you need an escort into the marina. If you accept, you will be billed.

Once you are docked at the marina, you will have to endure a lengthy process of clearing in with immigration and customs officers, health officials, agriculture inspectors, and coast guard officers. Relax, be patient, and offer a cold drink to anyone who comes aboard.

If you traveled to Cuba legally (with a Specific or General OFAC license) and you want to keep things clean upon your return to the United States, you must call the nearest Customs and Border Patrol office[22] (or visit the office in person) shortly after you dock in the United States. U.S. citizens do not need to contact Customs and Border Patrol in advance by radio. If you arrive back in the U.S. after Customs and Border Patrol operating hours (i.e., late at night), you need to call the toll free number (1-800-432-1216 or 1-800-451-0393). The person answering the phone will ask you some basic questions[23] and give you the address of the nearest Customs and Border Patrol office where you will need to present yourself and any passengers for a face-to-face interview within twenty-four hours[24].

If you sailed to Cuba without a permit, pull into a port or anchorage of your choosing and go about your normal business. Be prepared for a boarding at sea by either the Coast Guard or Customs and Border Patrol. If this happens, follow the same precautions outlined in Question number four, Section 1 of this manual.

7.   Are there any commercial passenger boats from third countries that sail to Cuba?

At the present time, there are no regularly scheduled commercial passenger boats from any country that carry passengers to Cuba. Some cruise ships do call on Cuban ports. For information about cruise ships, you will have to contact a travel agency outside the U.S. Pullmantur from Spain, Fred Olsen Cruise Lines from England, and Hapag Lloyd from Germany are three cruise line operators that have scheduled stops in Cuba. Two freighter companies that sail from Europe to Cuba are Hamburg-Sud Reiseagentur GMBH in Hamburg, Germany and Strand Voyages in London, England.

SECTION 3

WHAT TO BRING AND WHEN TO GO

1. Is there a good time or a bad time to visit Cuba?

Cuba will enchant you no matter what time of year you visit. If you want to avoid the hot months, which can be unbearable at times, don't go from July to September. If you want to avoid the wettest months, don't go from June to October. Hurricanes and tropical storms can strike from June to November, with intensity and frequency peaking in September and October. The coolest month of the year is February, when night temperatures during periodic and short-lasting cold fronts can dip (very briefly) into the forties. Temperatures during the day, however, hover in the seventies.

The high season for tourism in Cuba runs from December to April, but even so the throngs are generally confined to the major resorts (i.e., Varadero, Cayo Coco) and the popular areas of certain cities (Habana Vieja, Trinidad, Santiago de Cuba). Furthermore, no matter where you go in Cuba, nor what time of the year, the tourist crowds don't begin to approach the densities in other popular Caribbean tourist destinations. The main issue about the peak tourist season in Cuba is that airfare and hotel prices are twenty to twenty-five percent higher than other times of the year. This is also true for certain national holidays, such as July 25-27, the Celebration of National Rebellion (Cuba's Forth of July).

In July and August, the local beaches will be crowded with Cuban tourists taking their annual vacations.

Baseball fans will not want to miss an opportunity to catch a big-league game. The regular season runs from November to March, with play-offs in April. Admission fees—one nice feature of Cuban socialism—are only a few pesos (fifty cents or less).

For those interested in witnessing the Cuban brand of socialism being celebrated on a national level, the major political events and celebrations are Liberation Day (January 1), Labor Day (May 1), the Celebration of National Rebellion (July 25-26), the celebration of the founding of the Committees for the Defense of the Revolution (September 28), and the Day of Cuban Culture (October 10). The table on page 30 and 31 summarizes the most important annual events and their dates.

2. I have heard so much about the food and material shortages in Cuba as a consequence of the U.S. trade embargoes and other political and economic factors.[25] What should I pack for my trip?
As a tourist with dollars to spend you can find almost anything you need in the shops of the big cities. No city in the country, however, will match the choice and selection of products found in Havana stores, and be prepared for a serious drop in quality compared to U.S. and European standards. In some other shops (clearly aimed at tourists whims), you even will find brand names of American-made products like Cheerios™ cereal and Pringles™ potato chips. The prices of these brand name products, however, will shock you (three or four times as much as you would pay back in the States) as they have endured an expensive and circuitous route before finding their way to the store shelves.

Other items will be hard—if not impossible—to find.   This includes quality running or walking shoes, decent shaving razors, cigarette lighters, men's and women's underwear, bras, tampons or sanitary napkins, a good pair of socks, jeans, sunglasses, sunscreen, insect repellant, contact lens solution, jewelry, books in English, medicine, toothpaste, dental floss, rain jackets, quality tools, and disposable or cloth diapers and other baby items. The Cuban people get these things from friends and relatives who live abroad and send care packages via very expensive couriers.

If you plan to move around a lot in Cuba and you are not going to rent a car, I would suggest you limit your baggage to one backpack. You can still bring extra bags even if you don't rent a car because taxis and private cars for hire (with drivers) are available everywhere. The downside to this is that you will be spending a lot of extra money on transport costs, and you won't be free to make spontaneous changes in your itinerary (that involve walking) if you decide to leave the car behind.   Because I usually bring extra baggage packed with gifts for my Cuban friends, I have to leave the bags in my rented room in Havana before I am free to wander around the city—and only when I hand the gifts over to my friends who live in another province am I truly free to begin exploring areas of the country I want to see.

3. What am I NOT allowed to bring?
Desktop computers (laptops are O.K.), pornography, pre-recorded video-cassettes, fresh meat, canoes or kayaks over five meters (unless you arrive by boat), motorized vehicles, GPS units, as well as the obvious illegal drugs and explosives. If entering Cuba by boat, weapons must be declared and left with customs

HOLIDAYS AND SPECIAL EVENTS

(The letter 'x' next to the event indicates that the dates are not the same each year.)

JANUARY
1 Liberation Day
28 Jose Marti Birthday
x Feria de Artesanias (Pabexpo, Havana)

FEBRUARY
x Carnaval (Havana—weekend evenings)
24 Anniv of the 1895 War of Independence
x Jornadas de la Cultura Camaguena
x Havana International Jazz Festival (every two years)

MARCH
13 Anniv of 1957 Attack on Batista Palace
8 International Women's Day
x Festival de Monogolos y Unipersonales (Havana)
x Teatro de Titeres (Puppet Theater, Matanzas)

APRIL
4 Children's Day
19 Anniv of Victory at Bay of Pigs
x Semana de la Cultura (Baracoa)
x Music Festival (Varadero)
x Huela de España (Havana)
x Festival de Percusion (Havana)
1-15 Bienal del Humor (San Antonio de los Banos)
x Festival de Arte Danzario (Havana, Camaguey)

MAY
1 Labor Day
x Mother's Day (second Sunday)
x Romeria de Mayo (Holguin)
x International Guitar Festival (Havana—every two years)

JUNE
1-15 Encuentro de Bandas de Concierto (Bayamo)
x Father's Day (third Sunday)
x Festival de Boleros de Oro (Havana, Santiago de Cuba, Morón)
x Fiestas Sanjuaneras (Trinidad)

x Festival of Rural Cuban Culture (Las Tunas)

JULY

25-27 Celebration of National Rebellion

x Carnaval (Santiago de Cuba—end of the month)

x Fiesta Nacional de la Danza (Santa Clara)

30 Martyrs of the Revolution

AUGUST

13 Fidel Castro's Birthday

x Festival de Teatro (Havana, every other year)

x Beny More Festival (Cienfuegos—every two
   years)

SEPTEMBER

8 Virgen del Cobre (Santiago de Cuba)

x International Theater Festival (Havana—every
   two years, end of the month)

28 Anniversary of the CDR's

OCTOBER

8 Anniv of Che Guevara's Death

10-20 Day of Cuban Culture

10 Festival of Rumba Dancers (Matanzas)

x Festival of Contemporary Music (Havana)

x International Ballet Festival (Havana—last two
   weeks)

x Fiesta de la Cultura Iberoamericana (Holguin—
   end of the month)

28 Death of Camilo Cienfuegos

NOVEMBER

x Cultura Trinitaria (Trinidad, last two weeks)

x Festival of Caribbean Music (Varadero—end
   of the month)

x Contemporary Cuban Art competition
   (Havana)

27 Massacre of Students by Spanish Army

DECEMBER

2 Landing of the Granma

7 Death of Antonio Maceo

8-24 Parrandas de Remedios

17 Day of San Lazaro (Santiago de las Vegas)

x International Choir Festival (Santiago de Cuba)

x International Festival of Latin-American Film (Havana)

officials, and then claimed when you depart. The limits to importing alcohol, tobacco, medicine, cash, and gifts are discussed below, in question number five. All checked baggage is machine-scanned. If you find a large red sticker on one of your bags when you claim it, be worried: A customs officer stationed at the baggage claim exit will detain you for a search.

4. What else do you recommend I pack that might come in handy?
The following list depends, of course, on how much you plan to move around the island, how long you plan to stay, and your class of lodging.

battery chargers	Band-Aids
mosquito netting	extra batteries
mini flashlight	three-way plug
scissors	three-prong to two-prong plug adapter
insect repellant	mini plug-in light (i.e., a night-light)
string to hang clothes	
multi-tool	anti-fungus cream
water shoes	rain poncho or jacket
a large, heavy-duty garbage bag	no-see-um mesh jacket
antibiotic cream	anti-septic wipes
water purification tablets	washcloth

5. Are there any baggage restrictions I should know about?
If you are traveling to Cuba under the provisions of an OFAC license, your "accompanied baggage," which includes carry-ons, cannot weigh more than forty-four pounds per traveler unless otherwise authorized by written license from the Department of Commerce or the Office of Foreign Assets Control.[26] Exceptions to this baggage limit include informational materials and those traveling under Specific or General OFAC licenses as journalists or for religious and humanitarian purposes. If you do acquire a permit from the Department of Commerce or OFAC to carry more than the

forty-four pound limit, you will be charged per additional pound (from Miami the charge is approximately two dollars per additional pound).   Different airlines have different baggage policies regardless of the permit you get from OFAC, so it is best to check with the airline or TSP that booked your flight.

6. What customs rules do I need to know when I arrive in Cuba?

You cannot export more than $5,000 in cash (per person) from Cuba unless you submit a customs declaration form indicating how much over that amount you are bringing into Cuba. Also, foreigners are technically not allowed to import or export Cuban currency, but everybody does anyway. Cuban customs authorities almost never ask visitors to empty their pockets.

Gifts (anything that is clearly not your personal belonging) in excess of $100 are subject to a 100 percent customs duty.

You are permitted to bring in up to three liters of alcohol and a choice of 200 cigarettes, 50 cigars, or 250 grams of cut tobacco.

The following items are subject to special restrictions and must be declared: Telecommunications equipment, unprocessed food (fruits, meats, cheese and vegetables), live animals, flora and fauna specimens, and biological or pharmaceutical products of animal origin.

If you bring prescription drugs with you, keep them in their original containers, and carry a copy of the prescription form with you. I also recommended that you bring a signed and dated letter from the physician who prescribed the medication. In the letter, list the generic name of the drug, and have the doctor explain why the prescription is necessary.

SECTION 4

GETTING AROUND IN CUBA

1. Is it easy to rent a car in Cuba?
Yes, but rental rates can be steep, the availability of vehicles can thin out during the high season (December to March), and some car rental agencies practice shoddy reservations procedures—like not having a car for you when you arrive, even if you have a confirmed reservation. Botched reservations are less of a problem in Havana, where nine different State-run car rental agencies have offices. These are listed in the appendix on page 199.

Havanautos and Transautos have offices in many hotels and Servi-Cupet gas stations around the country, a convenience if your car suffers a malfunction. Transautos also offers some of the cheapest rates.

Prices run from about forty-five to seventy-five CUC per day, with discounts for weekly and bi-weekly rentals. Japanese and Korean economy cars (Suzuki, Daiihatsu, Toyota) are the most common vehicles available for rent, but you will also find French Peugots, Audis and Mercedes from Germany, and Skodas from the Czech Republic. You can pay a flat rate that includes unlimited mileage, or you can pay a lesser flat rate and add a per mile fee (usually .30 to .40 CUC) when you turn the car in. Insurance is extra—about ten to twenty CUC per day (depending on the car) and you will have to leave a deposit (200 to 300 CUC) in the form of cash or a blank, signed credit card slip. (The credit card can't be drawn on a U.S. bank.) The insurance policies all have deductible clauses ranging from 200 to 500 CUC. Some of the policies do not include theft, or liability coverage if the accident is your fault.

Gas is readily available in pumping stations in the cities and on the highways, but the stations are very limited in number compared to what one finds in the U.S. Medium-sized cities in Cuba will only offer one or two pumping stations. On the highways, the stations (called *Servi-Cupet* and *Oro Negro*) are spread about twenty to forty miles apart. A decent road map (available at the car-rental agencies and tourist information centers such as *Infotur*) will mark the locations of the gas stations with the symbol of a pump. Keep in mind that gas prices are two dollars or more per gallon than what Americans are used to paying at home.

For details about road conditions and driving hazards in Cuba, please turn to page 126 (Section 8).

When signing on the dotted line of your rental-car contract, follow these precautions:

- Make sure any pre-existing damages such as dents, scratches, missing equipment, and cracked windows are noted on the rental agreement form. When you return the car, take pictures of it from all four sides as evidence in case someone from the agency tries to slap you with a bill after you drop the car off.

- Check that all operating equipment such as turn signals, brake lights, headlights, speedometer, odometer, and windshield wipers are functioning, and that spare tires, jacks, mirrors, and radios are present.

- Find out if you will be charged for the gasoline already in the tank, and if you will get any credit for any gasoline remaining in the tank when you return the car.

- Park the car in guarded lots, or ask a security guard to watch it. You can also park your car in front of a bicycle *parqueo* and pay the attendant to watch it for you.

- If your car breaks down on the highway, don't abandon it as thieves will strip it of badly needed parts.

- If you lose the rental contract, you will be assessed a penalty, and you won't be able to drop the car off anywhere but the location where you first picked it up.

- Usually, cash is the only form of payment allowed for the refundable deposit if you want to drop the car off at a location other than the one you picked it up.

- Inquire about drop off fees.

2. Is it possible to rent a motorcycle or scooter in Cuba?

You will not find large motorcycles for rent anywhere in Cuba, but mopeds and scooters are available for rent at large resort areas. These cost about ten to fifteen CUC per hour and require a cash deposit and/or a passport.   Driving in Cuban cities—especially Havana—can be chaotic and downright dangerous if you don't know what to look for. Three-wheeled Coco-taxis, pedicabs, and Russian motorcycles with sidecars compete with taxis, trucks, and monstrous, conjoined buses. The lanes are not clearly marked, the side streets are filled with people walking IN the road because the sidewalks are very narrow, and most intersections use stop signs instead of traffic lights. The danger of driving in Cuban cities is multiplied several times over when you are perched atop a two-wheeled motorized vehicle—and one that feels foreign to you.

3.   Please help clarify the confusing and multi-tiered taxi system in Cuba.

First-time visitors to Cuba are always bewildered by the vast array of taxi services and networks crisscrossing the grid of Cuban streets and highways. The bewilderment is intensified when the visitor is refused rides in taxis that display signs in the windshield that clearly say "TAXI."

The following is a breakdown and description of all the types of taxi services, their rates, the areas they cover, and for whom they cater. The taxi-drivers in five of the eight categories listed are not legally allowed to carry foreigners, but they do anyway, if they feel their chances of getting caught are minimal.

- *Panataxis*: State-owned, metered taxis that only accept convertible pesos. These are like the "Yellow Cab" radio-dispatched taxis that roam around the cities in the U.S., but the cars are almost always small Ladas. The Panataxis usually have roof signs and the word "Panataxi" painted on the doors. Panataxis are the most common type of convertible pesos taxi on Havana streets, and also the cheapest convertible pesos taxi (a ten-minute trip across town will cost about three CUC). Rates are for the whole taxi, not per person, and you do not have to share it with other people looking for rides. If you are riding alone, however, the driver would probably be very grateful if you tell him you don't mind if he or she picks up another fare enroute to your destination. *Panataxis* are only found in the main tourist towns.

- **Peso *Ladas***: These look and function just like the Panataxis described above but are only licensed to carry Cuban nationals. Rates are in pesos. The taxis are yellow and black and have an odd Arabic script painted on the doors. They are also noticeably run down, are not radio-dispatched, and lack air-conditioning.

- *Colectivos*: Privately owned vehicles licensed by the State to carry Cuban nationals only. Rates, of course, are in pesos, and the car is always shared. The drivers of the *colectivos* (commonly called *maquinas*), do not offer door-to-door service, but instead pick up and discharge passengers along a set route. The *colectivos* are almost always hunkering old American cars from the 1950s or before. This is by far the cheapest way to get around town (ten pesos per person) if the driver is willing to let you board. If you look or talk like a tourist, they won't, but I often travel this way when I am with a Cuban friend who does all the talking.

- **Tourist Taxi**: State-owned taxis (*Turistaxi, Taxi-OK, Taxi Transtur*, among others) that are the only ones allowed to park at taxi stands in front of tourist hotels. They are the most expensive type of taxi, but also the nicest. Rates are always in convertible pesos and the final price is usually determined beforehand. The taxis look like private cars but most of them have a "T" painted on the door and blue license plates (instead of the yellow license plate of personal cars).

- *Coco-taxis*: Three-wheeled, egg-shaped, two-seaters that ride like golf carts. Designed for short hops (and sightseeing in Old Havana), but I have ridden these all the way to the airport. Rates are in convertible pesos and must be agreed upon beforehand.

- **Pedicabs**: Called *ciclo-taxis*, these are three-wheeled bicycles with a small rear seat and overhead canopy. Also for short distances (very handy for carting groceries and large packets), and the cheapest form of taxi—ten pesos for Cubans and a negotiated rate in convertible pesos for foreigners, about five to ten CUC per hour. (You can usually get them to come down on the beginning asking price if you think it is too high.) Riding these things is a relaxing way to sightsee. Don't feel bad for the drivers—they appreciate your business and like to chat. Not all *ciclo-taxis* are licensed to carry tourists. Make sure you verify whether the quoted price is in Cuban pesos (*moneda nacional*) or convertible pesos (*pesos convertibles*).

- *Maquina Particular*: Unlicensed, privately owned cars whose owners roam the streets and promote their services in underground social circles in an attempt to make a black market peso. Because of the scarcity of food and goods, the high prices combined with low salaries, and the limits to free enterprise in the country, many people do what they can to supplement their incomes; using one's car is one way to do this.

  Hiring a driver on the sly is ridiculously cheap; many are happy with twenty or thirty CUC (more than what they earn in a month working their State jobs) for a full day of chauffering.   To find a black market car and driver, ask around. Everybody has a relative or knows a friend of a friend who owns a car and will jump at the opportunity to make some extra cash. The downside to black market rides is that the driver risks stiff fines imposed by vigilant traffic cops, and the vehicles are usually in poor condition.

- **Interprovincial taxis**: These are shared taxis—usually privately owned and licensed by the State—that carry passengers on long drives between cities. Most are found at organized taxi stands near interprovincial bus stations. Each driver at the taxi stand advertises a specific destination and waits for the car to fill up before heading out. Rates are per person—about ten CUC, depending on the distance. Passengers do not have to share the taxi if they pay for the empty seats.   Everyone—Cubans and foreigners alike—pay in convertible pesos, but the drivers who are not licensed to carry foreigners understandably charge them a few convertible pesos more. Most of the taxis at the interprovincial stands are NOT licensed to carry foreigners, and many—especially if the passenger clearly looks like a tourist—do not want to take the gamble of a fine that will take them a week of driving to pay. Those who are desperate enough to take the chance will ask you to wait for them a few blocks away. Payment is not usually made until the driver delivers you to the promised destination.

4. Is it safe to hire a black market taxi?
Tourists in Cuba do not have to worry about being driven to a remote spot and robbed by a driver, a scenario that plays out with alarming frequency in other Latin American countries. (For more information about crime in Cuba, turn to Section 12.) The black market activity is so common in Cuba—necessary, in fact, for daily survival—that the danger is not in getting swindled but in getting caught.   In any event, whenever possible, procure illegal taxi services through referrals. And keep your eye on bags stored in the trunk—not just for thieves, but for gasoline that spills out of jugs during the ride.

5. What's the best way to get around the cities?
In Havana and other large tourist towns, I prefer the Panataxis, explained in question number one, above.   They are cheap, trustworthy, legal, knowledgeable, friendly, comfortable, professional, and numerous. In Havana, I once left a digital camera in the back seat of a Panataxi after the ride was over, and a different Panataxi driver was able to use his radio to track the

original driver down.

You won't find many Panataxis in the smaller cities. If you want convenience and don't mind paying the extra money, tourist taxis are the way to go. Personally, I use the horse-drawn shuttles (explained in the question number seven, below) or I ask around for a *maquina particular*, as described in the previous question.

6. Is the public bus system any good?

The great majority of residents in the large cities get around town using the public bus system. The network of routes is quite extensive, but the wait at bus stops can be long (except in Havana) and the buses themselves are often crammed full. Keep a tight grip on your purses, wallets, bags, and etcetera when you ride a crowded bus because pick pocketing is very common.

Public buses come in all shapes and sizes. Mostly, you will see the kind of city buses similar in size and shape to the ones used in large U.S. cities, but you will also find "road trains" (the bodies of two buses welded together, and pulled by a truck), and yellow school buses.

In Havana, you can buy a day pass for a tourist minibus shuttle that stops every hour at twenty-three different locations along a circuitous route of the city. The pass costs five CUC and can be purchased from the driver or at the tourist desk in large hotels. The shuttle is called *Vaiven Turistico* and you can contact the company that runs it at (7) 66-9713 or (7) 24-9626.

In rural areas, another type of bus used for public transport is the *camión*—a tarp-covered dump truck or flat-bed truck fitted with benches. Also, by law, all government vehicles with empty seats must stop to pick up people waiting at bus stops on rural roads. This includes dump trucks, cargo trucks, vans, and even jeeps. State inspectors called *amarillos* (meaning "yellow", because they wear mustard-colored shirts and trousers) are assigned to the rural bus stops and main intersections to flag down the empty State vehicles and to organize the queues.

The fare for buses that make frequent stops on a city route is twenty centavos. Express buses cost a little more—a sign in the windshield should indicate the price. Usually, you pay a conductor or drop the money in a box near the driver. If you board a bus through a rear door and it is too crowded to reach the driver to pay your fare, pass your money to the person beside you to initiate a sort of fireman's bucket brigade.

To learn about the rules and etiquette for queues at bus stops, turn to page 121 ("Standing in Line").

7. Are horse-drawn wagons in Cuba really used as public transportation, and are foreigners allowed to use them?

Horse-drawn wagons—called *coches*—are used as short-distance shuttles in most Cuban cities, but you won't find any in the metropolis of Havana. The *coches* cost one peso to ride, and passengers sit on benches running the length of the wagon. When a passenger boards a *coche*, he or she must hand the fare up the line of other seated passengers until it reaches the driver. This system of paying the driver is a quaint example of commuter etiquette that, for many visitors, provides additional evidence of the endearing bond of unity and cooperation among the Cuban people.

Technically, the *coche* drivers are not supposed to take tourists, but if you don't act like a gawking, joy-riding tourist and keep the talk to a minimum, they'll let you board.

Like the lively, festive train rides in Cuba, the mood on these *coches* can be quite jolly. Teen friends break into spontaneous song, strangers share vital information about the new policies of the rations, and men offer jokes that poke fun at the system and their predicaments. I once heard a man recite the following Limerick that left his fellow passengers in stitches:

> *Ayer fui a comprar boniato*
> *Y me dijo el bodeguero*
> *Tiene que traer primero*
> *El carnet del sindicato*
> *Hasta el Viejo Olegario*
> *Me dijo con mucho disimulo,*
> *Traiga dos fotos del culo*
> *Para el papel sanitario*

> (Yesterday I went to buy sweet potato
> And the ration clerk said
> First bring your State identity card
> Even old Olegario
> Said with much stealth,
> Bring me two photos of your ass
> For the toilet paper)

8.   How do you prefer to travel when you are going long distances?

I usually opt for the interprovincial taxis, mentioned above (question number three) because they are the fastest (except for domestic flights) and cheapest form of long distance travel. The drivers always stop for meals and breaks along the way, and those who travel this way can get an excellent education and insight on many Cuban topics through long conversations with drivers and other passengers who are forced to sit next to each other for hours at a time.

I also enjoy riding the Via Azul interprovincial buses for long distance travel because they are a step up in comfort (soft seats and more leg room), and the price is not much more than what you would pay for a shared, interprovincial taxi. The only drawbacks to traveling by Via Azul bus are that you need to reserve a seat in advance (not always, but recommended, especially during the high season), and the destinations and departure times are limited. For more information about long distance travel by bus, see question number ten in this Section.

For super-long distances, (i.e., Havana to Santiago de Cuba), I recommend a domestic flight. (See question number x, below). Traveling across the country in a shared car requires too many hours of cramped sitting. Also, domestic plane fares are very cheap—50 to 130 CUC, one-way to anywhere in the country.

9. Can you please explain how I can find an interprovincial taxi as I travel around the country, and what the procedures are for securing a seat (since many of them are not licensed to carry foreigners)?

You can find an interprovincial taxi at select interprovincial bus terminals and train stations.   The taxis—called *maquinas particulares interprovincial*—either line up at an organized taxi stand or loiter loosely near or across the street from the terminal entrance. Only specific terminals in each city are designated as interprovincial taxi hubs, so make sure you head for the right one (ask any local). In Havana, which has several main bus and train terminals, the one to go to is at the corner of *Avenida de Independencia* and *Avenida 19 de Mayo.*

Show up before seven p.m. to improve your chances of finding a car. Many drivers won't depart for a destination until the car has a full load, and the later in the day you turn up looking for a car, the fewer people show up looking for rides.

It is almost a guarantee that, if you look like a foreigner, before you even reach the terminal you will be assaulted by a pack of aggressive taxi salesmen fighting each other for your business. The salesmen—known as *boteros*—are paid a commission by the taxi driver for "finding" a passenger. In the case of foreigners, who are not very informed about taxi prices, the *boteros* try to get the potential rider to pay as much as possible above the going rate and pocket the difference. I simply wave them off and speak directly with one of the taxi drivers (who will be sitting behind the wheel or leaning against the car). Don't ask one of the *boteros* to take you to a driver!

The biggest problem foreigners have finding rides in interprovincial taxis is that most of the taxis are not licensed to carry foreigners. If your foreigner looks are obvious and the driver is willing to take the gamble of a fine levied by a highway patrol officer, he or she may ask you to wait some distance away until the quota of passengers is met. Otherwise, you may have to wait a while for a driver who does have a license to carry foreigners. If a licensed *turista* taxi does finally appear, you may get stuck paying for the entire car if another foreigner doesn't come along looking for a taxi to the same destination.

Fares from Havana to Santa Clara, Cienfuegos, and Trinidad are ten CUC per person for Cubans and about fifteen CUC per person for foreigners. You may have to travel in city-to-city legs if your final destination is longer than a taxi is willing to go.

10. What are my options for traveling long distance by bus?
You have four possibilities for long distance travel by bus:

- **Via Azul bus**: Well-maintained, air-conditioned buses that only accept convertible pesos. They make limited stops along the spine of the island (mostly tourist-friendly cities) and depart for destinations one to three times each day. The longest leg—from Havana to Santiago de Cuba (thirteen hours, 530 miles if you take the overnight express bus)—costs fifty CUC. In the high season, it is wise to reserve a seat in advance. Call (7) 881-1413 in Havana or visit their website at www.viazul.cu. A schedule of Via Azul departure times for various cities is provided in Appendix 17 on page 202.

- **Astro bus**: Peso currency buses with service to most cities. Most Cubans use the Astro system because they can't afford the Via Azul fares. As a consequence, the high demand creates a shortage of seats. Reservations must be made weeks in advance. Only a few seats on each bus are made available for foreigners who must pay in convertible pesos. As expected, the buses take a lot of wear and tear; the seats are hard, the air-conditioning is usually broken, and the buses frequently break down. If taking one of these buses is your last resort, and you haven't made a reservation, you need to show up in person at the bus station at least one hour before the bus is scheduled to depart. Because you pay in convertible pesos, you'll probably be able to get a seat. The Havana telephone number for Astro bus information is (7) 870-3397. (Note: Many of the run-down Astro buses are currently being replaced by newer ones from China.)

- **Tourist excursion bus**: In some cases, you may find it more convenient to sign up for a group excursion by bus, and then abandon ship when the bus arrives at your desired destination. For information about excursions, inquire at the tourist information desk at major hotels or contact one of the domestic tour operators listed in Appendix 18 on page 204.

* **Intermunicipal bus**: Buses that travel to specific cities within a province. Usually, you can only board these buses at the intermunicipal bus terminal, and the buses make limited stops to discharge passengers at the smaller towns along the way. Prices are always in pesos. Oftentimes, you will be handed a piece of paper with a number on it that indicates your place in line, and then you pay the conductor when you board the bus. Note that many cities have separate bus terminals for intermunicipal buses and interprovincial buses.

11. Do you recommend traveling long distance by train?

Travel time by train is often a little faster than the bus (but not faster than express buses), and cheaper if you board one of the slower *regular* trains. If you don't fly super-long distances (i.e., Havana to Santiago de Cuba) as I recommended earlier, I would choose an express (*especial*) train over travel by bus or interprovincial taxi. It's a little more expensive (sixty-two CUC from Havana to Santiago de Cuba) but you can chop a few hours off the travel time, and the first-class cars are very comfortable (and ice-cold from the air-conditioning—take a sweater). Slower, local (*regular*) trains to Santiago de Cuba cost thirty CUC and take fourteen hours to complete. (This is twenty CUC cheaper than riding the Via Azul bus.)

Another convenience of train travel is that the stations are located near the center of town (just like the Old West). This makes it easier to get to accommodations, shops, and other needed services.

Unless you can find a friend to purchase a ticket for you, you will have to pay in convertible pesos. Convertible peso-paying passengers are seated in comfortable, first-class cars (isolated from the suffering masses in the other cars) and can usually purchase tickets at the station without having to wait in line. Seats are almost always available for convertible peso-paying passengers, but if you don't want to take the chance you can purchase a ticket in advance at most train stations (ask for the FerroCuba office) and some domestic tour agencies (i.e., Infotur). You can also visit or call the main FerroCuba office in Old Havana, Calle Arsenal, between Cienfuegos and Apontes, (7) 861-4259. Their website is ferrotur@ceniai.cuz. A list of inter-city train departure times is provided in the appendix on page 201.

Train tickets for peso-paying passengers are only available on the day of departure, and sometimes the day before. The times for purchasing peso tickets varies with each station and are normally posted in the ticket window. The queue begins forming early. If you are able to acquire a peso ticket (fifty cents to Santa Clara, when converted to dollars), be prepared to cough up the convertible peso fare when the conductor on board sees that you are a foreigner.

More often than not, the express trains have dining cars, or hostesses selling food in the aisles, but don't expect much more than French fries and pork sandwiches.

The slower, *regular* trains are dirtier, smellier, crowded, and fitted with uncushioned wooden seats. The atmosphere, however, is livelier. People talk and joke with one another, men share their bottles of rum, and invariably somebody with a guitar shows up. When the train stops at a station, vendors come aboard selling sandwiches, coffee, candy, pre-peeled oranges, cheese, and homemade drinks. To buy a drink, you need to provide your own glass or cup. Sometimes the drink vendor provides a glass that has to be emptied quickly and returned. Some *regular* trains offer special first class seating compatible with the comfy arrangements found on first-class cars of the express (*especial*) trains.

Warning: Departure times for many trains are often at night, so the joy of sightseeing through the windows won't be possible. Also, delays are very common, and schedules often change without notice.

12.   Are there any public or commercial provincial or interprovincial boats or ferries in Cuba?

The only significant public or commercial ferry in Cuba sails between the Isla de Juventud and Nueva Gerona on the south coast. A few cities provide ferry shuttles across their harbors. In Havana, for example, you can ride the ferry from the pier at San Pedro and Santa Clara in Old Havana to the town of Regla across the Bay of Havana.

13. What are my options to travel the country by plane?

You can access any part of the country by plane (all major cities have airports) and fares are very affordable (50 to 130 CUC, one-way) but availability on short notice is tricky. If you can, book all domestic flights when you purchase your international entry. This will not only guarantee you a seat, but you can save up to twenty-five percent off the domestic leg.

If you aren't able to book a domestic flight in advance, it is best to appear in person at the main airline office in Havana as many of the local airline offices in other parts of the country are not hooked up to the computerized reservation system. (They confirm seats by phone.) If the lines are long at the main airline offices, you can save time by booking your flight through a hotel tour desk or a domestic travel agency (i.e., Havanaturs. A list of domestic travel agencies in Cuba is provided in the appendix on page 205). Cubana de Aviacion and Aero Caribbean are the main carriers, while

Aerogaviota and Aerotaxi operate smaller charter flights and air-taxi services.   The addresses, telephone numbers and websites for these airlines are listed in Appendix 20 on page 206.

Warning: Cubana de Aviacion is reported to be one of the most dangerous in the world.   The airline also has a reputation for delaying and canceling flights, and treating its customers poorly.

14. Can I rent a bicycle a bicycle in Cuba?

In Havana, there are three places where you can rent a bicycle. These are listed in the appendix on page 207.   Bicycles are also available for rent in Varadero (at hotels and along Avenida 1a) and some major tourist resorts.   In other cities, bike rental places are rare to nonexistent.   Rates are usually two CUC per hour or ten to twelve CUC per day.   Bicycle theft is a major problem in Cuba, so it is best to leave your rented bike in a bicycle *parqueo* (guarded yards operated by private homeowners) or in somebody's house. Bicycle rental places usually require a 250 CUC deposit.

15. Can I bring my own bicycle into the country, and do you recommend traveling the country this way?

Most airlines (including Cubana) offering flights to Cuba permit bicycles to be checked as luggage.   The weight of your bicycle is applied toward the baggage limit.   If you travel to Cuba legally (with an OFAC license), remember that OFAC rules, as discussed in Section 3, require that your "accompanied baggage," which includes carry-ons, cannot weigh more than forty-four pounds per traveler unless otherwise authorized by written license from the Department of Commerce or the Office of Foreign Assets Control.

You don't have to take your bicycle apart and pack it in a bag or box—you can simply hand it over to the check-in clerk who will attach a baggage tag to it.   Some airlines may ask that you remove the pedals or handlebars, but double-check the policies and procedures of each airline beforehand.   Baggage rules and requirements change frequently.

If you give your bicycle away or it is stolen while you are in Cuba, customs officers will make you pay an "importation" fee equal to one hundred percent of the estimated value.

Cuba has become famous for being the "bicycle capital of the world."   Only the lucky few have cars—due as much to government controls as the inability of the average Cuban to afford one.

The shortage of cars opens up the neighborhood streets and intercity roads to bicycle and pedestrian traffic, but the main arteries in the large cities are always dangerously clogged during the day.

A few main roads connecting some towns are also dangerous, especially when the road is the only access stringing a number of towns to a main city.   The touring bicyclist will get the most pleasure riding from town to town on the secondary roads.   Except on the main highway that bisects the island—and where bicycles are not allowed—shoulders are nonexistent. And you can forget about bicycle lanes.

Bring spares and parts you think you might need for your bike as they are impossible to find in Cuba. What few parts are available are for single-cog, clunky models manufactured in Cuban factories or purchased from China.

You can transport your bicycle in the baggage compartment of trains and the Via Azul buses, but it is best to confirm this with the ticketing agent before you buy a ticket. You may be better off finding a driver of an interprovincial taxi or *maquina particular* (discussed above, in question number three) who will let you put the bicycle in the trunk. Public buses do not have bike racks.

For information about bicycle touring and suggested routes, contact the Club Nacional de Cicloturismo Gran Caribe at (07) 96-9193, www.trans@ip.etecsa.cu (They are located in Old Havana at Lonja del Comercio #6D, Calle Oficios.) Bicycles Without Borders, a Canadian non-profit that sponors a bicycle repair workshop and rental business in Havana, can also help you plan a route. Contact them in Toronto at (416) 364-5329 or visit their website at www.bikestocuba.org.

16. Do you recommend hitchhiking?

Hitchhiking is so widespread in Cuba that the government passed a law requiring all State vehicles with empty seats to pick up people waiting at bus stops, major intersections, and highway exit ramps. Inspectors are assigned to these spots to flag down the vehicles and to organize the queues.

Obviously, since everybody else hitchhikes, you don't need to suffer any insecurities about doing so yourself, but your competition will be fierce. Personally, I think hitchhiking is a tough way to get around the country, especially when all the other methods of internal transportation are so inexpensive. The Cuban people hitchhike out of desperation, and most of them would think you're crazy if you told them you hitchhike for pleasure.

If you have a thing for getting around this way, don't stick out your thumb to ask for a lift—just wave your arm.

Also remember that, by law, a Cuban person is not allowed to carry foreigners as a passenger in his or her private car, so don't be surprised if someone refuses to give you a lift while accepting others.

17. Please explain the cruising rules if I want to cruise Cuba by private boat.

After you have cleared in with authorities at an international port of entry (see question number six on page 25), you can request a cruising permit from the port captain. The permit (called a *Permiso*

Especial de Navegacion) costs fifty CUC. When you apply for the permit, you must present a list of your intended stops or ports of call along the coast. A document called a *Despacho* will be drawn up. At each stop along the way, your old *Despacho* will be retained by the port captain and a new one will be issued. You are not allowed to leave any port without a *Despacho*.   Doing so invites fines, prosecution, and expulsion.

In case you deviate from your official list of stops, I strongly recommended that you request a form called a *Permiso de Salida* (sometimes substituted for a *Guia de Recala*).   This form lists potential stops and an ultimate destination.   Also ask the port officials to indicate on the form that you have their permission to anchor out in between stops.

It is important to inform each port officer of your departure time at least a day in advance.

Generally, vessels flying foreign flags will only be permitted to call on sanctioned ports with marina facilities for tourists. You will not be able to go ashore—even in a dinghy—at small towns and ports.   Some industrial ports are off-limits to pleasure boaters. Study your charts and cruising guides for other restricted areas such as practice ranges and military installations. With a *Permiso de Salida*, you can skip a planned stop, but you risk serious consequences if you attempt to go ashore at points not listed on your *Despacho*.   This rule doesn't apply to anchoring off outer islands located off the mainland.

SECTION 5

WHERE TO STAY IN CUBA

1. What are my (legal) options for accommodations in Cuba?
Cuba is the third most popular tourist destination in the Caribbean (behind the Dominican Republic and Puerto Rico) with two million visitors each year. Canadians, Italians, Germans, and Spaniards are the largest group of foreigners visiting. The priority that the Cuban government places on its tourism industry has resulted in a variety and scope of lodging options for visitors that rivals other popular tourist destinations in the hemisphere. Below is a breakdown of accommodation categories, ranging from world-class hotels in ritzy resort areas to dirt-cheap rooms in private homes. The appendices from page 208 to page 240 list many of the lodging options by city.

- **Hotels.** Readily available and voluminous in quantity, but vary greatly in price, quality, and amenities. Question number eight on page 54 discusses hotel options in greater detail.

- **Resorts.** Located in all quadrants of the island—especially along the coast and on nearby *cayos* (small islands off the mainland)—and comparable in quality and scale to those found in the Bahamas and Mexico. Many of the resorts succeed in harnessing the character and flavor of the country that is unique to its culture, traditions, and natural beauty. Resorts in Cuba are indicated in parentheses in appendix 24 on page 231.

- **Bungalows and Villas.** Called *cabañas* in Spanish. All have the potential for charm, but there are inconsistencies from one location to the other. Most *cabañas* have shared living rooms and kitchens, and some have no cooking facilities at all.

- **Marinas.** Boaters who dock at marinas save money on airfare and hotel stays but the drawbacks are 1) They are isolated from the true nature of people and culture in Cuba in the same way that guests are isolated when they take up

- residence at hotels and resorts. (This actually may not be a drawback, depending upon one's idea of a vacation.) 2) The marinas are not within walking distance of the sights and attractions in the cities, therefore, marina residents end up spending as much money on taxis as the cost of renting a room in town. 3) The amenities and standards at marinas are sub-par by international standards.   In addition, the number of large, full-service marinas in Cuba is very limited (three in the whole country). On the plus side, boaters who pull into one of the many small ports while cruising have more of an opportunity to explore some of the off-the-beaten-path places that landlubbers miss, and there is no substitute for anchoring inside a secluded cove on the coast to experience the breathtaking beauty of Cuba's pristine marine and shore life.

- **Peso Hotels.** These hotels are for Cubans who can use their much-devalued national currency to pay for a room. (The average wage in Cuba is fifteen to twenty dollars per month.)   As one would expect, the cleanliness and conditions of the rooms can be—but are not always—disappointing. Many peso hotels will not allow foreigners to book a room, and if they do, it won't be at the peso rate. Peso hotels, though, are a good option for travelers on a tight budget as rates—for foreigners—are about ten to fifteen CUC for a double room.   Don't expect air-conditioning, hot water, refrigerators, televisions, or clean sheets.

- **Posadas.** No frills, State-run "love" motels created as an alternative for romantic couples who have a hard time getting any privacy in their own over-crowded homes.

- **Houses.**   Houses are available through several State enterprises (i.e., Gaviota, S.A.), but can be expensive. Many of the State-managed houses are reserved for high-ranking government officials, diplomats, and foreign dignitaries and are located on prime real estate (such as former mansions, beachfronts, and retreats in garden settings).   Licensed, privately owned houses are more difficult but not impossible to find since most rental licenses only allow the property owners to rent a maximum of two rooms in their home.   There is a fair share of privately owned homes for rent at the popular beaches (except Varadero and other exclusive resort towns).   These cost about fifty CUC per day and are fully functional with complete kitchens, clean bedding, air-conditioning, hot water, and televisions.

- **Apartments.** Like the houses mentioned above, you can find apartments for rent through State enterprises. With a little bit of effort, privately owned apartments can be found, but technically the owners are only allowed to rent out rooms. They rent the whole unit out anyway—usually for forty or fifty dollars per night. What often happens is that the family living in the apartment stays somewhere else (with friends or other family members) until the renters leave. Padlocked closets, well-used dishes, and baby pictures hanging on the walls suggest this.

- **University Dormitories.** Most campus housing is off-limits to non-students, but a handful do make an exception during semester breaks or if some rooms are unoccupied by students during the school year. Rates are low but the rooms are generally Spartan, and bathrooms, kitchens, and living rooms are shared. The appendix on page 208 lists some of the dormitories known to rent to non-students.

- **Sports Hotels.** This is another category of State-subsidized housing where visiting teams stay during competitions and league play. (All sports in Cuba—both professional and amateur—are State-managed.) As with the university dormitories mentioned above, a few exceptions are made at the sports hotels to rent to non-athletes when time and space permits. Again, the quality is not great, but the rates are very affordable.

- **Rented rooms in a private home.** This is the Cuban version of Bed and Breakfasts, but with an intimate twist: The rooms are (usually, but not always) in the actual homes of individuals and families, so it feels like you're living with a Cuban family. This is an excellent way to get an insight on how Cubans live, although not necessarily a complete insight since these licensed homes are regulated and inspected by State authorities for cleanliness, comfort, and safety. Renting a room in a private home (called a *casa particular* in Spanish) is also the cheapest form of lodging: Prices run from fifteen to twenty-five CUC per night. The rate is usually quoted per room, not per person, but this needs to be confirmed before you take the room. Note: In the resort town of Varadero, and other select tourist areas, the renting of rooms in private homes is forbidden. Question two and three below discuss *casas particulares* in greater detail.

- **As a nonpaying guest in a private home.** See question number four below.

- **Camping.** Described in question number nine.

2. What accommodation arrangements do you prefer to make when you are in Cuba?

If I'm staying put for a while, I often stay with friends in their homes. To do this, though, you need to get permission (and pay a fee) from the immigration authorities. I know—it's an outrage. It's like having to get permission from the Department of Homeland Security to have a friend from abroad stay with you at your house in the U.S.— AFTER your friend has already been admitted into the country. A fee must be paid to the *Estado* if the homeowner is approved to have you as a guest, and the homeowner risks hefty fines if she or he doesn't follow this procedure. Question four below explains how you and the homeowner can apply for this permission.

If I am traveling around Cuba with friends, I like to rent a whole house or apartment that is privately owned and licensed by the *Estado* to rent to foreigners. The advantages for this are obvious: Privacy, the freedom to come and go at any time of the day or night, and a place to store groceries and cook, which is a lot cheaper than eating out for every meal. The drawback is that it is difficult to find a house or apartment on short notice. There aren't that many around, and those that do exist are often booked. It's no fun riding around in the fading light with a small group and a couple of kids in tow and not knowing if a roof and beds are going to be found.

If I'm traveling around with a friend or by myself, I prefer to rent a room in a *casa particular*. They are plentiful, conveniently located, cheap, you don't have to book in advance, you can pay-as-you-go, the home-cooked meals are better than most restaurants, the service is highly personal, and you can get an intimate insight of family life and neighborhood relations. Obviously, if you are the type of traveler who needs space and privacy, a room in a private home is not going to work. The next question below explains how to find a *casa particular*.

3. How can I find a *casa particular*?

In the larger cities, you can stroll around the perimeters of the historic districts and look for the "room for rent" signs near the front doors. These signs have a blue, inverted anchor or a pyramid symbol, and the words *"Arrendador Divisa"* ("Foreign Currency Renter") or "Arrendador Inscripto" ("Registered Renter") printed at the bottom—see the illustrations on page 66b. (Red-colored signs indicate rentals for Cubans only.) You can also ask anyone who lives in the neighborhood. If they don't know, they can point you to someone who does. I have asked people at a pizza stand, a bartender at a beach hut, two teenagers sitting on a doorstep, a lady sweeping the sidewalk, and many taxi-drivers and not once has anyone ever said "I don't know." Try asking a stranger in the U.S if he or she knows someone who has a room for rent in their house for the night and see what kind of facial expressions you get.

If you look like a tourist and you're walking in a tourist-frequented area of town, you don't even have to look for someone who can find you a room—a person with a room will come looking for you. The same thing happens at bus terminals and train stations. These roaming room vendors try their best to earn a few extra pesos for the day by taking a commission on the boarders they bring in to property owners. While they are at it, they will also try to sell you cigars, girls, rum, lobster dinners, chauffeurs, souvenirs, a Santeria priest, an English version of the national paper, Cuban pesos, an authentic army cap, a Che Guevara coin, and anything else you need.

Appendix 23 on page 209 provides a list of names and telephone numbers for privately owned properties that offer rooms or entire units for rent. These addresses change often as licenses are not renewed and people move. An annually updated booklet of *casas particulares* is available online at www.cubatravelpro.com, or you can request one by mail at: Casa Particular, P.O. Box 4510, Key West Florida, 33041.

While the rates for the rooms in private homes do not fluctuate much, the cleanliness and appeal do. Stick to recommendations by people you know or have rented from before. Some rooms may have air-conditioning while others only have fans. With a little luck, you might get a toilet or a hand sink with your room, but more than likely, you will have to share a bathroom with the rest of the people in the house. Don't be disappointed if you find that there is no running hot water in the shower—most Cubans heat water in a pot on the stove for their bathing. The better-kept *casas particulares* have tiny electrical holding tanks attached to the shower head that produce somewhat heated water, but with diminished pressure. (These miniature electrical tanks are against the law in the U.S.)

The proprietor will offer to prepare meals for you, but don't feel obligated. Breakfast costs about two CUC, lunch or dinner from five to seven CUC. You will find that home-cooked meals are far superior to meals at tourist restaurants and hotels.

Most proprietors will offer you coffee several times throughout the day and will decline your attempts to pay for it. Feel free to store items in their refrigerator but make sure you don't take up all the space. Don't drink the water from the tap. Every *casa particular* in which I've stayed keeps a pitcher of pre-boiled, cold drinking water in the fridge or in plastic bottles in the freezer.

The proprietor will also be able to launder your clothes (for a fee) or else know someone who can. The people who run these *casas particulares* are excellent resources of information. They can tell you where the best restaurants are, where to catch a bus, where the nearest money exchange place is, how to use the payphone, etcetera. The proprietors can also find you a trustworthy driver to take you to the beach or the airport, and if you are looking for a *casa particular* in another city, they can usually refer you to one or ask someone who knows.

When you first check in, you will need to show them your passport and sign a receipt. Payment in full in advance is always appreciated, but it is also O.K. to pay day-by-day. Often, you will not get a key—somebody will always be on the premises to let you in, regardless what time of the day or night you return. Although you can bring guests in, always ask first. Do not under any circumstances bring someone in to stay overnight in your room. As a licensed establishment, the proprietors must register anyone staying overnight. If they don't, they could be fined or have their rental permit revoked. Besides, *the casa particular* is their home and you need to respect their space and their privacy.

Be careful about getting a room with a window to the street. It may be nice and quiet when you check in at night, but it'll be quite a shock for you in the morning when rush hour traffic hits the road and the kids race off to school.

4. Am I allowed to stay in private homes and claim I am a nonpaying guest?

Not without permission from the immigration authorities. The reasoning is a bit complex and up for debate. Some say that the Cuban government discourages contacts between foreigners and the Cuban people in order to minimize capitalist influence on the socialist mindset. Others say that the government does not want outsiders to see the reality of life in Cuba—or for Cubans to see the reality of life on the outside. Officially, the authorities argue that, in most cases, foreign "friends" who stay with Cubans in their homes pay the property owners money under the table. This, the authorities say, robs the State of potential income and places the money in the hands of the individual, an inequity that violates the socialist principles of parity. Another official explanation why foreigners are not allowed to stay in private homes is to protect the visitor from unforeseen hazards and dangers.

To obtain permission to stay in a private home as a guest, the homeowner needs to appear in person with you at the nearest immigration office within twenty-four hours to apply for an A2 visa (see the appendix on page 192 for locations of immigration offices). Bring your passport and tourist card. The homeowner will need to bring his or her State-issued identity card. You must tell the immigration officer exactly how many days you will be staying at the private home, and then you will have to pay a fee of anywhere from fifty to two hundred dollars. Permission is not always granted, and you might be referred to another immigration office to file your request.

5.   What will happen if the homeowner doesn't get the permission to have a foreigner as an overnight guest?
Eventually—trust me on this—word will get out and a housing inspector will stop by. You will have to pack your things immediately and leave, and the proprietor will be issued a fine. The fine for first time violators is 1,000 pesos—an amount equivalent to two and a half-months in wages. If the money is not paid within thirty days, the fine will double, and if that is not paid, the owner of the property must serve a jail sentence equal to one day for every peso of the fine. Repeat violators will eventually have their homes taken away from them.

6.   Do you recommend that I talk to the *jineteros* (roaming, black market street vendors) who approach me on the street and offer to find me a place to stay?
The roaming room vendors are generally trustworthy but, as I mentioned before, you can just as easily find a *casa particular* by asking somebody who lives in the area or by scouting the neighborhood yourself. The *jineteros* tend to be very aggressive sales people and don't easily take no for an answer. If you let one latch on to you, he or she might be tough to shake. Also, they are very territorial and once you agree to use their services, street code requires that other *jineteros* must keep their distance from you. In a sense, you unwittingly become the *jinetero's* property.

7.   Is a Cuban national allowed to stay with me in my hotel room or rented unit?
If you rent a room or an entire house or apartment that is privately owned, you must register your guest with the proprietor. Usually there is no extra charge, since the rate is per room, not per person. You are also allowed to have a Cuban guest stay with you in your State-run *divisa* (foreign currency) hotel or resort, but you must register your guest and either pay an additional 70 or 75 CUC per guest or upgrade to a double room if you only have a single. Peso hotels cater to Cubans, so you won't have any problems there.

8. Please tell me about the hotels in Cuba and how I can book a room in one.
All hotels in Cuba are owned by the government. Many of the better hotels are managed by well-known foreign hotel companies such as Sol Melia from Spain and SuperClub in Jamaica, and they are on par with international standards. You can get some good bargains

by booking an air-and-land package with a travel agency outside the U.S.   See the appendix on page 185 for a list of these travel agencies.   Except during the high season in Havana and Varadero, hotels in Cuba are rarely fully booked.   I mention this because it is often cheaper to book a room on the spot rather than reserving one through an agency.   Also, reservations made with travel agencies in Cuba are often misplaced or not forwarded to the hotel.   This paves the way for something of a shock that awaits you when you arrive at the front desk and find that the hotel has no record of your reservation and the place is full.   Trying to get a refund will probably send you on a wild goose chase because nobody wants to take the blame.

Hotel rates are higher from December to April, and from July to August, but rates in some hotels do not change at all.

The list of hotels in the appendix on page 231 classifies your options into five main categories: super cheap, cheap, medium-priced, high-class, and super high-class Many of the hotels listed in the "cheap" category are peso hotels mentioned earlier (hotels where Cubans can pay in their national currency).   These hotels probably won't have air-conditioning, hot water, refrigerators, televisions, or clean sheets, and you may have to pay in convertible pesos what the Cubans pay in pesos.   If this happens, complain that the price is too much and try to haggle.

9. What are my options for camping in Cuba?
There is only one national network of campsites in Cuba.   It is called *Campismo Popular* and to reserve a site you need to show up at one of their offices in the larger cities.   Campsites are usually located at beaches and in the mountains.

The campgrounds, however, do not have designated areas for pitching tents.   Instead, everyone sleeps in rudimentary cabins.   If you insist on staying in your tent, you'll probably be allowed to do so, but you'll have to pay the cabin rate anyway.

Many of the campsites are only open during Cuban holidays, at which point the cabins fill up, so don't take the chance of showing up at the site unannounced.

While the Cuban people pay in pesos for a cabin, foreigners will be charged about ten CUC (per cabin, not per person).   Many of the guests at the campsites are groups of students (i.e., from the Communist Youth Movement) or model State employees enjoying a subsidized vacation as a reward for their hard work.

A listing of *Campismo Popular* offices by city is provided in the appendix on page 241.

If you want to camp in places outside of the *Campismo Popular* sites, you still need to apply for a permit.   Do not pitch a tent on private land as that will get the owner of the property into trouble for "renting without a license."

SECTION 6

MONEY MATTERS

1. What is the common currency used in Cuba to buy things?
Two types of currency are used for cash transactions in Cuba: Cuban pesos and the convertible peso. In some tourist resorts, the euro is also legal tender.

The Cuban peso is the national currency that the Cuban people use to pay their bills, deposit into bank accounts, and—whenever possible—shop. All wages and salaries are also paid in pesos.

The word "peso" is the most common term used by the Cuban people when quoting and inquiring about prices in Cuban peso shops, but you will also hear people refer to the peso as *"moneda nacional"* and *"pesos Cubanos."* Pesos come in notes of one, three, five, ten, twenty, fifty, and one hundred. Coins come in one and three-peso form and are further divided into centavo coins (one hundred centavos equal one peso) of one, two, five, twenty, and forty. The one-centavo coin is sometimes called a *kilo*, the five-centavo coin a *medio*, and the twenty-centavo coin a *peseta*. An illustration of all the Cuban paper currency is provided on page 66c. The symbol displayed next to prices quoted in pesos is "MN" or "CUP." Ten pesos would be "MN 10.00," and twenty centavos would be "MN .20" or "20 centavos." Sometimes the "$" symbol is also used to indicate Cuban peso prices.

The convertible peso is used on a much broader scale in Cuba. The great majority of household items, clothes, shoes, appliances, electronics, and other popular consumer goods are only available in State-owned stores that only accept convertible pesos. Convertible pesos are also the only currency accepted at all tourist restaurants and hotels. The parallel economies of the Cuban peso and the convertible peso is necessary because much of the Cuban people's food, goods, and services is subsidized by the government (in Cuban pesos), yet the government is forced to pay world-market prices for desperately needed imports. Because the Cuban peso is so devalued, Cuba must use its hard currency earnings from tourism, foreign investment, and exports in order to pay for the imports.

Paper denominations of the convertible peso come in one, two, three (a popular Che Guevara souvenir), five, ten, twenty, fifty, and one hundred convertible peso bills. Coins come in denominations of one, three (also Che Guevara), five, ten, twenty-five, fifty centavos (the same term used for Cuban centavos), and one convertible peso. One hundred convertible centavos equal one convertible peso. An illustration of the convertible peso paper denominations is provided on page 66c. The word "peso" is also commonly used by the Cuban people when referring to the convertible peso. If you are not sure which currency someone is referring to, simply ask if it is *"moneda nacional"* or *"en divisa."* *Divisa* means "convertible currency." Other common terms used by the Cuban people when referring to the convertible peso include *verde, guano, fula and chavitos.* The symbol used for the convertible peso is "CUC," thus ten convertible pesos is "10 CUC" or "CUC10," and ten centavos *en divisa* is ".10 CUC" or "10 centavos CUC." As with the Cuban peso, the "$" symbol is sometimes used to indicate convertible peso prices.

Convertible pesos are not exchangeable on world markets.

2. Can I use dollars, euros, or other foreign currency to buy things in Cuba?
While some foreign currency can be exchanged for Cuban pesos or convertible pesos (see question number five, below), foreign currency is not used in transactions with the exception of euros in some tourist resorts. In 1994, the U.S. dollar was the main hard currency in circulation, but it was replaced by the convertible peso ten years later.

3. Can foreigners use the Cuban peso to buy things?
Yes, but the products and services available in the Cuban peso are limited. Things that foreigners can buy with Cuban pesos are fresh fruits, vegetables, and other items at farmers'markets; pizza, rolls with pork or cheese, deep-fried corn batter, homemade juices, ice-cream, pastry, homemade candy, peanut bars, coffee, and other things at private stalls; public transportation; and a limited selection of food and beverages offered for sale at Cuban peso bars and restaurants. Because the Cuban peso is so devalued, it is much cheaper for foreigners to change their foreign currency into Cuban pesos and purchase things in Cuban pesos whenever they can. Buying things from Cuban peso businesses is also a helpful boost for the owners. The government, however, does not appreciate the competition of privately owned businesses (limited to sole proprietorships) and prefers you spend convertible pesos that eventually end up in State hands.

4. How many Cuban pesos does one U.S. dollar buy?
In January 2009, one U.S. dollar brought twenty-five Cuban pesos.

To put that into perspective, a homemade pizza purchased at a privately owned stall might cost you six Cuban pesos, or about thirty cents. Homemade ice cream and small snacks such as a paper cone of roasted peanuts cost about one Cuban peso. A bottle of Hatuey beer (brewed in Cuba) at a Cuban peso restaurant will cost about twelve Cuban pesos.

5.   Can the Cuban people use convertible pesos or foreign currency to buy things in Cuba?
Yes, they can, and the government prefers that they do because it promotes a flow of foreign currency into the country (especially from relatives and friends who send them money from abroad) and channels the hard currency into State-owned businesses. (Only State-owned businesses are permitted to charge convertible pesos for products and services.)

6. Can all foreign currency be exchanged in Cuba?
Only the following foreign currencies can be exchanged in Cuba: The U.S. dollar, Euros, the British pound, Canadian dollars, the Swiss franc, Mexican pesos, and the Japanese yen.

7. What foreign currency has the best exchange rate in Cuba?
The Cuban banking system uses the U.S. dollar market rate (almost one-to-one with the convertible peso) as the yardstick with which to exchange all foreign currency, so no currency is going to have a better exchange rate than another.

8. What are the current rates and commissions to exchange U.S. dollars and other foreign currency into convertible pesos?
In January 2009, Cuban banks and exchange houses offered the following exchange rates:

1 U.S. dollar	bought	.8960 CUC
1 euro	bought	1.2583 CUC
1 Canadian dollar	bought	.9339 CUC
1 Swiss franc	bought	.8367 CUC
1 Mexican peso	bought	.8623 CUC
1 Japanese yen	bought	.0098 CUC

In addition, those who use U.S. dollars to buy convertible pesos must first pay a ten percent surcharge before the exchange is made. So in the end, one U.S. dollar will buy

$$1.00 \text{ USD} - 10\% = .90 \text{ USD} \times .8960 \text{ CUC} = .8064 \text{ CUC}$$

Those who use other foreign currencies to purchase convertible pesos are not assessed a ten percent surcharge, but they may be asked to pay a small commission.

Updated exchange rates for convertible pesos can be found online at www.banco-metropolitano.com.

9. Do you recommend that I change my dollars into a different foreign currency before I go to Cuba?
Only if you can get a really good exchange rate and avoid steep commission fees. Even if you do, the savings will not amount to much.

An example, using January 2009 exchange rates: If you exchange one U.S. dollar at a rate of .70 euros to the dollar with a 3.95% commission fee, you would receive

$$1.00 \text{ USD} - 3.95\% = .96 \text{ USD} \times .70 = .67 \text{ euros}$$

Then, when you exchange the .67 euros for convertible pesos at the going rate of 1.2583 CUC to the euro, you would end up with .84 CUC (minus any commission, if applicable).   Since (as shown in question number seven, above) one U.S. dollar nets you .80 CUC (after the ten percent surcharge), you would gain .04 CUC for every dollar if you exchanged U.S. dollars for euros before traveling to Cuba. The net gain, in dollars, is about five cents.

Again, the key is to get a very good exchange rate and avoid steep commissions when you exchange U.S. dollars for any foreign currency prior to exchanging the foreign currency for convertible pesos.   Expending the effort (i.e., phone calls, research, driving time) to find a good exchange rate may not be worth the few cents on the dollar you gain.

10. Can you tell me about any tricks in the currency exchange game that can help me stretch my spending power?

- If you are traveling to Cuba from Mexico, Europe, Canada, or Japan, shop around for a bank or exchange house that will give you a good rate (to change U.S. dollars) and a low commission fee.

- Buy (with U.S, dollars) euros, yen or other foreign currency (accepted at exchange houses in Cuba) a year or more in advance of your Cuba trip in the hopes that the foreign currency you buy will gain on the dollar. This is purely speculative and may end up causing you losses if the dollar gains instead.

- Purchase more convertible pesos than you will need, then when you return home, sell the extra convertible pesos to people on their way to Cuba. Again, this may work against you if the dollar gains on world markets. (Note: Cuban law does not allow anyone to export or import Cuban pesos or convertible pesos, but customs officers almost never ask travelers to display the contents of their pockets. Coins, however, have to be deposited in trays so as not to set off alarms when you pass through metal detectors.) If you travel to Cuba without an OFAC permit, this trick has an added (very dangerous) risk that U.S. customs officers will find the Cuban money in your pocket when you return home.

- Save your extra convertible pesos for a future trip. The ten percent fee of changing U.S. dollars to convertible pesos will certainly not come down, and may go up.

- Buy, at the same one-to-one rate offered by Cuban exchange houses, leftover convertible pesos from people departing Cuba.

- Wells Fargo online (www.wellsfargo.com) is said to offer some of the best rates to exchange dollars.

- See question number eighteen in this Section for details about foreign-issued, pre-paid debit cards that eliminate the ten percent surcharge on exchanging U.S. dollars for convertible pesos.

11. Where can I exchange money while I am in Cuba?
All foreign currency can be exchanged at many tourist hotels, most banks, international airports, and official exchange bureaus called *Cadecas.*

The main bank with extensive services for foreigners as well as nationals is the privately operated Banco Financiero Internacional, with eight branches throughout the country. Four other banks offering services for foreigners are Banco de Credito y Comercio, Banco Internacional de Comercio, and Banco Metropolitano, and the international branch of the Banco Nacional de Cuba. The Banco Popular de Ahorro is primarily a savings institution for nationals, but some branches in the smaller cities that lack a large international bank will cater to tourists.

The *Cadecas* tend to keep longer hours (i.e., 8:00 a.m. to 10:00 p.m.) and are more strategically located in shopping districts and tourist-frequented areas. Often, there are separate lines at the *Cadecas* (and some banks) for those who want to change foreign currency into convertible pesos and those who want to change convertible pesos into Cuban pesos or vice-versa. At *Cadecas* where there is only one queue, security guards and ushers often guide foreigners to the front of the line.

12. Will I be charged any commissions or service fees when I exchange money at any of the banks, hotels, or exchange bureaus?

As explained in question number seven in this Section, those who use U.S. dollars to buy convertible pesos must pay a ten percent surcharge, regardless of where they exchange their money. Beyond that, you are not supposed to be charged any additional commission or fees for exchanging your money. If a hotel clerk or *Cadeca* teller tries to charge you any fees on top of the ten percent skim, take your business elsewhere.

The airports and hotels tend to offer less favorable exchange rates. The Banco Financiero Internacional has been known to offer the best rates, but the *Cadecas* are also reasonable.

Warning: Whenever exchanging money, always work out the numbers ahead of time and ask for a printed receipt. Even bank tellers are known to pull a few punches. Coins are not accepted for exchanges, and neither are torn or marked bills. Check the watermark on the high-denomination convertible pesos as counterfeits (supposedly from South America) are becoming more common.

13. Do you recommend exchanging money on the black market?

Most black market money exchangers are trustworthy and do provide a useful service when other (legal) exchange options are closed or far away. They can also save you time waiting in line. As expected, the black market exchangers will probably offer a slightly less favorable rate or commission, but the difference, especially when changing small amounts of money, is not going to be dramatic.

Black market money exchangers operate quite openly on the streets (especially near *Cadecas* and shopping districts) and are not frowned upon or overly persecuted by the authorities. However, many dishonest black market exchangers do try to pull fast ones on tourists (one Cuban peso is not the same as one convertible peso!), and snatch and run tactics occur daily. If you do need to exchange money on the black market, operate out in the open, don't pull out too much money at once, and work out the numbers ahead of time.

14. Are there any limits as to how much cash I can bring into or take out of Cuba?

As explained in Section 3, you cannot leave Cuba with more than $5,000 in cash in your pocket (per person) unless you submit a customs declaration form (upon arrival) indicating how much over that amount you are bringing into Cuba. Also, foreigners are technically not allowed to import or export Cuban currency, but a few pesos aren't going to get you in trouble.

15. Can credit cards be used in Cuba?

Not if they are issued by a U.S. bank or other U.S.-based financial institution. Credit cards issued by other countries are accepted, but the holder needs to make sure that the card is not outsourced to a U.S. company.

If you use a credit card, a surcharge of two to five percent will be added to the bill. Also, the credit card company that issued the card may charge a small fee for transactions that take place in Cuba.

Mastercard and Visa seem to be the best cards to use in Cuba, but Diners Club, Cabal, Transcard, Banamex, Carnet, Eurocard, and JCB are accepted in some places as well.

Relying solely on credit cards for all your travel expenses is not recommended as computer glitches, broken card readers, bad phone lines, and depleted paper supplies interfere with a business' ability to complete a transaction.   Only State-owned businesses (i.e., hotels, tourist restaurants, and car rental agencies) can accept credit cards; *casas particulares* and other privately run operations are not set up to do so.

Cash advances are possible off some credit cards at banks and ATMs in Cuba (ATM availability is discussed in question number seventeen in this Section), but to date, only non-U.S. Visa cards can be used at ATMs. Other non-U.S. credit cards such as Mastercard can be used for over-the-counter withdrawals. Cash advances of up to 5,000 CUC off non-U.S. credit cards are possible at Banco Financiero Internacional branches.

16. What about debit cards?

Debit cards can also be used in Cuba, but again, as long as they are not issued by a U.S. bank, subsidiary, or financial institution. Visitors to Cuba seem to use debit cards more often than credit cards. It is reported that those who use Visa debit cards in Cuba are not charged an interest fee by the credit card company.

Several Canadian-based companies offer a unique type of pre-paid debit card that can be used to access cash at more than 6,500 locations in Cuba, including banks, ATMs, *Cadecas*, and hotels. Deposits can be made into the account by using cashier's checks, money orders, and credit cards. For more details about these handy cards, see question number eighteen in this Section.

17. Are traveler's checks accepted in Cuba?

American Express, Thomas Cook, and Visa traveler's checks are accepted at many hotels, restaurants, and *divisa* shops. They can also be cashed at all *Cadecas* and most banks. For some odd reason, the restriction against traveler's checks issued by U.S.

banks and financial institutions does not apply in Cuba. Refunds for lost or stolen traveler's checks, however, cannot be made in Cuba—you have to wait until you return home to file a claim. Eurocheques are not accepted anywhere in the country.

Fees for using or cashing traveler's checks range from two to four percent. Hotels usually charge the highest fee.

Do not fill in the date, place, or payee on the traveler's checks when you use them or they will be rejected.

Because the traveler's checks cannot be refunded in Cuba if lost or stolen, and because of the fees charged to issue them and cash them, using a debit card or a front-loaded credit card (issued by a company from a country other than the U.S.) to make cash withdrawals from banks or ATMs (discussed below) is a better option. Also, read question number eighteen below for ways to beat hefty fees and surcharges on credit cards.

18. Are there any ATMs in Cuba?
Yes, but they are not compatible with international debit/bank card systems such as Cirrus or Switch. However, Visa cards (not issued in the U.S.) and cash cards issued in Cuba by Cuban banks can be used to withdraw cash at ATMs. Currently, the ATMs are only available in major cities and tourist resorts. A small fee, similar to the ones assessed by card issuers worldwide, is assessed to make ATM cash withdrawals.

19. Does there exist a type of pre-paid debit card that can be used in Cuba and can be loaded from the U.S.?
As mentioned in question number fifteen in this Section, a number of foreign-based companies offer a unique type of pre-paid debit card that can be used to access cash at more than 6,500 locations in Cuba, including banks, ATMs, *Cadecas*, and hotels. Deposits can be made into the account from the U.S. by using cashier's checks, money orders, and credit cards. A fee is charged to make deposits into the account, but the final cost of using the card is almost always less than the cost of using credit cards and traveler's checks. Also, the rate of exchanging U.S. dollars to convertible pesos is often better, and because the funds are transferred from a foreign country, users of the pre-paid cards avoid the ten percent surcharge on U.S. dollars exchanged in Cuba.

Generally, it is cheaper if you use cashier's checks or money orders to make deposits into the account instead of using credit cards. For example, using a credit card to make a $1,000 deposit into a pre-paid card account set up by one particular company results in 810 CUC, while using a $1,000 money order or cashier's check to make a deposit results in 860 CUC. The fee for purchasing the money order or cashier's check needs to be taken into account when comparing final costs.

Two companies you can contact to set up a pre-paid card account are Caribbean Transfers (www.caribbeantransfers.com) and Transcard International (www.transcardinter.com, telephone 905-660-5558), both from Canada.

20. Can I set up a bank account in the U.S. or another country so that I can access my money from a branch office in Cuba?

There are no banking relationships between the U.S. and Cuba, but it is possible to set up a bank account in other countries in which funds can be withdrawn from or deposited in a Cuban bank. The Banco Financiero Internacional in Cuba is the main bank that handles accounts originating from foreign countries. It has two locations in Havana: Inside the Hotel Tryp Habana Libre at Calle L between 23rd Street and 25th Street; and at Linea No. 1 and O Street. Other Cuban banks that handle commercial and personal accounts originating from foreign countries include the Banco de Credito y Comercio, Banco Internacional de Comercio, and Banco Metropolitano, and the international branch of the Banco Nacional de Cuba.

21. Is it possible to wire money to Cuba from the U.S.?

Current embargo laws only allow a "person subject to U.S. jurisdiction who is eighteen years or older" to send a maximum of 300 dollars in any three-month period to immediate family members. "Immediate family member" is defined to include "only a spouse, child, grandchildren, grandparent, sibling of the remitter or that remitter's spouse, as well as any spouse or widower of the foregoing." In addition, remittances cannot be made to certain government officials and current members of the Cuban Communist Party.

Western Union is the only U.S.-based money wiring company authorized by the OFAC to wire money to Cuba.

Transcard International, the Canadian-based pre-paid card company mentioned in question number eighteen, also offers an inexpensive, secure, and convenient way to send money to Cuba. Funds are sent to a named beneficiary who can collect the money at a designated bank, ATM, or *Cadeca*. Ask them about the Quickcash service or log on to their website at www.quickcash.com.

SECTION 7

THE THRIVING BLACK MARKET

1. Is it true that there is a significant informal (black market) economy in Cuba that operates in conjunction with the legal economy?

For millions of Cuban people, making a living and obtaining basic necessities illegally is a matter of survival. In *Cuba In Focus, A Guide to People, Politics, and Culture* (Interlink Publishing Group, 1999), Emily Hatchwell and Simon Calder write: "Unlike in other Latin American countries, the black market in Cuba is not the preserve of the marginal classes, but is responsible instead for circulating goods and services among all sectors of society. People trade as much on the black market as they do in the state sector."

In order to appreciate the significance of these statements, a little background on the economic situation in Cuba is necessary.

Life for the average Cuban family is a Herculean struggle. Newspaper substitutes for toilet paper. Bar soap is used as shampoo. Breakfast is a bread roll or a fruit fly-covered banana. When bedtime rolls around, padding is spread on available space on the floor, and family members, including relatives from both sides of a marriage, sleep several per room.

In the streets, long lines of people spill out of ration distribution centers, and dilapidated public buses, packed to the seams with commuters, groan under the excess weight. Bicycle traffic and horse-drawn covered wagons (less visible in tourist towns like Varadero and Havana) replace taxis and buses to alleviate the consumption of budget-crippling oil imports.

When gleaming, air-conditioned tourist buses speed across the country's principal highway from the exclusive resort of Varadero to the metropolis of Havana, curious passengers see farmers in straw hats driving teams of oxen hauling ploughs to turn up the soil in small fields.

Cuba's current economic difficulties are rooted in the total economic collapse that occurred in the early 1990's when Russia, Cuba's main trading partner, was forced to cut subsidies and trade as a result of its own demise.

But the loss of trade with a single country is not the sole culprit in the Cuban people's struggles. Outside economic analysts point their fingers at many contributing factors, some having a greater impact on living conditions than others. These factors include the U.S. trade embargo; a government monopoly on industry; restrictions to free enterprise; a cumbersome and inefficient model of government and industry planning and management based on centralization and vertical command; a lack of diversification in production and an over-dependence on one or two cash crops (sugar and tobacco) for export; and the socialist philosophy itself that many claim inhibits competition and productivity.

One crucial factor has been left off this list because it merits a deeper analysis of its own. This is the fact that two totally separate and parallel economies function simultaneously in Cuba: one that revolves around the hard cash convertible peso (pegged to fluctuations of the U.S. dollar) and the other that revolves around the Cuban peso (artificially fixed). The Cuban people are paid in Cuban pesos, while the State pockets the vast majority of hard cash received from exports and tourism. The average salary in Cuba is about 400 pesos, or sixteen dollars when exchanged at market rates. Many things in the peso economy such as food, rent, electricity, transportation, medical care, and education are all heavily subsidized by the State (see page 66a for an overview of the ration system) and paid in pesos, but the great majority of basic necessities (underwear, paper goods, refrigerators, toothpaste, shampoo, toilet paper) are only available in hard currency stores at world market prices. This is because Cuba has to import most of its consumer goods, as the country, for one reason or another, is unable to produce these things at home.

This means that people earning sixteen dollars a month have to pay eighteen dollars to buy a pair of decent shoes, two dollars for laundry detergent, six dollars for a gallon of gas, a dollar for toothpaste, several hundred dollars for a fridge, and so on.

It is this discrepancy of rock-bottom incomes and sky-high prices of basic necessities, combined with all the other factors of production or lack thereof, that forces people to turn to the black market to find ways to boost their income and obtain the things they desperately need. Workers pilfer lumber, eggs, and cigars from the factories so they can sell them on the street or enjoy them at home. Doctors moonlight as unlicensed taxi-drivers. Families offer illegal rooms and meals in their homes to tourists who pay with the much sought after convertible peso. Just one convertible peso is equivalent to two days of work at a Cuban peso paying job, and for this reason street hustlers are particularly aggressive—and annoying—in seeking out tourists to offer any and all imaginable products and services the visitors might need (including girls and drugs).

RATIONS IN CUBA

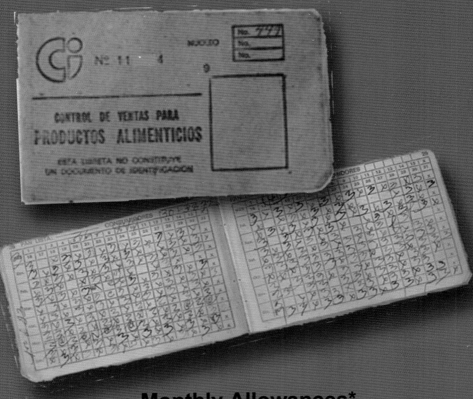

Monthly Allowances*
(When available)

Product	Quantity	Price (MN)
Rice	6 lbs	.70/lb
Beans	11 oz	.32/lb
Meat** (Can be fish, beef, pork, ground beef with soy, chicken, sausage, pork, or ham)	1/2 to 1 lb	.70
Vegetable (Usually sweet potato or plaintain)	10-15 lbs	.40/lb
Eggs (September to December only)	8	.20 ea
White sugar	3 lbs	.15/lb
Raw sugar	3 lbs	.10/lb
Milk (Children under 7 and the elderly only)	1 litre	.25/litre
Coffee (Distributed twice per month)	4 oz	.20/oz
Bar of Soap	1/2 bar	.25/bar
Bread Rolls (1 roll per person per day)	1 roll	.40/roll

Other subsidized items that are occasionally or almost never available for purchase include oil, toothpaste, laundry detergent, butter, lard, candles, and canned tomato paste.

*Per person, 2009   **Meat products distributed only twice per month

DOOR SYMBOLS FOR LICENSED FOREIGN CURRENCY
ROOM RENTALS IN PRIVATE HOMES
(*CASAS PARTICULARES*)

ARRENDADOR INSCRIPTO

ARRENDADOR DIVISA

TOURIST CARD ISSUED BY CUBAN IMMIGRATION OFFICER
OR AIRLINE TICKETING AGENT

PAPER CURRENCIES CIRCULATING IN CUBA

CONVERTIBLE PESOS (CUC)   **CUBAN PESO (MN)**

Announcing Service From

STOCK ISLAND
KEY WEST-HAVANA

Passenger—Automobile and Cargo

FERRY SERVICE

S/S "CITY OF HAVANA"

SOUTHBOUND DEPARTS: Stock Island, Key West, Florida — 10 A.M.   ARRIVES: Havana, Cuba — 5:00
TUESDAY — THURSDAY — SATURDAY

NORTHBOUND DEPARTS: Havana, Cuba — 10 A.M.   ARRIVES: Stock Island, Key West, Florida — 5:00
MONDAY — WEDNESDAY — FRIDAY

500 Passengers   **125 Automobiles**   **Air Conditio**

BUS CONNECTIONS VIA GREYHOUND TO OR FROM MIAMI

SPACIOUS LOUNGES   PRIVATE CABINS, PARLORS   ESCALATOR TO PASSENGER DECK   MODERN SNACK BARS   TROPICAL GIFT SHO

BEVERAGE BAR   SIX CONTINUOUS HOURS OF MUSIC   TROPICAL DAY OCEAN CRUISE   CUBAN CUSTOMS AND IMMIGRATION INSPECTION ENROU

THE LARGEST SHIP OPERATING FROM FLORIDA TO CUBA

For Further Information Contact Your Travel Agent or

WEST INDIA FRUIT & STEAMSHIP COMPANY, Inc.
KEY WEST TERMINAL COMPANY, Inc.

AGENTS
KEY WEST, FLORIDA

P.O. Box 671, Stock Island   PHONE: CYpres

Key West Citizen newspaper ad, April 4, 1956. Round-trip fares cost $23.5 per person and $75.00 per automobile. A private cabin was $10.00 extr The crossing took seven hours. (Courtesy of the Key West Citizen.)

2. What kinds of goods and services are available on the black market?

Just about any product or service that can be sold to augment incomes, and anything in demand that is difficult to obtain via the legal venues. Food available in Cuban pesos and through the ration system is quite limited, so if anyone can get their hands on some stolen eggs, chicken, or cheese, they'll have an easy time unloading them. The Cuban government forbids the sale of a long list of food products such as milk, bread, beef, coffee, butter, oil, chicken, and fish at peso farmers' markets, so people with connections to producers of these commodities market them via secret networks.

It is the same story with basic household goods. Blankets, shoes, light bulbs, shampoo, dinner plates, and cooking pots are intercepted somewhere between the cargo ship and the shelves of convertible peso shops and end up in kitchens and bedrooms of people who more than likely didn't spend a whole month's salary to buy them.

The most lucrative trade in the black market is in products and services for tourists. While some tourist services such as rooms and meals in private homes are permitted, the government tries to ensure that most of the hard cash derived from tourism goes to State enterprises. The restrictions on private tourist trade and the high value of the convertible peso creates a huge incentive for the illicit sale of everything from taxis to cigars, girls, rum, lobsters, Cuban pesos, an authentic army cap, a show at the Tropicana, and tickets to a baseball game.

Selling things on the black market is not limited to small items. Entire homes and automobiles are sold on the sly because Cuban law prevents citizens from doing so legally.

3.   Is the black market exchange of goods and services tolerated by the State authorities?

To a large degree, it has to be tolerated because the government knows it is the only way many people can obtain things and supplement their incomes. Even the lawmakers themselves have to engage in black market transactions (they usually do so through intermediaries). After forty-eight years of socialist indoctrination, a monopoly on industry, and restrictions to free enterprise, the Cuban government and the Communist Party have become masters at using the black market as a safety valve to release any building pressure that might explode into outright revolt.

4. Do you recommend I buy black market goods and services?

The pressure to buy things and services on the black market is not as great for visitors from the U.S. and other wealthy nations who earn dollars and euros because prices for products and services in the legal Cuban economy are still very affordable. Also, the Cuban government, aware of the importance of remittances from the tourist trade, does everything within its power to make sure that visitors get what they need. If this smells like apartheid, or a paradox of class in a nation committed to socialism, it might be.

Still, if you are a budget traveler and you want to stretch your money, or you simply like the idea of a bargain, obtaining goods and services on the black market will save you tons. Instead of paying eighty convertible pesos for a hotel room in Varadero (where *casas particulares* are not allowed), you can find a willing black market homeowner to rent you a room for twenty. Rather than pay a tourist taxi to take you to Santa Clara for the official rate of fifty convertible pesos, you can ask a black market driver to take you in a shared *colectivo* the same distance for ten. Instead of eating out all the time and paying convertible pesos at State-sanctioned restaurants, it is a cinch to locate someone plugged into the black market network who will cook meals for you and accept payment in Cuban pesos.

You must be careful, though, from whom you choose to buy contraband products and services. Everybody buys and sells on the informal market, yes, but most people are familiar with those with whom they trade, while you, as a newcomer, will not be. Always try to enlist a Cuban person you know to help you through the deal. In a world where people are struggling, money is tight, and food is scarce, rip-offs happen and scams are prevalent. In particular, the naïve tourist is a favorite prey for the less honest segment of the population.

Below is a list of the most common scams that unfold in black market deals:

- Money exchangers exchanging your dollars for the Cuban peso at the same rate as convertible pesos.

- Sellers of any product or service claiming that dollars are not worth anything anymore, or claiming that they have no idea what the dollar is worth when you try to use dollars to buy something. They know very well what the dollar is worth; they are just gauging your knowledge of the facts to see if you are an easy prey.

- People overcharging you for tickets to sporting events such as baseball games and boxing matches. Prices for professional baseball games (completely subsidized by the State) are sold for three Cuban pesos (fifteen cents) on a first-come, first-served basis.

- Fake cigars: Authentic cigar boxes and labels are stolen

from authentic factories and often packed with fakes. Real *Cohibas* go for two or three hundred convertible pesos for a box of twenty-five, and if someone who claims they obtained a box from a relative who works at the factory and is willing to let you have it for a bargain price of fifty dollars, be suspicious. Cigars rolled by amateurs with a lesser quality leaf proliferate in Cuba and can be purchased for a few Cuban pesos (fifteen cents) apiece.

- "Pure" Cuban coffee purchased on the black market may be mixed with foreign substances to beef up the volume. The best coffee beans are exported as a cash crop and the Cubans usually get an inferior brand as part of their monthly rations.

- Someone offering you a deal on gasoline may have added kerosene (or worse, water) to it to stretch the supply.

- The famous Habana Club rum offered by black market vendors may be substitutes in authentic bottles.

SECTION 8

PRACTICAL INFORMATION

1. Where can I buy groceries?

Foreigners can buy groceries at stores where only convertible pesos are accepted and at farmers'markets where only Cuban pesos are accepted. The convertible peso stores are officially called *Tiendas Panamericanas* but the Cuban people refer to them as *el chopin* or *divisa* shops. (*Divisa* means 'foreign currency.') These *divisa* stores are everywhere but don't expect the quality and selection to be anywhere near what you see in U.S. supermarkets. Many items such as ground beef, steaks, fish, and eggs are simply not available (what little there is in the country goes to tourist restaurants and hotels), and fresh fruits and vegetables are sold only at the farmers'markets.

The farmers'markets are a little harder to find—ask any local where one is—but if harvest periods are decent, they will have bananas, mangoes, papaya, limes, yucca, *malanga* (taro—tastes like a potato), calabaza (a squash), avocados, cucumbers, onions, tomatoes, string beans, lettuce, rice, black beans, and fly-ridden pork. Many food items—especially those that are rationed—are not allowed to be sold at farmers'markets. These include beef and fish products, eggs, cheese, chicken, and coffee. Bring your own bag. Hurricanes that slice through the country have an immediate and drastic effect on selection and availability.

In the larger cities there are a limited number of shops that sell freshly baked Cuban loafs or rolls. It is the same bread offered in *divisa* shops, but you can pay in pesos (ten or so) and save money. Store times, however, are erratic, and the bread, when it is baked, sells out quickly.

You will often see casual (unlicensed) vendors on the street or stopping house-to-house hawking everything from tomatoes to light bulbs. The police tend to turn a blind eye to these black market vendors (even the police buy black market things—but usually through an intermediary) unless the vendors are suspected of selling beef or lobster products. Jail times for doing so are stiff.

Depending on the time of year, sometimes you will come across a crowd of people buying freshly harvested farm products being sold from the back of trucks. There is no set location or schedule for these farmers markets on wheels, but if the items are seasonal products, such as corn or avocados, you can be sure the products will sell fast.

In each neighborhood, certain households develop a reputation for being the local (illegal) purveyor of basic food items, such as beans, rice, coffee, eggs, and oil. I find it endearing when I'm visiting someone at their house and a little girl shows up with a cup or a plastic bag in her hand and asks to buy some rice or beans. Black market food sales are common in every country where food is scarce, wages are low, and prices are high. It could happen in the U.S.

One last note about buying groceries in Cuba: You will often see people buying groceries at a dimly lit, hole-in-the-wall shop and discover that it is not a store but a *bodega* where locals fetch their monthly rations. You won't be able to buy anything there. You can tell if it's a *bodega* if you see a price list displayed on the back wall and people holding little brown booklets about the size of a passport.

2. What tips can you give me on eating out?

Read the information on page 120 in Section 12 of this manual for a discussion on some of the unique social rules and customs you will encounter while eating out in restaurants in Cuba.

For some reason, the food served in most restaurants is unimpressive. One theory for the poor quality is that, instead of offering traditional Cuban recipes, the tourist establishments try to emulate the international fare foreigners are accustomed to eating in their own countries. To the Cuban chef, this change from the usual Cuban meal of rice, black beans, and pork is exciting enough in itself, so less emphasis is placed on the way the food is cooked.

Also, the fact that most restaurants in Cuba are owned and managed by State enterprises—and the fact that work is guaranteed to all Cubans—cuts into the competitive nature of a good restaurant and eliminates the requirement for an establishment to turn a profit. (Funds from other departments can be moved around.)

The scarcity of quality food products is another major factor that contributes to sub-par meals in restaurants. Canned peas and carrots are served as side dishes to the main course. Catsup is used as a sauce for pizza and spaghetti. Shredded cabbage is used for salads instead of lettuce. Lemon juice and salt substitutes for homemade dressings. I have even seen the yolk missing from the eggs in omelets. If you expect meals to be as good as or better than what you'd find in the highly competitive restaurant business in

Europe and the U.S., you'll be quite disappointed.

This is not to say that good restaurants don't exist in Cuba. They're just hard to find. Ask taxi-drivers, front desk clerks, and proprietors of *casas particulares* where their favorite places are and chances are those places will become your favorites too.

In my experience, the best meals are prepared by the proprietors of *casas particulares* and in small, privately owned restaurants called *paladares*. Many of these *paladares* are run right out of the dining room of homeowners.   The meals at these places are essentially prepared the same way the proprietor prepares meals for his or her own family, so you are getting a truly authentic dish.

Excellent buffet spreads can be found at the better hotels managed by foreign companies. (If you are not a guest at one of these hotels, you may be required to purchase a day-pass in order to remain on the premises.) If you're on the road, find out where the sightseeing tourist buses stop for lunch or dinner.

In Havana, I have found a couple of good Chinese restaurants in the small area known as the *barrio Chino*. Again, the quality is nowhere near what you'd find in the U.S., but if you hit the right place the food will be adequate, and the prices are amazingly low (two-to-three CUC for an entrée). Try Restaurante Tien-Tan, at San Nicholas and Cuchillo. Another place I like is on Dragones (#364, up a flight of stairs to the second floor) that serves huge mounds of stir-fry noodles or fried rice and, surprisingly, a large selection of very good pizza. The soups, egg rolls, and fried wonton (called *maripositas*) are also quite tasty.

3.   Are there any restaurants where I can pay in the Cuban peso?

There are, but most of them have very little to offer (rolls with a slice of pork, rum) and they are unkempt. Peso restaurants that have any ambiance and a greater selection of menu items are a rarity and will probably require reservations because they are popular with the Cubans who can't afford to eat in the *divisa* restaurants. In Havana, you can find self-service lunch counters inside peso department stores, but again the offerings are going to be slim. On a display board on the wall behind the counter of these self-service places, pieces of paper with menu items written on them are removed or added as the items are sold out or added throughout the day.

On Cuchillo Street in the *barrio Chino*, there is a stand that sells large servings of take-out, stir-fried rice for a few pesos—about thirty cents.

Everywhere you go—even in the small towns—you will see tiny snack stands operating out of a window of a private house. Everything for sale at these licensed stands must, by law, be homemade. The best things to buy at these stands are freshly baked, personal-size pizzas, stuffed meat or vegetable turnovers, croquettes, and Cuban-style hushpuppies called *frituras*. Items like these cost about six or seven pesos, or about thirty cents when you convert the peso price to dollars. Other things you can buy at the stands are Cuban coffee, juice drinks, yucca crackers, peanut candy bars, and ice cream. In the winter and spring months you can often find a stall with a press that squeezes the juice out of sugarcane. Served chilled, these all-natural juices are delicious.

Some very clean and comfortable peso cafés—many with air-conditioning—are intentionally hidden from tourists for the obvious reason that the government would rather foreigners spend convertible pesos at State-owned establishments. These hidden cafés do not have signs out front and are either tucked between some buildings down a side street or entered through an unmarked door and up a flight of stairs. Have a local take you to one of these places—otherwise you'll probably be charged in convertible pesos at a one-to-one rate of the Cuban peso price.

See the next question below for the name and location of the only vegetarian restaurant in the country (that I know of) that accepts payment in pesos.

4. Do vegetarians have difficulty finding decent meals?
Cubans are obsessed with meat. The fact that they can't get much of it accentuates their obsession. In spite of this, vegetarians will have no problem finding adequate fare if they look in the right places. Peso restaurants aren't going to be much help, but the *divisa* restaurants in tourist areas should be able to offer salads, rice, black beans, and vegetables. Yucca is almost always available in the *divisa* restaurants, and avocado can be either added to the salad or served as a side dish. As mentioned earlier, pizza is available in restaurants and at snack stands, and the Chinese restaurants in Havana offer a wide selection of fried rice dishes and noodles with vegetables. If you're staying at a *casa particular*, the proprietor will probably be happy to prepare you a vegetable and potato stew with red beans, white beans, or chickpeas; corn tamales; a cold pasta salad; deep fried *malanga* hushpuppies; boiled yucca; fried plantain chips or cakes; and the standard rice with black beans.

Watch out for servers who assure you that the black beans or the vegetable soup doesn't have meat when in fact they do, a discovery you'll make after you've taken a few bites and notice small pieces of pork in the dish:

"You said there wasn't any meat in the dish," you complain.

"There isn't," the server retorts.

"Then what's this?" you ask, pointing to the pork pieces.

"That's just for flavor," the server replies, still not comprehending what your fuss is all about.

Try the following places in Havana that offer vegetarian fare:

- Restaurante Biki at Infanta and San Lazaro in Vedado (near the University). This buffet-style place is actually quite good, but don't go at the end of the evening when the food in the chafing pans has dried up. Restaurante Biki is the only peso vegetarian restaurant I have seen in Cuba.

- Café Hanoi at Brasil and Bernaza in Habana Vieja. Not a vegetarian restaurant, but has a fair share of menu items to chose from and offers combination dishes at very affordable prices. You will enjoy the tables in the garden area.

- Restaurante Naturista at Linea and Calle C (Vedado).

- Restaurante El Carmelo de Calzada at Calzada and Calle D (Vedado).

- Restaurante La Terraza Vegetariana at Calle M between 23 and 25 (Vedado).

5. Are there any health issues I should be concerned about?
Visitors to Cuba are not in any more danger of contracting a serious illness or disease than in the U.S. and other developed countries. All the inoculative diseases that plagued the rest of the world prior to the 1960s have been eradicated,[27] and no vaccinations are required to enter, unless you arrive from South America, in which case you need to show proof of a yellow fever inoculation. Your biggest health threats in Cuba are sunburn, upset stomachs reacting to unfamiliar bacteria, food poisoning, dehydration, and diarrhea. All of these can be avoided if you take the right precautions. (See question six, below.) Mosquito-borne illnesses and diseases are not a concern, but it is wise to cover up and use repellent if you venture into the countryside. You will thank yourself if you pack a mosquito net (useful against pesky flies, too), and I never travel without a no-see-um mesh jacket which you can find online.   (Forest City Surplus, Ltd. in Canada sells a nice one for about fourteen dollars. Their website address is www.fcsurplus.com.)

For more information about recommended vaccinations and other health concerns when traveling abroad, contact the Center for Disease Control and Prevention at (877) 394-8747 or their website at www.cdc.gov/travel.

6. You mention taking precautions against upset stomachs, food poisoning, and diarrhea. What are these precautions?
Don't let the following list of precautions frighten you. I chow liberally at restaurants and private homes all over the country without adverse effects.   There's a difference between being

cautious and being paranoid.

- Acclimatize yourself gradually to new foods.

- Be suspicious of the hygienic conditions of non-tourist restaurants (especially the food-cutting surfaces and dishwashing methods).

- Take antiseptic wipes and a dry washcloth to clean drinking glasses, plates, and silverware at questionable restaurants.

- Beware of undercooked meat and seafood items at non-tourist restaurants.

- Don't buy fresh meat at farmers' markets, if it's not refrigerated.

- Avoid food items at snack stands that are not wrapped or refrigerated.

- Check the color and smell for the age of oil used for deep fried foods.

- Don't swim in freshwater rivers downstream from large towns, farms, and cattle grazing fields.

- Read the next question below, about drinking the tap water.

7. Is it safe to drink the tap water?
Although many people will tell you that the tap water is O.K to drink, most Cubans take the precaution of boiling it first. If you don't have the ability to boil the water, I recommend purchasing bottled water or treating the tap water with *Sanosil* or other purification tablets. When you buy bottled water, check to make sure the seal hasn't been broken. Don't put ice made from non-boiled water in your drinks, and watch out for homemade fruit drinks mixed with tap water. Although restaurants and bars in Cuba use ice cubes for alcoholic drinks, ice is almost never served with water, juices, or soft drinks.

At restaurants, uncooked greens and vegetables used in salads probably are rinsed in tap water. There's not much you can do about this. You're just going to have to make a choice between risking a little stomach discomfort or going hungry.

Make sure plates, utensils, and glasses are thoroughly dried after being rinsed.

8. Where should I go if I need a doctor?
In many cities, including Havana, Varadero, Cienfuegos, Trinidad,

Playa Santa Lucia, Guardalavaca, and Santiago de Cuba, there are designated clinics for foreigners (see the appendix on page 250 for addresses) but if you speak some Spanish and don't mind waiting in line, you can visit a clinic (called a *policlinica*) that services the Cubans.   Initial visits at the *policlinicas* are usually free, and prescriptions—if available—are only pennies to the dollar. To find a *policlinica* nearest you, ask any resident in the neighborhood to direct you.

The designated clinics for foreigners—managed by Servimed, a department of the State tourist enterprise Cubanacan Corporation—are staffed with English-speaking nurses and doctors.   A consultation will cost you about twenty-five CUC.

In every neighborhood—as well as at work places, schools, and farming cooperatives—residents can call on the house of a designated community doctor whose main role is not so much treatment as identification of illnesses, medical guidance, and promoting sanitary conditions in the home and in the neighborhood.

Most tourist hotels and resorts have a first-aid nurse on duty.

9. Where should go if I need hospitalization?
Hospitals—both public and foreigner-specialized—are listed in Appendix 26 (page 250) by province.   Servimed oversees a successful medical tourism industry that offers a wide range of surgical procedures and medical treatments at very affordable costs.   These treatments include eye surgery, dentistry, plastic surgery, drug addiction, heart surgery, organ transplants, skin disorders, paralysis, bone deformities, and high blood pressure. The main hospitals that provide these services are in Havana and include the *Hospital Nacional Hermanos Ameijeiras* in Central Havana and the *Clinica Central Cira Garcia* in Miramar.   The facilities in these tourism hospitals are superior to those found in public hospitals, a reality that causes critics of the Cuban government to cry apartheid.   Others argue that the superior care and conditions in tourist hospitals is a perfectly logical genesis of a fundamental law of economics that states that the more one spends, the better the products and services (you get what you pay for)—a fact of life that is far more prevalent in the U.S. and other market-driven societies.   The Cuban government, obviously, can't afford to provide, free of charge, every man, woman, and child the best medical care money can buy—no government on the planet can do that.   It is valid to complain, though, that for complex reasons— some not in its control—the Cuban government fails miserably to guarantee even a minimal standard of health care for its citizens. Conditions at public hospitals can be shockingly primitive.

Note: American film director Michael Moore's recent attempt (in his movie, *Sicko*) to argue that health care in Cuba is just as good as that found in the U.S.—and free to boot—is inaccurate.   The footage shot in the movie depicts top-notch hospital conditions that are an exception in Cuban hospitals, not the norm.

Turn to page 124 for an explanation of some unique hospital protocol and etiquette you can expect if you find yourself a patient at a public hospital in Cuba.

10. Who should I call in a medical emergency?

If you are near a telephone, dial 106 or 116 for the police, and 105 or 115 for the fire department.   The telephone number for an ambulance varies with each city.   In Havana, it is 55-1185. Remember that the operators do not speak English.

If you don't have a telephone—many households in Cuba do not—ask a neighbor where the community phone (*teléfono communitario*) is. A community phone is a telephone in a private residence where the proprietor, as a means of extra income, is in the business of letting people make calls for a fee.

If luck is on your side, and there is a working pay phone nearby, you can dial the operator or the emergency numbers without having to insert money into the slot.

Also, remember that all neighborhoods have a designated community doctor who can be fetched to help.

If you are in a tourist-frequented area, you should be able to find a police officer patrolling the streets.

By nature, Cubans are Good Samaritans, and in an emergency, more often than not, someone has already called for help before you do.

As in the U.S., emergency rooms at all hospitals are open twenty-four hours a day and are available to all foreigners.

If you have a serious medical emergency, the Cuban doctors and/or State authorities may insist on evacuating you, at a major cost to you, to the U.S.

11. Are over-the-counter medicines and prescribed medicines available in Cuba?

Yes, but in very limited quantities. Many Cubans have to get friends and relatives living abroad to send them medications. Even basic over-the-counter drugs such as aspirin-free pain relievers, diaper rash ointments, and anti-fungal creams are next to impossible to find in local pharmacies.   You will have better luck finding medications at the Servimed tourist hospitals, but if they have the medication in stock, be prepared to pay more than what you'd pay for it in the U.S. as the medicine has probably been imported.

12. Is it possible to use my health insurance in Cuba?

Yes, if your health insurance policy has a clause that states that your medical expenses abroad are covered. If your existing plan does not have such a clause, you may be able to purchase supplemental travel insurance from your existing insurance company or from a separate travel insurance company. A list of travel insurance companies and air ambulance services is available on the U.S. State Department website (www.travel.state.gov).

The trade embargo laws forbid U.S.-based travel insurance companies to pay Cuban hospitals for service provided you without OFAC authorization. This means that, in most cases, you'll have to put the money up yourself for any medical bills and be reimbursed by the insurance company when you return home (and after all the fact-checking and authorizations have been completed). Two complications arise in this scenario: First, many people aren't going to have that kind of cash on them to pay up-front for medical treatment. Second, whether you have an OFAC license or not to travel to Cuba, you will violate embargo laws if you pay Cuban hospitals for services rendered without prior OFAC authorization. (Remember, the maximum allowable per diem rate for OFAC-licensed travelers is $188.00.)

There are two solutions to circumvent the aforementioned complications. One way is to purchase travel insurance from a foreign country. If you do buy a policy from a foreign travel insurance company, make sure they will pay the Cuban providers directly rather than reimburse you after you've put the money up yourself.

In any event, Cuban Servimed hospitals usually will require payment up-front[28]. This presents a problem if the medical treatment you need requires immediate attention.

The best solution to all of this is to purchase medical/travel insurance from a Cuban travel insurance company. The cost of the policy—about five dollars per day—keeps you well within your maximum allowable per diem rate if you are traveling with an OFAC license. And payments for any medical treatment you require are made by a Cuban insurance company to a Cuban provider—an arrangement that OFAC doesn't—and can't—prohibit. Details on where and how to buy medical and travel insurance from a Cuban medical insurance company is provided in the appendix on page 255.

Wherever you decide to buy travel insurance, make sure the coverage includes expenses for emergency evacuation by air ambulance. Also, be aware that many U.S.-based and foreign travel insurance companies will not sell you a plan if you don't have an existing health plan, and often the travel insurance company will pay only for expenses above those already covered by your regular insurance company.

Note: There is no case on record in which OFAC has prosecuted U.S. citizens for exceeding the maximum allowable per diem rate when they pay Cuban hospitals for emergency services. If this happens to you, you will be the first.

13. Is there a U.S. consulate office in Cuba where U.S. citizens can go for assistance?
Although diplomatic relations between the U.S. and Cuba were severed in 1961, the U.S. government maintains a consulate office for its citizens through the Swiss embassy in Havana. (The Cuban government has a similar arrangement for its consulate office in Washington, D.C.) U.S. citizens in Cuba who need help with lost passports, legal wrangles, and contacting family members in an emergency can visit the U.S. consulate office (officially known as the U.S. Interest Section, American Citizen Services Unit) on Calzada, between L and M Streets in Vedado (near the seawall). The number to call is (7) 833-3551 through 3559, and the fax number is (7) 833-1084.   Office hours are 8 a.m. to 4:30 p.m. Monday through Thursday and 8 a.m. to 3:30 p.m. on Friday. For emergency assistance after hours, call the duty officer at (7) 833-3026.

If you have traveled to Cuba illegally and need consular assistance, DO contact the U.S. Interest Section—the American staff there has gone to great lengths to assure their fellow citizens that it is not the consulate's standard procedure to report blockade runners to the OFAC authorities back home. U.S. citizens visiting the Interest Section will not be asked to show their OFAC licenses.

14. Are there any tourist information offices in Cuba that I can visit?
Yes, but they are generally confined to the three largest tourist-friendly cities of Havana, Varadero, and Santiago de Cuba. In these and other cities, many of the main tourist hotels have a tourist information desk in the lobby.

Havana

- HAVANATUR—Travel agency: Books flights, accommodations, rental cars, and tours. Calle 2 No. 17, between Avenida No. 1 and No. 2. (in Miramar) Tel (7) 33-2273, (7) 33-2877.

- ASISTUR—A reservations office, tourist information office, and a visitor assistance office to help visitors resolve problems and emergencies they may encounter during their stay. Prado 254, Habana Vieja, Tel (7) 62-5519, (7) 63-8284, (7) 33-8527; fax, (7) 33-8087.

- INFOTUR—In Old Havana at 521 Obispo or at the cruise terminal on Avenida del Puerto. Also at Jose Marti airport. Sells maps, guides, and books and can help you rent a car or find lodging.

- CUBATUR—Specializes in group and private tours. Calle F No. 157 between Calle 9 and Calzada (in Vedado) Tel (7) 33-4155, (7) 33-3529.

- POTOTO TOURIST SERVICES—Personalized assistance from a dependable fellow who can help you find a *casa particular*, a driver, one-on-one guided tours, and answer your questions.   Tel (7) 870-6359.   He is featured in www.cuba-junky.com.

- CUBA LINDA—Travel agency operated by former CIA agent Phillip Agee. Tel: (7) 553-686; fax: (7) 553-980. Also on the web: www.cubalinda.com.

Santiago de Cuba

- INFOTUR—Calle Heredia, at the corner of Calle San Pedro (Plaza de la Catedral). Tel (22) 2-2222

Varadero

- CENTRO DE INFORMACION TURISTICA—Avenida Primera on the corner of Calle 23. Tel (45) 66-6666, (45) 66-7060.

- CUBATUR—Calle 38 between Avenida Primera and Playa, Tel (45) 6-4143.

- HABANATUR VARADERO—Avenida Playa No. 3606, between Calle 36 and Calle 37.

15. What advice can you give me about traveling to Cuba with children?
Given the stories one hears about the repression, communism, the disaffected masses, the poverty, and the U.S. illicitness of travel to Cuba, it is understandable that parents may have reservations about taking their kids into the country. The truth is, in terms of crime and physical injury, it is more dangerous to walk with your child in a U.S. or Mexican street than a Cuban one. Even traditionally tourist-friendly nations, such as Great Britain and France, consistently rank in the top ten worst countries for per capita violent crime, such as assault, murder, and rape, while Cuba doesn't even break the top fifty.

As mentioned many times throughout this manual, the Cuban people are very social and maintain an intimate, communal sense of belonging and unity on a national level as well as in their immediate neighborhoods.   Cuban children often wander by themselves through the streets—even in the big cities—because their parents are not gripped by the alienation and distrust of strangers common in other cultures.

That ubiquitous entity known as *el Estado*, through its efforts in education, nutrition, and physical health, even if tainted with political bias, also understands and appreciates the value of its youth.   Clear evidence of this can be seen in the fact that street children— prevalent in many other Latin American countries—are non-existent in Cuba.

After school and on weekends, the neighborhood streets are crammed with kids playing stickball, shooting marbles, and jumping hopscotch squares.   In the parks, especially near the larger farmers'markets, children ride carts pulled by goats and miniature horses.   Impromptu appearances by a silly clown are common, and in every town—on a certain day, at a certain time—puppet theaters, story-telling, and other forms of entertainment are organized by staff members of community "cultural" departments.

Havana itself is an endless playground for children of all ages. Ice cream, drink, and snack stands beckon on every block.   In the summer, the older kids swim in holes cut into the rocks off the seawall, and shirtless little boys race homemade scooters up and down the Prado.   Shopping districts such as Calle Obispo in Old Havana, Calle San Rafael in Centro Habana, and the arts and craft booths near the *Catedral* are great places to stroll.   The excellent beaches east of the city are only twenty minutes away.   A full day can be spent at the national zoo where tour buses venture into safari-like animal reserves.   And a visit to the national aquarium will delight young marine fans who can get up close and personal with sea turtles and watch trainers frolic with sea lions.

If you travel to Cuba with an infant, keep in mind that you will have difficulty finding decent baby items in stores.   This includes disposable and cloth diapers, baby dishware and utensils, diaper rash cream, and baby shoes and clothes.

Finally, it will facilitate entry and departure processing if you take copies of your child's birth certificate or adoption papers showing that you are the legal parent or guardian (or a letter granting you permission from the parents or guardians to travel with the child).   If a child is traveling with only one parent, a letter of permission for the child's travel from the absent parent is recommended.

16. Please tell me about using telephones in Cuba.

Telephone service in Cuba is overseen by *Etecsa*, a joint venture of the Cuban government's Ministry of Information and Communication and the Italian phone company *Telecom Italia*.   *Etecsa* has made great strides upgrading and modernizing Cuba's previously primitive telecommunications service, but a little patience might still be required (for those accustomed to the high level of phone efficiency and technology found in the U.S.) when trying to place local, long distance, or international calls within, to, or from Cuba.

Public pay phones. You will find two types of pay phones on the streets (note: many will be out of order): Phone booths that are equipped with readers for phone cards and only accept convertible pesos, and phone booths that only accept Cuban peso coins. For obvious reasons, convertible peso phone booths are more prevalent in tourist areas, and peso phone booths are more prevalent in residential areas. Sometimes, you will see one of each located side-by-side. While it might be more convenient to use the convertible peso telephone booth, it is always cheaper to place calls from a Cuban peso phone. When using coins for a coin-operated Cuban peso phone booth (harder to find because they are being phased out), listen for the continuous tone before inserting your money. If you don't hear a continuous tone, the phone is out of order. A screen will display the words "*inserte moneda.*" After you insert the coin, the screen will tell you to dial the number ("*marque numero*"), and as the call is put through, you will see a series of dots travel across the screen. When the person at the other end of the line answers, a visual countdown of the monetary balance will begin (indicated by the word "*credito*" on the screen), and you need to insert additional coins before the countdown reaches zero. You will not receive any change for unused portions of the balance, so don't insert more coins than you need for the call. If you have a balance remaining after you've ended the call and you want to make another call, do not hang up. Press the button marked "R." The screen will tell you to "*marque numero*" again. If you have a balance remaining after you are finished making calls and you see another person waiting in line to use the same phone, it is standard practice to hand the telephone to that person rather than hang up. It's a nice touch in Cuban etiquette and further demonstrates the national climate of sharing which is so common in the country. Note: The mimimum coin denomination that you can use to initiate a call is twenty centavos. Any denomination can be used to add more minutes. Also—and this will confound the hell out of you if you're not aware of this ironic quirk—the one-peso coins with Jose Marti's likeness will not work to initiate calls. Only the one-peso coin with the star works.

Magnetic phone cards for public pay phones that are outfitted with card readers can be purchased at State phone centers (described below), the main post offices, and some of the tourist information centers explained in question number fourteen in this Section. If you are in Old Havana, you can stop by the *Etecsa* office in the *Lonja de Comercio* building off the Plaza de San Francisco.

- **Directory Assistance:** Dial 113.
- **Operator assistance:** Dial 110.
- **International operator assistance:** Dial 09.
- **Making local calls:** It is not necessary to dial the city code.
- **Making long distance calls within the country:** You must dial "0," followed by the city code. (City codes are listed in Appendix 28 on page 256.)
- **Making international calls from Cuba:** Dial 119 from pay phones, wait for the tone, and then dial the country code, the city area code, and the local number.   (The country code for the U.S. is "1.") From a hotel phone, you need to dial 88 instead of 119, followed by the country code, the city code, and the local number.
- **Collect calls:** Can only be made from residential phones. Dial 661212.

State-operated telephone centers: Just about every municipality in Cuba has a State-run telephone center or office where people can go in person to place calls through a real live operator.   These peso telephone centers are officially known as *Telepuntos* or *Servicio Telefonico (Nacional* or *Internacional* or both), but most Cubans call the centers a *centro de telefono del Estado* or a *centro de llamada*. Some of these telephone centers are small shacks or booths crowding a sidewalk, and some of the centers occupy storefronts or actual offices in a building. Also, you will find a telephone center in main post offices. All of the State-operated telephone centers are capable of placing long distance calls within Cuba, but not all of them will be able to place international calls. The phone clerk will put the call through, and then inform you of the charges after you end the call. Payment is usually made in pesos.

Residential phones: Private telephones in residences are still the exception rather than the norm in Cuba, but just about everyone has a friend or a relative who has one.   All *casas particulares* licensed to rent rooms to foreigners will have a phone. This is not only good business sense, it is also one of the considerations when housing inspectors grant rental licenses.   Homeowners pay a monthly flat rate for the line and are billed by the minute for long distance and international calls. When you make a long distance call from a residential phone, you need to dial zero first so that an operator can inform the homeowner how much he or she was billed for the call. Here's a neat trick: To see if the ringer on a residential telephone is working properly, dial 110, and then hang up.

Community Telephones (*Telefono communitario*): These telephones are essentially residential telephones described above, but the homeowner, as a means of extra income, lets people place and receive calls for a small fee. The cost of the call is determined as described above—by dialing zero first and requesting the total charges from the operator. There is no charge to receive a call at a community telephone. Community telephones are not only convenient (and necessary in emergencies), they are yet another tie in the communal bond of the Cuban people; the community telephone concept forces neighbors to share, to help each other, and to go to each other's houses. Owners of the community phones are constantly running down the street to fetch a neighbor who is receiving a call.

Hotel Phones: Only the best hotels have phones in each room, but all hotels can place calls for you from the front desk or a telephone located in the lobby. Usually, the receptionist or hotel operator will obtain a line for you from the staff phone, and then transfer the open line to a separate telephone nearby where you can dial the telephone number yourself. Confirm the rate per minute before you ask the receptionist to place the call or give you an open line.

Telephone Area Codes for Cuban cities: These are one to three digit numbers that precede the local number. See appendix 28 on page 256 for a complete listing of these city codes.

Calling Cuba from the U.S.: Dial the international access code (011), the country code for Cuba (53), the city code, and the local number. Getting through to Cuba from the U.S. (and vice-versa) is more difficult than getting a line through to other countries because toll remittances by U.S. phone companies to Cuban-based telephone companies are restricted by the trade embargo.

17. Can I use a cell phone while I am in Cuba?
You can, but if you have cellular service with a U.S. company, you're going to have to rent a cell phone or buy a new simcard and sign up for a short-term subscription with *Cubacel* (telephone 80-2222 in Havana, Calle 28 No. 510 bewteen Avenida 5 and 7). Simcards are expensive in Cuba (80 to 120 CUC) and minutes cost somewhere around .40 CUC each. International calls from your cell phone in Cuba will set you back three to five CUC per minute. Some cell phones and plans offered by other companies in countries such as Canada and Italy do work in Cuba, but the range, speed, and features vary depending on what area of Cuba in which you send or receive calls. I have heard that Canadian-based Rogers cell phones used in Cuba can send and receive text messages to Rogers cell phones in Florida. Dial 05 before dialing the number when calling a cell phone within the Cuban borders.

18.   Where can I mail letters and packages?   Is there postal service between Cuba and the U.S.?
All cities have a main post office located in or near the city center. Some of the large tourist hotels also have a post office where you can buy stamps and mail letters and packages, but the rates in these hotel post offices will be in convertible pesos.

Satellite peso post offices are also scattered around town, but their services will be basic. You can drop letters and postcards in mailboxes on the streets. Letters will reach their destinations— domestic or international—but expect the delivery times to be a lot slower than you're used to in the U.S. If a letter is urgent or important, you might want to consider sending a fax instead. Assume that any mail you send can and will be opened by Ministry of Interior agents looking for information and activity that is illegal or a threat to national security.

And, yes, the Cuban and U.S. postal services will deliver any mail sent or received between the two countries, but there are many restrictions.   The U.S. Postal Service will not send packages weighing more than four pounds, and even then, the contents are usually limited to books and informational material. In conformance with trade embargo laws, you cannot send valuable items, dutiable articles, or money in any form without OFAC or Commerce Department approval.   Also, for some odd reason, musical letters or cards that play a sound recording are not permitted. If you want to send something other than paper items from the U.S., you'll have better luck stuffing an International Priority Mail Flat Rate Mailing Envelope. Private courier services operating out of both countries are a good option for sending large packages, but the fees are stiff. You can send and receive packages to or from Cuba via a third country if you can find someone to re-stamp and forward the packages. If you need speed for your mail going out of Cuba, the international courier company DHL Express has drop-off locations in many Cuban cities. Mail handled by DHL Express is sent to the U.S. via daily flights to Mexico. Also, try Cubanacan Express in Havana at Avenida 5 #8210 between Calle 8 and 84. (Tel: (7) 204-1578).

19. Where can I send or receive a fax message? At most hotels, some of the telephone centers described above, and many of the tourist information and assistance offices listed in question number fourteen in this Section (Asistur, in particular).

20. Is Internet readily available in Cuba?
Yes, but out of reach for many Cubans because of the cost involved compared to their very meager salaries. The price of computers and monthly Internet plans are on par with U.S. prices, a roadblock

for many Cuban people who make the average income of less than twenty dollars (when converted from pesos) per month. Many Cubans send and receive e-mails via their computers at work, but this tactic is usually against company policy and can get them in trouble.

If you have Internet provider software installed on your computer (i.e., Yahoo e-mail), you can purchase pay-as-you-go Internet cards from *Etecsa*, and then plug into a residential line and Internet away. Otherwise, you can use the computers at most hotels and any of the limited number of Internet cafes located in major tourist areas. The pay-as-you-go Internet cards are available at *Etecsa* offices, some of the large tourist hotels, and select tourist information centers such as Infotur.

Note: Homeowners who do not already use the Internet may be nervous about letting you use their phone lines to access the Internet for extended periods of time because they know telephone surveillance technology can quickly determine somebody in the house is using the Internet. This is an issue because Internet usage in private homes must be authorized.

Again, be careful what sites you log on to and what information you send over the web while you are in Cuba, as Internet users are monitored by government agents. (Messages sent through the service provider network are scanned by surveillance software for certain trigger words.)

You may suffer slow service and connection problems while browsing on the web because Cuba uses satellite technology instead of fiber optics to transmit Internet signals. A fiber optic line is being laid currently from Venezuela, and when it is completed in the next couple of years, Internet connections and speed will improve.

21. Is it possible to use my wireless Internet service while I am in Cuba?
Not as you travel around the country, but a few select hotels such as the *Melia Cohiba* and the *Saratoga* in Havana offer the service. Ongoing upgrades in technology and the recent loosening of restrictions on Internet and computer usage no doubt will expand wireless accessibility with every passing month. Log on to the *Etecsa* website at www.etecsa.cu and check for updates.

22. What are the business hours in Cuba?

Shopping: In general, 9:30 a.m. to 5 p.m., Monday through Saturday, but many shops stay open later. Some shops close for a siesta break from 12:30 p.m. to 2 p.m. Often, shops will close every other Saturday.

- Government offices: 8:30 a.m. to 5:30 p.m., Monday through Friday. (Many government offices close for lunch from 12:30 p.m. to 1:30 p.m. Some offices are open on Saturday.)

- Post Offices: 8 a.m. to 6 p.m., Monday through Saturday. (Some of the main branches stay open until 10 p.m.)

- Pharmacies: 8 a.m. to 8 p.m. (Certain pharmacies take turns staying open twenty-four hours)

- Banks and currency exchange offices: 8:30 a.m. to 3 p.m., Monday through Friday (with lunch from noon to 1:30 p.m.) and Saturday from 8 a.m. to 10 a.m.

- Museums: In general, 9 a.m to 5 p.m., Tuesday through Saturday and 8 a.m. to noon on Sunday.

- Tourist offices at hotels: 8 a.m to 8 p.m. daily.

23. Where can I find a bank and a currency exchange office?
Question number eleven on page 60 discusses banks and currency exchange offices in Cuba.

24. Can money be wired to and from Cuba?
As discussed in Section 6 (question number twenty-one), U.S. trade embargo laws restrict remittances to Cuba from the U.S. However, wiring money to Cuba from other countries (through banks or through money wiring companies, such as Western Union) and vice versa is easy, but U.S. citizens are still subject to the trade embargo laws even if they are not physically in the U.S. More information about wiring money to Cuba is provided on page 64 (question number twenty-one) in Section 6.

25. Where can I do my laundry, or arrange to have it done?
It may surprise you to learn that there are no Laundromats in Cuba. Cubans wash all their clothes at home (often by hand) or pay individuals who operate personal laundering services to wash their clothes for them. Wherever you stay, it is almost a guarantee that the homeowner or proprietor will be able to make the arrangements to have your clothes laundered. Also, you can take your dirty clothes to a hotel laundry service. Rates are usually per article of clothing and are shockingly expensive by Cuban standards.
    One well known, privately owned laundering service in Old Havana is Lavanderia El Guillermo at Maximo Gomez No. 521 between San Nicolas and Indio (07-863-7585).

26. Where can I get photos developed?

In the cities, a chain of photo shops called Photo Service offers film and digital developing services and a very little in the way of camera equipment and supplies. I think there are only two or three of these shops in the entire city of Havana (population, two million), an indication that few Cubans can afford the convertible pesos prices of film developing. The few Photo Service shops that exist can't do much more than print four-by-sixes.

27. Will I need any electrical converters or adapters to plug in my laptop, battery charger, and other electrical appliances I take with me?

No, as voltage (110 volts) and plug styles are the same as in the U.S.   Some hotels in Cuba have a 220-volt outlet for air conditioners, so make sure you don't plug any of your appliances into it or the appliance will burn out. Outlets in Cuba do not have a third prong for the ground, so take a three-prong-to-two-prong adapter if any of your appliances have a three-prong plug. Also, take a surge protector if you take a laptop with you—power outages are common, and many houses are outfitted with limited outlets and breakers, causing overloads on circuits.

28. Is it possible to use a hotel swimming pool even if I don't have a room at the hotel?

Yes, most hotels will let you—and your Cuban friends—use their pool, but you will have to pay for a pass. The pass can cost anywhere from three to twenty CUC and often includes meals and/or drinks. The following is a list of hotels in Havana that offer pool passes:

- **Hotel Nacional**, Calle O y 23, Vedado.   Fifteen CUC, includes 15 CUC worth of food and drinks.   Great food, lovely setting with views of the Straits.

- **Hotel Riviera**, Malecon y Paseo. Three CUC.

- **Hotel Kohly**, Avenida 49 y 36A, Playa. Quiet location with an affordable snack bar, bowling, and gym.

- **Hotel Sevilla**, Trocadero #55, Habana Vieja. Twenty CUC includes food and drinks. You might be able to get in for five CUC without the food part.

- **Hotel Deauville**, Avenida de Italia y Malecon. Eight CUC.

- **Marina Hemingway**, Avenida 5ta y Calle 248, Santa Fe.

Twelve CUC, but might be waived if you can convince the guard at the gate that you are entering to eat at one of the restaurants.

- The **Hotel St. John's** (Calle O #206, Vedado) and **Hotel Vedado** (Calle O #244 between 23 and 25, Vedado) also sells pool passes but the fees are not known.

SECTION 9

TACKLING SOME VERY SENSITIVE POLITICAL QUESTIONS

1. Do the Cuban people support their government?
Without question, the 1959 Revolution was a popular one because of its promise of social justice and independence from foreign domination. In the years following Fidel Castro's triumphant march into the capital, the new socialist government chalked up impressive gains in education, health care, housing, land appropriation, and employment. Millions of Cubans living in abject poverty were pulled out of their pits of despair and given the same rights and opportunities enjoyed by those in the middle and upper classes.

Fifty years later, most unbiased political analysts—and the Cuban people themselves—say that the Revolution is in ruins. It bears little resemblance to its former glory, and its major accomplishments have taken a backward dive. Serious shortfalls plague the main pillars of social welfare upon which the Revolution stands—or stood. Outsiders who are able to spend time with Cuban friends and families will uncover widespread disillusionment and bitterness with the government and its leaders. In private—never in public—your average Cuban mutters words of helplessness and frustration that they are not free to choose their own destiny. They feel bound by the strict laws and ideological principles that socialism demands. The rebellious youth shout their discontent in lyrics of rock songs and bent old men in their shanties curse Fidel and Raul under hot, tobacco-and-coffee-flavored breath.   There is never enough to eat, they say.   The State salaries don't cover basic needs. Houses are falling apart and lack plumbing. The hospitals lack medicine and basic equipment. They are tired, they say, of sacrificing themselves and their personal freedoms for an ideology that, despite its good intentions, has failed to deliver.

A communist sympathizer will tell you differently.   But a sympathizer's support for the current system seems biased for a few reasons. For one, people who pledge themselves to the socialist or communist cause are given preference when it comes to selecting candidates for study and jobs in their field of choice. For another, communist sympathizers are more likely to obtain bonus rewards for their dedication, rewards such as nicer homes, cars and travel privileges. These bonuses substantially improve their quality of life and standard of living. Naturally they are going to say the system works—for them.

As for the other ninety-two percent of the population, they trudge on, hoping that things will improve or somehow take a different tack. Most feel powerless to fight for change for fear of being branded an enemy of the State or losing State-doled benefits that are already inadequate. Those who don't want to wait around yet another decade for things to get better look for ways to leave. I can't tell you how many times people approach me asking me to help them find a way to get out. They explore all possible routes: sponsorship for travel visas, marriage, help with migration paperwork, even illegal flight. Many take the ultimate risk by building rafts and other floating contraptions and set out across the Florida Straits.

2. Is Castro hated in Cuba or is he a hero?
In the early years of the Cuban Revolution, Fidel Castro was the embodiment of a savior to the great majority of the Cuban population. He was not just a hero, he was a living legend who, against insurmountable odds, kicked out a corrupt dictator (Batista) who was buoyed by big American business and the mafia. On the follow-through of his victory, Castro toiled tirelessly to keep his country on a sovereign path and improve the lives of his people. But Castro lost the broad support of his country when he turned to harsh methods to further—or protect—his dream of an ideal society that he tried to build using the blueprint of Karl Marx's theories of socialism. He banned free press and political plurality, illegalized free enterprise, and ditched the constitutional checks and balances of an independent judicial system. In spite of his brilliant leadership skills, he made some horrible blunders like illegally expropriating American businesses operating in Cuba, selling his country's soul to communism without a referendum, dangerously over-depending on Russian trade and subsidies, and allowing a lack of diversity in the Cuban economy. Today, most of the Cuban people I meet tell me that the years of sacrificing themselves and their basic rights and freedoms has not been worth it. In contrast to the early years of the 1959 Cuban Revolution, Castro supporters now appear to be a very small minority of the population. The short answer to the question above is that Castro is a hero in some ways and a villain in others.

3. Are most Cubans members of the communist party?
It is estimated that there are about 500,000 to 800,000 Party members, or less than eight percent of the population. It must be

noted that many Cubans declare their allegiance to the Party not because they agree with the ideology but to obtain perks (job promotions, travel outside the country, houses, cars) that improve their quality of life.

4. Is the Socialist Revolution working?

Just days after Castro and his revolutionaries took control over the fiscal and political operations of the country, drastic, bold, and innovative social programs in housing, health care and education were carried out. These dramatic new programs erased almost overnight the broad gap of inequity between the poor and the wealthy few that existed under the previous democratic, albeit corrupt, governments. Rents were reduced fifty percent across the board.   Electricity rates were cut.   Racial discrimination was abolished. In the cities, most schools were temporarily shut down so that students and teachers could travel to the rural areas to teach the illiterate how to read and write. Hospitals and clinics were built where previously there were none, and all medical graduates were required to complete two-year internships in the countryside.

  Things were looking up. The advances for the country as a whole seemed worth the sacrifices in individual rights and freedoms that socialist ideology asks of its constituents. In particular, Cubans were giddy with their first true taste of independence in the nation's history. If the old system had to be tossed out the window and replaced with a brand new one—even if it carried the label of socialism—most seemed willing to go with it.

  Unfortunately, a domino sequence of events in the late Eighties and early Nineties wiped away almost all of the fantastic gains of the Revolution and left it smoldering in a deflated heap.   Internal corruption and a subsequent purge of government and military followed a sharp turn toward orthodox communism. Then, in 1989, communism in eastern Europe collapsed completely and the Soviet Union, Cuba's main trading partner, was forced to cut subsidies and much of its trade with the country. Cuba plunged into the darkest depression in its history and Castro was forced to allow emergency social, economic and political measures that knocked the nation off its socialist course toward his nemeses of capitalism, the U.S. dollar, (limited) private enterprise, the corruptive element of tourism, and foreign investment. The economy improved, but the measures brought back many of the capitalist symptoms that the communist party and the socialist government had labored forty years to eliminate. Class differences re-emerged in Cuban social circles. Inequities in wealth returned. Conditions of apartheid took hold in tourist-only beaches and hotels.   Prostitution became rampant again.   And taxation, absent since 1963, was imposed on businesses and salaries utilizing the dollar currency.

  Castro has always said that Cuban socialism is unique, a work in progress, subject to change and adjustments according to the needs of the State and the orders of the Party. Fundamental socialist tenets, however, have never been up for negotiation. In the end, though, regardless what political brand name the Cuban government gives itself, if the success of the Cuban Revolution is measured by its ability to provide its people with a minimum standard in the areas of housing, education, employment and health care, most Cubans (if they were free to speak their minds) would probably tell you that the Revolution has failed them.

5. The U.S. government maintains that Cuba is a totalitarian police state that relies on repressive methods to maintain control[29], and the U.S. media frequently run stories detailing the Cuban government's consistent track record of human and political rights abuse. Most of the Cuban people who have fled the country back this up. Is all of this true?
Most Americans[30] would be appalled if they had to subsist within the constraints of some of the harsh laws that the Cuban people must tolerate on a daily basis. The Cuban Constitution lacks many of the basic rights afforded Americans in their own constitution.   Other rights in Cuba (free speech, due process, the right to assemble) are frequently curtailed, blatantly violated and even subject to nullification[31]. When I am in Cuba, I often witness or encounter the repression in action and it makes my blood boil. Blatant censorship and misinformation in the State-controlled television and newspapers is a daily ritual. I couldn't believe my ears one evening when I heard a Cuban doctor being interviewed on TV about his humanitarian assistance to a poor region in Nicaragua say that with all of its millions of dollars, "The United States does nothing for the Nicaraguan people." Another example: During the Elian Gonzalez incident, the Cuban media frequently ran photos of a sad-faced boy peering through what looked like prison bars but were really the bars of a fence enclosing the yard of a house. And all sorts of bad things were said about Elian's custodial relatives in the U.S. Castro himself went on national TV and said that Elian's great uncle had a criminal record and was a child molester.

Proponents of the socialist Revolution (and there are many of them) justify the constraints on personal freedoms as a necessary trade-off for independence from imperialist enemies and to protect the socialist gains (free medical care and education, guaranteed housing and work) of the Revolution. In addition, they say, a true socialist society requires that the rights and needs of the individual take a back seat to those of society as a whole.

There are no death squads in Cuba that come in the night and yank suspected counter-revolutionaries out of bed, and people are not carted off to Siberia for challenging the authority.   The repercussions for speaking out against the system, or even for indifference or non-participation in Revolutionary politics, are more subtle but equally effective: Rations are suspended, jobs are lost, promotions are blocked and benefits are denied.   Local Rapid Response Brigades are mobilized to picket in front of a rabble–rouser's house, and the children of the offending parents are ridiculed by their teachers at school.

6. Are the Cuban people free to express their political opinions that differ with the opinions of the current party in power without fear of retaliation? They are not.   Actual laws in the Criminal Code of Cuba forbid disrespecting, insulting or offending (with the spoken word or in writing) "the dignity of an authority or a political, social or institutional organization of the Republic[32]." Another law criminalizes any "appearance of support for U.S. policies against Cuba[33]." Many Cuban human rights activists are in jail today for daring to criticize the government or its policies.

A staunch communist I met in an Havana park defended the restrictions of free speech because it prevents opponents of the Revolution from saying "false things." People have the right to say whatever they want, he insisted, "as long as it's in their own house."

But even in their own homes, Cubans who voice their dissent talk in low voices and glance furtively over their shoulders as if the walls had ears.

7. Is there a freedom of press in Cuba?
All television production, radio transmissions and newspaper publication in Cuba is tightly controlled by the government. Private ownership of press, radio, television and other means of communication is prohibited by law[34].   The persecution and imprisonment of independent journalists in the country is probably the most publicized and visible form of the repression taking place today. The journalists are jailed on bogus or trumped-up charges such as "sedition," "subversion," "disseminating enemy propaganda," "the spreading of material of a subversive character," "attempting to destabilize the country" and "attempting to destroy the State." Prison sentences are lengthy—up to twenty-eight years. If a defiant, independent journalist somehow eludes jail, he or she must put up with daily threats to their lives, intense surveillance by State security, harassment by police-led mobs, and denial of basic needs and services (such as rations and health care).   Denial of these needs forces the independent journalist to depend on support from outside the country, often from sources in the United States. This provides the Cuban government with a justification to charge the independent journalists with other crimes like treason and aiding and abetting the enemy.

8. Is there freedom of religion in Cuba?

Shortly after the triumph of the Revolution in 1959, Castro's regime took measures to neutralize organized religion's power and influence in the country. These measures include the expulsion of Roman Catholic priests, the confiscation of all property held by the church, and the transfer of control of all schools associated with a church to the government. This was essentially a strategic maneuver to stifle dissent and reactionary opposition within the church's membership (many of whom belonged to the wealthy upper class and had the most to lose) to Castro's new government. In addition, the Roman Catholic Church's leaders vehemently objected to many of the drastic socio-political changes that stripped it of its power and redistributed its wealth. Church services were never prohibited, however, and everyone is still free to practice the faith of their choice.

Pope John Paul II's visit to Cuba in 1998—which turned into a tongue-lashing for Castro and a spiritual boost for many Cubans—resulted in an increase in the State's tolerance for religion in general and a subsequent increase in the number of church-goers. Still, Churches are not permitted to preach in public and operate schools, but many Cuban people say that they are not aware of any persecution or repression of the church leadership or their members. I personally know many Cuban people who attend church on a regular basis and they all tell me they are happy with the way things are progressing in terms of their right and freedom to practice their faith.

9. Do the Cuban people have the right to assemble peacefully and petition their government for a redress of grievances?

Like the independent journalists who dare to print the truth about the injustices of their government, many human rights activists in Cuba are arrested, harassed and sentenced to lengthy jail terms for demonstrating peacefully, participating in meetings to discuss government injustices, and petitioning the government for change. Activists are charged with violating laws in the criminal codes of Cuba that forbid acts that are in contradiction "with the norms of the socialist morality[35]," are "contrary to the goals of the socialist State," "socialist legality," "the people's decision to build socialism and communism[36]," and demonstrate "collaboration in the ideological war against our homeland[37]." Unions, civil and professional organizations, and human rights groups that operate outside the sphere of government-controlled organizations are denied legal status.

Although Cuba is a member of the United Nations and is a signatory to the United Nations Universal Declaration of Human Rights, many international human rights organizations condemn the Cuban government annually for not abiding by the rights and freedoms outlined in the Declaration.

In late 2007, the Cuban government agreed to set a timetable to sign two U.N. covenants that would hold them to a number of important civil and economic rights and allow regular visits by the U.N. Human Rights Council.   This is good news for human rights in Cuba, but many critics are unimpressed and predict that the Cuban government will continue its track record of saying one thing and doing another. In addition, the critics say, the effectiveness of the accords is diluted because Cuban authorities, by the terms of previous U.N. covenants, will still have the right to question a monitor's credentials and refuse them entry.

10. Is there political plurality?
Only one political party in Cuba is given a license to wield legislative and executive authority within the political framework of the country, and that is the Cuban Communist Party. Other political parties are forbidden to organize. Anyone affiliated with a political party other than the Communist Party is considered a counter-revolutionary and will be prosecuted (in a communist judicial system). Cuba's current constitution establishes the Cuban Communist Party as the "highest guiding force of the society and the State."   Other laws in the Criminal Codes of Cuba nullify the rights and freedoms guaranteed in the Constitution if they are contrary to "the people's decision to build socialism and communism[38]."

11. Do you see signs of racial inequality and injustice in Cuba?
Cuba is one of the most racially integrated countries I have ever visited. In the neighborhoods, at the markets and on the job, the coexistence of the races seems natural, not even an issue. From what I see, the Cuban people display nothing but respect and consideration for each other regardless of their skin color or heritage. In Cuba there are no race riots, organized "black power" protests or "black" areas of town that exist in many other countries, including the United States and other so-called free and developed nations.

Certainly, Cuba's ugly history of racial injustice and prejudice parallels that of the rest of the white man's world in the United States and Europe, but the Cuban people seem to have been able to shake the racial demons of the past much more quickly, more effectively, and more completely than other nations struggling with racial divides.

Many experts on racial issues contend that Cuba has been able to eliminate or reduce racial injustice quicker and with less strife than other countries due to a number of factors. These include: The high rate of intermarriage between Hispanics and blacks; a steady increase in the proportion of blacks and mulattos in the overall population (officially 1/3, some say fifty percent); a lengthy history of integration of black cultural traditions (including music, lore and art) into Cuban society; and drastic changes in the socio-economic structure of the country that are rooted in fundamental socialist principles of social rights, classlessness and the equal distribution of property and wealth. Prior to the 1959 Revolution, black people and people of color in general were relegated to the bottom end of the socio-economic ladder; they worked the menial jobs; they lived in the worst neighborhoods; they lacked decent housing; they did not have access to private schools as did thirty-percent of the white kids at the time (public schools suffered for lack of funds and staff); and they were more likely to be illiterate and unemployed. All the social rights guaranteed by the Cuban Revolution—in education, housing, employment and medical care—almost instantly pulled them out of their economic hole and brought them at least closer to par with the rest of the population.

Still, many experts on racial issues say Cuban society is not the utopia of racial equality that some, including Castro himself, claim. Symptoms of discrimination and racial injustice persist. Some of these symptoms surfaced after the limited free-enterprise measures to resuscitate the economy were implemented in the Nineties, and some of the symptoms linger from the past. For example, there is compelling evidence that white or light-skinned people are frequently chosen over black-skinned people to work in the more visible positions in hotels and tourist areas. These positions are more in demand and usually more lucrative because of a more comfortable work environment and contacts with foreigners who donate needed items and tip in hard currency that is worth far more than their own country's peso. Other claims of racial discrimination include: Black men who approach foreigners on the street seem to be detained and questioned by the police more often than white men; a disproportionate number of blacks sit in Cuban jails; there is a less-than-equal representation of people of color in high levels of government; many of the older Cuban whites have a negative attitude toward inter-racial marriage; and the Cuban government is unwilling to acknowledge that these symptoms of discrimination and racial injustice exist or the government is not doing enough to promote needed public debate on these issues.

For me, personally, when I travel to Cuba I don't see black, white or mulatto; I see Cuban.

12. What is the state of women's rights in Cuba?

The Cuban government and its lawmakers have labored tirelessly to guarantee equal rights and active participation and representation for women in society including in politics, the workforce, education and social programs. Articles in the Cuban Constitution demand that women have the same opportunities as men "in order to achieve full participation in the development of the country." Statistics indicate that the legislation is not just so many words:

Women in Cuba constitute sixty-two percent of university students; sixty-one percent of attorneys; forty-nine percent of judges; forty-seven percent of Supreme Court judges; and thirty-five percent of parliamentary seats in the Cuban National Assembly, a percentage that places Cuba sixth out of 162 countries as far as government representation is concerned.

Other Cuban laws provide for special needs and rights of the nation's women including abortion (free), maternity leave (one year with full pay) and family codes that require equal participation and rights of the husband and wife in family and home life.

As in most societies, some double standards exist within the dynamics of the personal relationship of many (but by no means all) Cuban couples. These double standards, which favor the men, are rooted deeply in old attitudes of machismo and include extramarital affairs (O.K. for the guys, taboo for the women) and the wife carrying more of the load in cooking, childcare and housework (on top of holding down full-time jobs).

13. What is the government and general social attitude toward homosexuality?

Legislative protection and general social tolerance for homosexuality in Cuba was nonexistent until the decade of the Nineties—way behind the times compared to the changes in policies and attitudes regarding homosexuality and same-sex relationships in the U.S. and other nations.

But Cuba seems to be catching up. Today, the climate toward gays, lesbians, bisexuals, and transgender people in Cuba today is pretty much what one would find in any civilized, politically-correct nation. Consensual sex between people of the same gender over age sixteen has been legal in Cuba since 1992. Same-sex marriages or spousal relationships, however, are not recognized in any court, and there are very few gay clubs or beaches. (Gay organizations are forbidden, as are gay magazines.) In many cities, specific areas of town—such as section of a seawall or the corner of a park—are known gathering places for gay people. In Havana, the gay hangout is on the Malecon and La Rampa. Also common are regularly scheduled gatherings at private homes (known as '*fiestas de diez pesos*') where guests are charged a nominal admission fee. In 2004, the Cuban government gave the National Center for Sex Education permission to carry out public educational campaigns on homosexual issues.

14. If things are so bad in Cuba, why don't the people take up arms and revolt? Why don't they launch another revolution like they did in the 1950s?

I asked that same question to a Cuban rafter who was picked up at sea by a Russian freighter and eventually made it to Key West,

Florida, by way of Guantanamo, Michigan, and Miami.   He said, "With what are they going to fight? Machetes and baseball bats?" It is against the law for Cubans to possess firearms, and even if enough of them did, the network of reporting suspicious activity is so wide—down to every block of the neighborhood—they'd be stopped before they left the house. Protests in Cuba do happen, but always with heavy-handed repercussions by the police, the armed forces, or security agents. The only way for a revolt to succeed is if the leadership comes from within the ranks of disaffected officers who command respect from their units. The last time that came even close to happening, the General (Arnaldo Ocha Sanchez, in 1989) was quickly put on trial for bogus charges and executed.

The Cuban government could be toppled if large numbers of forces and weaponry came from outside Cuba. There are many Cuban exiles who would love to see this happen. (They tried a small-scale invasion at the Bay of Pigs in 1961, but failed miserably.) However, a large-scale invasion of Cuba is unlikely because the Cuban government's worst enemy—the U.S.—does not view Cuba as a military threat. That, however, would change in a heartbeat if the Cuban government were ever to obtain nuclear or long-range missiles. The scenario of war with Cuba came very close to playing out during the Cuban missile crisis in 1962 when the Soviet Union began installing missile launching pads on Cuban soil. Only when the U.S.S.R. Premier Nikita Khrushchev agreed to end the installation project—on the condition that then U.S. President John F. Kennedy promise not to invade Cuba—was the crisis defused.

Change in Cuba will have to come from an internal sequence of events. It might be abrupt (and bloody) or it might be gradual (and peaceful). Not even the Cuban people themselves know. My personal feeling is that the Cuban people will learn to coexist with a hybrid of a social and political structure that melds the contradictions of socialist thought and free-market economics. The government will loosen some of its control over the market system and ownership of industry. Shackles to personal freedoms and basic rights will loosen, and things will improve. But many of the laws and philosophies that shape the unique brand of Cuban socialism will never be tossed.

15.   Castro and the Cuban government blame the U.S. trade embargoes for their country's economic troubles—not market trends or their own mismanagement. But there are plenty of other countries with which Cuba can trade.   Can the U.S. embargoes really be blamed for Cuba's woes?
Without a doubt, the U.S. trade embargoes deprive the Cuban government and the Cuban people of substantial amounts of desperately needed U.S. dollars, food, equipment, raw materials,

trained professionals, and other necessities. But most economic analysts agree that the U.S. trade restrictions against Cuba are not the main culprit for Cuba's economic woes. They blame:

- A cumbersome centralized system of production and distribution (all industry is owned by the State, and therefore most Cuban people are State employees).

- Low productivity on the job (due to government controls on low salaries and the guarantee of work for all).

- A lack of incentive for industries to make a profit. (Since the government owns everything, it could move funds around.)

- A precarious over-dependence on too few export commodities. (Sugar accounts for about seventy-percent of income from exports.)

- The ban of free enterprise and market-based trade. (Among other things, this limits the amount of foreign currency that could be pulled into the market.)

- The flight of professionals from the country.

- An overburdened debt owed to a host of other countries.

Cuba has plenty of resources, analysts say. The country has a thriving tourism industry (ranking third among destinations in the Caribbean), and the tropical climate combined with the fertile land should permit the country to feed its own people.

Despite the government's unconventional ways of doing business, most Cubans were actually able to get by reasonably well until 1989 when the Soviet Union, Cuba's main trading partner, collapsed. Russia could no longer trade oil for sugar at favorable prices, and overnight Castro's regime lost the five billion dollar-per-year safety net that allowed it to run its internal finances inefficiently.

Amid the din of blame-throwing, it is interesting to note that the U.S. is now the fourth largest exporter (mostly in agricultural products, medicine, and humanitarian aid) to Cuba. Furthermore, the total remittances of people in the U.S. sending money to friends and relatives in Cuba amount to about one billion dollars per year—almost as much as the annual tallies for hard currency from tourism.

16. Why, then, does the Cuban government continue to blame the United States embargo for its economic hardship?
As mentioned, the U.S. embargo does create some shortages and suffering for the Cuban people. And because of the skyrocketing

cost of oil, it would be much cheaper for Cuba to ship from the resource-rich U.S. which lies only ninety miles across the Florida Straits. On a purely propaganda level, there are many who say that the embargo also gives the Cuban government a handy scapegoat to blame for the Revolution's failings.

The following is a list of arguments that suggest that the U.S. trade embargo, rather than punishing the Cuban government, actually helps it:

- Foreign governments who disagree with the embargo are moved to extend aid and support to Cuba.

- Instead of bringing democracy to Cuba, the U.S.'s penalizing and isolating policies forced the Cuban government to turn to the Soviet Union for help. The strong trade relationship that ensued eventually encouraged the Cuban government to adopt the U.S.S.R's communist model of government.

- In Cuba, the U.S. embargo establishes the U.S. as the "enemy of the Cuban people" (believe me, they teach this in Cuban grade schools) and emboldens Cuban nationals to rally around a common cause to defend its independence and sovereignty.

- The embargo provides "proof" (used in the Cuban government's propaganda campaigns) of U.S. imperialism and the U.S. attempts to dominate the hemisphere and influence sovereign Cuban policy.

- The embargo undermines civil and human rights in Cuba by giving the Cuban government a pretext to enforce military law on its citizens. The embargo assault on Cuba's economic welfare—and thus the country's stability—makes it easier for the Cuban government to justify imprisonment, expulsion, and punishment of those who stand in the way of the government's agenda.

- Some of the embargo laws (the Helms-Burton Act, for example) are aimed at punishing other countries (Canada and European nations, in particular) that want to trade with Cuba. This creates animosity, resentment, and alienation of allies who don't appreciate the U.S. government telling them when and with whom they can trade. A few countries have even created their own laws that make it illegal for their citizens to ABIDE U.S. trade embargo laws.

SECTION 10

SOME CUBAN LAWS YOU SHOULD KNOW

1. Are the laws that govern Cuban society very different from the state and federal laws that govern Americans in the U.S.?
In many respects, the contrast between the concept of justice in the Cuban legal system and the concept of justice in the U.S. legal system is shockingly stark. If you read the last Section, you are already aware of some of the major differences between the constitutions of both nations.

One way to understand the Cuban brand of justice—and the authorities who enforce it—is to realize that many of the country's laws are designed to protect the rights of the State and society as a whole over those of the individual. This is a simple fact of Marxist-Leninist socialism, the philosophy of governing that has guided Cuban society for almost half-a-century. In the U.S., the reverse is true: U.S. laws are passed to ensure the unalienable rights of the individual (among which are life, liberty, and the pursuit of happiness). Paraphrasing the U.S. Declaration of Independence, governments in the U.S. derive their powers from the consent of the governed, and when the government becomes destructive in securing these rights, the people have a right to alter or abolish it and institute a new government.

Other fundamental principles of socialism and communism shape Cuban law. A few of these principles include the belief that society should be classless; the belief that the government should be the sole owner of industry, production, and distribution; and the belief that only one political party (the Cuban Communist Party) should have the power to pursue these socialist principles.

2. Can you list some of these Cuban laws that are vastly different or nonexistent in the U.S. so I can avoid getting myself or others into trouble with the authorities?
Here are the most important ones:

- Cubans are not allowed to have foreigners as overnight guests in their homes without permission from the immigration authorities.

- Cubans are not allowed to carry foreigners in their personal vehicles.

- Cubans are not allowed to go out on boats—either as drivers or passengers— without State permission.

- A Cuban person risks fines and jail for approaching a foreigner on the street.

- It is against the law to insult or offend, with the spoken word or in writing, the dignity of an authority or a political, social, or institutional organization of the Republic.

- It is against the law to show support for U.S. policies against Cuba.

- Private ownership of press, radio, television, and other means of communication is prohibited.

- It is against the law to demonstrate collaboration in the ideological war against the homeland.

- It is against the law to own or possess a firearm.

- It is against the law to sell or transfer real estate property without oversight of the State.

- It is against the law to sell or transfer automobiles.

- Communicating subversive information to a foreigner or journalist who later publishes the information can result in charges of "disseminating enemy propaganda."

- Law enforcement officers are not required to obtain search warrants to enter and search private homes and property.

- A person may be arrested without being charged with a specific crime.

- Detainees can be held for nine months or longer without a trial.

- MININT (Ministry of the Interior) authorities can place individuals under house arrest without a judge's order.

- Warrants are not required for authorities to search mail and wire-tap telephones.

- Satellite television dishes are illegal.

- Listening to Radio Marti and other foreign radio stations is against the law.

- Private enterprise is limited to certain self-employment endeavors only.

- Only State enterprises are allowed to have employees.

- Privately owned businesses are not allowed to sell any item or product not personally prepared or made by the owner of the business.

- Some food products such as milk, eggs, cheese, and any product obtained through the ration system are not allowed to be used in the production and sale of items offered by privately owned and operated businesses.

- The government imposes hefty tariffs and fees on many self-employment occupations to limit excessive income and competition with State businesses.

- Only State enterprises are permitted to charge foreign currency or convertible pesos for services or products. Privately owned businesses can only charge Cuban pesos for their products or services.

- While private access to computers and Internet is legal (since 2008), the government imposes stringent application procedures and hefty rates and fees to limit Internet use.

- Producing pornography is illegal.

- See questions number three and six in Section 3 for a list of things you are not allowed to bring into or take out of the country.

- Prostitution is illegal.

- The minimum age for consensual sex is sixteen for Cubans, eighteen for foreigners.

- Anti-social behavior such as not working, not going to school, joining a gang, and living on the street is punishable by work-camp stints.

- Black market street hustlers who harass tourists are often detained and carted off to the police stations where they will be written up. Multiple infractions result in jail time or work camps.

- Those who participate in human rights groups, political parties other than the Communist Political Party, and unsanctioned press activities are often arrested on bogus charges.

- The Cuban Constitution establishes the Communist Party of Cuba as the "highest guiding force of the society and the State." Even the Supreme Court is subordinate to the Communist Party.

- Witnesses to crimes and accidents are required to cooperate with investigators and may be forced to delay or cancel planned activities and scheduled departures.

- If you are treated at a tourist-friendly Servimed hospital for a medical emergency and do not have medical insurance or the money to pay the bill, you may be prevented from leaving the country until the matter is resolved.

- Cuban adults must carry their national identity cards with them at all times and foreigners are expected to carry photo identification with them at all times or they risk detention.

- In some cases, *victims* of passport theft are jailed until authorities have completed their investigation. If your passport is stolen, report the theft to the embassy before reporting it to the police.

- It is against the law to photograph military or police buildings, military or police personnel, factories, State port facilities, airports, and many public bus or train stations.

- Although consensual sex between people of the same gender over age sixteen has been legal in Cuba since 1992, same-sex displays of affection (holding hands, kissing) in public are forbidden.

- Passengers who ride in vehicles driven by persons under

the influence will be prosecuted.

3. Are foreign visitors to Cuba subject to the Cuban laws, even if the laws contradict the laws of their own country?
Yes, although in cases involving less serious offenses, foreigners are often reprimanded or deported rather than channeled through jails and court proceedings.   Cuban accomplices of foreigners involved in criminal acts are dealt with far more severely.

4. Are the penalties for breaking the laws comparable to the penalties imposed in the U.S.?
Jail sentences are often far harsher than what one would expect in the U.S. Maximum penalties, for example, are:

- Ten years for possession of small amounts of marijuana.
- Five to eight years for insulting the dignity of an authority of the Republic.
- Five years for selling beef on the black market.
- Thirty years for drug dealing.
- Ten years for killing a cow belonging to the *Estado*.
- Twenty years for assaulting a tourist.
- Life for habitual pimps.

5. Does the Cuban Constitution guarantee the same rights and protections guaranteed in the U.S. Constitution?
As discussed in Section 9, many rights and freedoms guaranteed in the U.S. Constitution are conspicuously absent in the Cuban Constitution. Some freedoms, such as the freedom of speech and the freedom of the press, are promised in the Cuban Constitution, but under one important condition: That they not interfere with the objectives of the socialist society.   Article sixty-two of the Cuban Constitution states: "None of the freedoms which are recognized for citizens can be exercised contrary to what is established in the Constitution by law, or contrary to the existence and objectives of the socialist state, or contrary to the decision of the Cuban people to build socialism and communism."

6. Is the due process in the Cuban court system reasonable?
Not by U.S. judicial standards.   In Cuban legal proceedings, hearings can go a little TOO fast, and in other cases, detention while awaiting trial can drag on for months.   The ability of the defense lawyers to adequately represent their clients is seriously compromised by rules that unfairly favor the prosecution. Defense lawyers, for example, do not have the same access to their clients and records that the prosecution does.   The right to appeal in Cuban courts is almost nonexistent.

7. Does the death penalty exist in Cuba?

The death penalty can be and has been handed out to those found guilty of violent crime, espionage, treason, hijacking, smuggling resulting in accidental death, and drug trafficking.

8. What are the jail conditions like?

By all accounts, much worse than conditions in U.S. prisons. The Cuban government does not allow independent human rights monitors to conduct visits to its prisons, but testimony of former prisoners and family members of former prisoners paints a grim picture of life in a Cuban jail. A 2006 report published by Human Rights Watch concludes that Cuban prison practices fail in many aspects to comply with the United Nations Standard Minimum Rules for Treatment of Prisoners, an international treaty of which Cuba is a signatory that establishes the guidelines on the treatment of prisoners. Former prisoners speak of filthy cells swarming with bugs and mosquitoes, disciplinary beatings, lack of medical care, overcrowded cells, and subsistent rations of food containing fish innards, bugs, and putrefied blood. Visits to inmates by family members are severely restricted—sometimes to two hours every two or three months. Pre-trial detainees are forced to share cells with convicts, and inmates are forbidden to possess many basic items such as bedding, clothes, and writing material.

SECTION 11

THE COMMUNIST POLICE

1. The Cuban government gets an awful lot of bad press in the U.S. media regarding the repression of its people. Should I be concerned about the possibility that I could end up in a Castro jail eating rice and chopped-up bugs?

There really is an ever-present 'Big Brother's Watching You' atmosphere that pervades daily life in Cuba but don't cancel your plans to visit the country because of this. Foreign visitors to the island won't see signs of the repression at first because they are given preferential treatment and they don't have to subsist within the daily constraints like the Cuban people do.

In addition, the Revolutionary police aren't really interested in you unless you're leaving a trail of counterrevolutionary activity or you're supplying dissidents with weapons to overthrow the government. This may sound like obvious advice, but you need to understand that the Cuban government is a lot more paranoid about getting overthrown than most governments because the number of disaffected citizens in Cuba is much greater than in other countries, and because, according to Castro, a giant superpower next door has been trying to topple them for years.

Keep in mind that there are many punishable offenses in Cuba that don't exist in the U.S., and regardless of your citizenship, while you are in Cuba, you are subject to Cuba's laws. Go back to Section 10 and read up on some of these unique Cuban laws if you skipped it.

Also, the penalties for breaking certain laws in Cuba can be a lot harsher than the penalties for breaking similar laws in the United States and elsewhere. But as long as you behave yourself, you'll be fine.

Reading these last few Sections that discuss the police and the repression in Cuba may give you the impression that Cuba is a nerve-wracking place to visit, and you won't be able to relax. This is really not the case—for tourists, anyway. Millions of people visit Cuba each year and have a wonderful time, namely because the

Cuban government does a good job of keeping the fantasy world of tourism and get-away vacations apart from the realities of daily life for the average Cuban person. The stress of repression increases the more you associate and get to know—in an intimate way—a Cuban and his or her family. But, while the stress may increase, so do the rewards. As I said before, the Cuban people are the friendliest and most sociable on the planet.

2. Do government security agents or police units monitor my movements while I'm in Cuba?

I don't want to sound like an alarmist or a paranoid conspiracy theorist, that is just not my nature, but Cuban intelligence and law enforcement agencies monitor your movements within the country from the moment you pass through the immigration window at the airport until you step off the plane that carries you out of the country. The highest duty (and "honor") of all State security agents and Revolutionary police members is "defense of the socialist motherland"[39] and protecting the "people's decision to build socialism and communism."[40] This duty is carried out utilizing a massive, all-encompassing and centralized infrastructure that employs a dizzying number of intelligence and police agencies and departments whose orders filter down from the desk of the head of the Ministry of Interior in Havana.

One tactic used to carry out this duty is to minimize the Cuban people's contact with foreigners in order to avoid "corrupting their minds" with capitalist ideas and to prevent Cubans from getting riled up when they are reminded of all the things they don't have (that people in other countries do). Misinformation on the government-controlled television and in the national newspapers is very effective in countering the information that the Cubans may get from talking to foreigners.

Along with the cooperative efforts of the multitude of civilian networks and government agencies discussed in question number three, below, the tracking of all foreigners' movements in Cuba is accomplished in another rather straightforward way: *Casa particular* owners must provide the Ministry of Interior the names of all guests (within twenty-four hours of check-in). Similar protocol is followed when foreigners rent cars, check into hotels, purchase bus and train tickets, and pull into a port by boat.

3. What intelligence or law enforcement agencies might be monitoring my activity while I'm in Cuba?

The Ministry of the Interior is the umbrella government agency that oversees all intelligence and police operations in the country. The provinces do not have their own law enforcement agencies with separate powers and laws like the states and counties in the U.S. do—everything is centralized. Cuba's Ministry of the Interior would be like the Department of Homeland Security in the U.S. overseeing all police and intelligence operations in every state and county along with coordinating the CIA, the FBI, the Coast Guard, Border Patrol, Immigration, Customs, S.W.A.T. teams, prisons, fire departments, ambulances and special rescue operations.   Each of these departments in Cuba has a neighborhood or municipal chief that reports to the provincial chief.   The head of the Ministry of the Interior is subordinate to the thirty-one-member Council of State, whose president (Raul Castro) is the head of the Cuban government.

The national police department in Cuba is called the *Policia Nacional Revolucionaria* (PNR).   Through the municipal and provincial chiefs, the PNR oversees the day-to-day policing operations including street patrol, crime investigation, crime prevention, traffic patrol, juvenile delinquency and special security (i.e., for public events, diplomats, tourist areas, hotels and other businesses).

While run-ins with any one of the neighborhood officers of the PNR will propel your name up the ranks to the files of the municipal and provincial chiefs, your biggest concern—as far as Big Brother watchdogs monitoring your activity and tracking your movements— is not a PNR officer (who is conscripted into compulsory service like the recruits of the armed forces), but undercover intelligence agents (operating out of the Ministry of the Interiors' State Security division) and local members of the Committees in the Defense of the Revolution (CDRs).

The CDRs are civilian neighborhood watch groups created shortly after the triumph of the 1959 Revolution to consolidate broad citizen support for the Revolution and the communist government. Every block in every village and city of the country has a CDR and the members of the CDRs consist of the residents of the houses on the block.   Their purpose, in Castro's own words, is to provide a "system of collective revolutionary vigilance so that everyone will know who everyone else is…what they devote themselves to, who they meet with, what activities they take part in."   Along with reporting suspicious illegal activity and anti-revolutionary behavior, the members of the CDRs hold regularly scheduled meetings and work in groups to clean and patrol the streets, campaign for education and health needs, and participate in other "volunteer" activities.   Non-participation is suspect.

A Consular Information Sheet compiled by the U.S. State Department's Bureau of Consular Affairs (apparently, they're pretty good spies themselves) warns that licensed taxis available near hotel areas "are often driven by DGSE (General Directorate for State Security) agents, or the drivers report to the DGSE as part of the regime's efforts to follow the activities of foreign visitors."   It should be expected that intelligence agents also work under the guise of Cubana check-in clerks, retail store clerks, and prostitutes. The U.S. State Department also warns that Cuban State Security eavesdropping on telephone conversations and their interception of regular mail and Internet communications is a common practice. Many of the Cuban people you meet will say the same thing.

The undercover State security agents are supplemented by paid local informers, lackeys, and *chivatas* (neighborhood snitches)—the most hated of all informers because they are seen as two-faced back-stabbers by those who have been betrayed.

On several occasions I have been busted by the Ministry of Construction housing inspectors and the Ministry of the Interior immigration officers for staying at private homes that did not have the permits for renting rooms out to foreigners. I was asked to pack my things and leave immediately. My claim that I was not paying for the room fell on deaf ears. The owners of the homes were assessed stiff fines (which I paid for them) and were threatened with confiscation of their property. The homeowners told me that more than likely the housing inspectors and the immigration officers were tipped off by members of the block CDR.

Brigadas de Respuesta Rapida (Rapid Response Brigades) are another sinister civilian auxiliary outfit (usually composed of communist party members) whose function is to mobilize against subversive elements in the neighborhood that pose threats to order. They are often called in to counter peaceful protests or demonstrations and coached by plainclothes Ministry of the Interior "anti-counterrevolutionary" agents. The Rapid Response Brigades have been known to assemble as an intimidating mob in front of the houses of dissidents, human rights activists, independent journalists and others suspected or accused of anti-revolutionary behavior, a tactic that is effective in alienating suspected anti-revolutionaries from the rest of the community and discouraging others from following their example.

4.   What tips can you give me to avoid run-ins with the Revolutionary police and other Ministry of the Interior agents?

- If you're going to stay in private homes that are not licensed to rent to foreigners, only stay with people you know well who have clout in the community to challenge the system. Otherwise, saving ten or twenty bucks on a bargain illegal room is really not worth the risk of heavy fines and confiscation of private property that the homeowners face.

- If you're going to stay in private homes not licensed to rent rooms to foreigners, get a phone number, call in advance, meet with the owners away from the property to discuss the arrangements, and have someone take your bags in and

out of the house ahead of time.
- Dress Cuban. Blend in. Be discreet.

- If you're not carrying baggage when you ride the cabs, have the taxi drop you off a block or two from your destination so that the undercover informants and local CDR snitches can't follow your movements that easily.

- If you're not doing anything illegal, go about your day and enjoy yourself. Nobody is going to care what you do. Stop being so paranoid.

- Guys, don't discuss sex as a business deal with a girl; get to know her a little bit before you go at it. Take her out to dinner, meet her family, spend a day at the beach with her. Even if a girl is in a relationship with you for the money, she'll take the time out to be with you and like it because she probably doesn't get the opportunity to be treated that often.

- Girls, I'd say the same thing goes with picking up the Cuban men.

- Gay guys and girls, ditto for picking up the gay Cuban guys and girls.

- Aliens and two-headed monsters…

5. What will happen if I am arrested?
Like everywhere else, you'll be handcuffed and helped into a squad car. Most subjects are driven to the local precinct where a report is filled out and the subjects are locked in a jail. People charged with capital crimes such as drug trafficking, murder, or corruption of a minor bypass the local precinct and are chauffeured to top security bureaus of interrogation.

In all likelihood, you won't be read any rights or told why you are being arrested. The authorities don't even have to tell you where they're taking you. One thing is for sure, though—as a foreigner, you'll get a lot more consideration for due process than the Cuban people normally do.

At some point, you'll be brought before a judge for a bond hearing and trial date, but there is no finite timeline for this. Unlike the due process requirements in the U.S., detainees snared in the Cuban justice system can be held for nine months or more without a trial. In one case, an American citizen arrested on a drug charge was detained for eighteen months before his trial began. Judges enjoy tremendous discretionary power, even if the written laws establish otherwise.

The authorities are not obligated to let you call or send messages to friends, family members, attorneys, or any other kind of assistance, but they'll usually put in a call to the U.S. Interests Section in Havana if you ask them. The authorities aren't obligated to allow regular visits by friends or family either.

In a consular information sheet published on its website (www.havana.usinterestsection.gov/arrests), the U.S. Interest Section in Havana offers the following advice to U.S. citizens jailed in Cuba:

- If you or any American citizen are arrested in Cuba, ask the authorities to notify a consular officer at the U.S. Interests Section immediately.

- We cannot get you, or anyone, out of jail (because you are subject to Cuba's laws), but we can help protect your legitimate interests and ensure that you are not discriminated against.

- We can also provide a list of local attorneys, visit you in jail and, if you wish, contact members of your family on your behalf. We can also transfer money, food, and clothing to prison authorities from your relatives for your benefit.

Legal eagles also advise that detainees request that all depositions and body searches be made in front of an independent witness.

Two organizations in Cuba that offer legal advice and assistance in many areas (including marriage and business ventures) are the *Consultoria Juridica Internacional* (Calle 16 No. 314 between 3rd and 5th Avenue in Miramar, Havana, telephone 07-204-1318, website www.cji.co.cu) and the *Bufete Internacional* (Avenida 5ta No. 16202 in Miramar, Havana, telephone 076-204-6749, website bufete@bufete.cha.cyt.cu).

SECTION 12

SPECIAL HAZARDS AND SOME WORDS OF WARNING

1. How safe—or dangerous—is Cuba crime-wise?
In terms of violent crime, Cuba is not only the safest country in Latin America, it is the safest country in the entire western hemisphere. In Havana, late at night, I often walk from Chinatown or *Habana Vieja* to my rented room in the slummy area of *Centro Habana*. Blackness blankets the neighborhood because most street lamps are either busted or burned out. Shadows smear the unpainted walls of the derelict buildings. Craters of asphalt erosion disfigure the streets. The smell of rotting food rises from overflowing dumpsters parked at the corners. Yet, I am not gripped by a feeling of an impending attack by a rapist or a drug addict lurking in the shadows the way I might be if I found myself in a blighted area of a large city in the U.S. It's hard to explain this peculiar lack of threat on a dark street of a Havana slum to anyone who hasn't experienced it, but additional details of the neighborhood help fill in the picture: Neighbors chatting in open doorways; the sight of families gathered around a TV in their *sala* as one passes an open, ground-floor window; salsa music beating from a second-floor balcony; and laughing children darting in and out of the shadows.

That said, petty crime such as purse-snatching and pick pocketing is a growing problem in Cuba, so don't let your guard down at any time during your trip. Don't flaunt your expensive watches, don't sport the gold chains around your neck, and don't wave your money around. I wear cheap, thrift-store clothes (never shorts) and grow a mustache when I'm in Cuba so that I can blend in with the crowd. If you are light-skinned and there is nothing you can do to hide your foreigner looks, you're just going to have to be a little more careful about where you go and who you meet. Here are some suggestions:

- As much as possible, avoid slinging a backpack over your shoulders.

- Don't wear those bulky fanny-packs either.

- Keep your money in a pocket sewn on the inside of your clothes or in a money belt hanging down your leg inside your pants.

- Hold on tight to all your valuables in crowds—especially on crowded buses.

- Men, if you don't want to attract *jinetero* sharks, don't wear shorts. (You'll notice that Cuban men almost always wear long pants when they are out on the town.) Street hustlers and thieves can spot a tourist a mile away when he is light-skinned, wearing shorts AND carrying a backpack.

- Ladies, hang onto your purses tightly; don't hang them on the back of a chair or place them by your feet when you're sitting at a café.

- Don't wear a bulky camera around your neck as you stroll around town. Keep it in a bag or carry a small digital camera in a buttoned or zippered pocket.

- It is almost as safe as Fort Knox, Kentucky to leave your bags and valuables with the owners of the private house where you rent a room. However, do not leave valuables lying around a hotel room (particularly, the smaller valuables that can be pocketed) as it only takes one hotel staff member out of hundreds to succumb to the temptation of a crime of opportunity.

- Don't leave washed clothes hanging unattended on clotheslines, even if you pay somebody else to wash them. When I did this on two separate trips to Cuba, I had to borrow some pants from a Cuban man who didn't have much of a wardrobe himself.

- Don't leave your things unattended at the beach.

- Park your car, motorbike, or bicycle inside private property or in guarded lots, or pay someone to watch it. Mirrors, hubcaps, and tires are favorite targets of thieves.

2. Besides the purse-snatching and pick pocketing mentioned above, what other scams and punches do petty criminals pull on unsuspecting tourists?
Don't let this rather long list of common scams give you the idea that

everybody in Cuba is after your money. Most Cubans are genuinely friendly and talkative because of a strong sense of communal bonding and trust they have with each other—not because they are after your money. Many Cuban people become even more talkative and inquisitive when they discover that you are a foreigner. They hunger for information and perspectives from the outside. Nonetheless, because of the serious economic difficulties in the country and the huge disparity of wealth between foreigners and Cuban citizens (the average salary in Cuba is twenty dollars per month), petty criminals will be drawn to you like sharks to chum. The following are some typical and not-so-typical scams perpetrated on unsuspecting tourists:

- Crooked store clerks or black market vendors trying to convince you that U.S. dollars aren't worth anything anymore or that convertible pesos are worth the same as the national peso (*moneda nacional*).

- Being charged convertible pesos in shops where the prices are marked in the national peso—paticularly in *moneda national* shops located in areas frequented by tourists.

- Roaming newspaper vendors trying to sell you the *Granma* daily for a convertible peso instead of the national peso. (Even though the words "20 CTVS"—twenty centavos—are printed at the top of the front page, the Cuban people themselves pay one national peso for the paper. If you give them a convertible peso, you will have paid one dollar and twenty-six cents for something that only costs five cents.) The special foreign language versions of the paper, however, cost more.

- Similar vendors trying to sell you a "special" three-peso Che Guevara coin for one convertible peso. These coins are common in the national peso circulation and are worth exactly three Cuban pesos (fifteen cents).

- Money exchange tellers attempting to charge you a service fee for changing money. There is no fee for changing money except for the standard ten percent off the top when you change dollars to convertible pesos. (See Section 6, 'Money Matters')

- Groping sticks and fishing poles snagging valuables through barred windows.

- Taxi-drivers trying to charge you more than the metered

rate. If the meter is not working, confirm the price BEFORE you get in the cab.

- Customs officials trying to confiscate your possessions or charging you fees for "importation." Familiarize yourself with the regulations (see question number five in Section 3).

- Baggage handlers at airports going through your stuff.

- Check-in clerks at the airport attempting to charge you overweight fees. Know the weight of your luggage before you have it weighed. At the smaller airports in Cuba, weights are sometimes taped to the underside of scales.

- Sleazy bars and cafés using fake menus to charge you more than the going rate.

- Bartenders padding your running tab.

- Cigars supposedly swiped from the Cohiba cigar factory at which the mother of the man trying to sell them to you supposedly works. Chances are, the cigars are counterfeit.

- Counterfeit convertible peso bills.

3.   What particular annoyances have you encountered during your visits to Cuba?   Do you have any pet peeves you can share with me?
The most irritating and persistent annoyance for visitors to Cuba—especially those who are not able to hide their obvious tourist features—is going to be the incessant pestering of **street hustlers** and roaming black market vendors using their best marketing skills to sell you something: Sex, a room for rent, a meal, cigars, rum, CDs, Cuban pesos, transportation and even instant caricatures. It drives me mad, especially when I'm trying to enjoy a relaxing *café con leche* at a sidewalk café. This is why I put so much effort into looking and dressing like a Cuban person. I don't wear my watch on my wrist while I'm strolling through the historic area of Old Havana because at every block someone will come up to me and ask me the time; rarely is the person asking the question interested in the time—he or she just wants to hear me talk to see if I'm a foreigner. (Street hustlers don't harass other Cubans.)

Most street hustlers will leave you alone if you politely decline to engage in any business transactions with them. Some will persist by putting the business aside—temporarily—and trying to get a conversation going. If they can hold onto you long enough (they'll invite you for a café at their home), they feel that eventually they'll find some way to get you to part with some of your cash. If a street hustler won't leave you alone after repeated attempts to shake him, you have no choice but to get firm.   A line like, "Please stop bothering me" ('*Por favor, no me molestes mas*') usually works. Street hustlers are arrested by the police all the time for harassing tourists, so if you've depleted all your other options of shaking your unwanted company, simply ask him to guide you to the nearest "*policia*."

   Boteros are another nuisance closely related to the street hustlers. These are the 'middlemen' who assault you *en masse* as you approach a taxi stand. Their goal is to procure passengers for the taxi-driver who gives the *botero* a commission. The *boteros* will try to get you to pay as much as possible over and above what the taxi-driver charges. My solution is to wave them all off and speak with the taxi-driver personally.   The problem is, it's hard to differentiate between the taxi-driver and the *botero* because they dress alike.   If you have used a local cab to take you to the interprovincial taxi stand, you can ask the first taxi-driver to talk to the interprovincial taxi-driver directly. Another solution is to collect business cards from the taxi-drivers so you can procure their service by phone.

4.   Please enlighten me on some of the social rules and customs that are unique to the Cuban way of life.
Attitudes, beliefs, social rules and customs in Cuba have been shaped by centuries of Spanish rule, African culture imported with the slaves, heavy U.S. influence during the first half of the twentieth century, and Marxist-Leninist ideology for the last forty-eight years. Naturally, factors such as geography, climate, the economy and natural resources all have their own roles in shaping attitudes and behavior in Cuban society. In the last few years, an increase in tourism and the introduction of limited free-market practices have had a rippling effect in every *barrio* and farm community on the island. For better or for worse, all of these influences have tagged Cuban culture with a reputation for tumultuousness and unpredictability.   Scholars of Cuban history and society often describe the situation in Cuba today as an ongoing social experiment. This might explain, at least in part, why many visitors to the island are often struck by impressions of the Cuban people that include such terms as vibrant, social, *joie de vivre*, exotic, sensual, explosive, emotional, expressive, and great capacity for feeling.

   The following highlights some of the more important social rules unique to Cuban culture that visitors to the island need to heed if they want to avoid any discomfort, awkwardness, or unpleasantness when socializing:

TALKING POLITICS
- Don't ask someone a pointed political question in the presence of others. ("Do you like Castro?"; "Do you support the Communist Party?") To avoid being branded a counterrevolutionary, the person being asked these questions in front of others has no choice but to verbalize support for the political system even if it is contrary to his or her beliefs. Admitting support for the system could easily alienate a person from others who oppose the system.
- Don't say negative things about the Cuban government or its officials, and don't divulge who has uttered negative comments about the Cuban government. Word will get around and soon you or your source will be labeled a dangerous enemy.
- Don't get into heavy political discussions with people you don't know.
- If you show support for communism and Castro, you will make a lot of enemies.
- If you criticize communism and Castro, you will make a lot of enemies.
- If you have to use the name "Castro" in a discussion, you need to say it in a low voice. The Cuban people often prefer to use gestures when referring to the brothers—by either stroking an imaginary beard or touching their fingers to a shoulder to indicate high-ranking insignia.

AT THE MARKET
- Many of the larger shops have entrance-only and exit-only doors. Don't be taken aback when an employee of the store won't let you in while lots of other people are inside shopping. You're probably entering through the wrong door.
- If you know you are entering through the right door and an employee of the store still won't let you in, it's probably because the place is too full and they are only letting one person in as another leaves.
- Most stores will not let you bring other bags in with you. There is usually a window or counter nearby (called a *guarda-bolsas*) where you can check your stuff before you go in.
- You may one day walk into a store where people appear to be buying things like chicken parts and ground coffee and find that the clerk won't sell you anything. The place is probably not a shop but a *bodega* where locals go to pick up their allotted rations.
- Some shops sell things in the national peso currency and some shops sell things in euros or the

convertible peso. Usually the national peso shops offer a smaller selection of things that are used or of very poor quality.
*   At the farmers'markets (where the currency and price tags are in the national peso, and where you can usually find a good selection of fresh fruits, vegetables, rice, beans, and pork) you will have to bring your own bag.

AT THE RESTAURANT
*   At many local *circos* (public dance halls) where rum and homemade fruit drinks are often the only beverages offered for sale, you have to bring your own glass.
*   Except at the better tourist hotels and restaurants, restrooms do not have toilet paper. Bring your own.
*   At many of the national peso restaurants—especially the sit-down ice cream parlors—tables are shared. Yes, you read right—you do not get to have your own private table. Not only are you expected to share a table with strangers (this could be a good thing or it could be a bad thing), the server will also take everybody's order at the same time and the food will be delivered at the same time. You are not required to talk to your table mates, though.
*   If you expect service, quality, and standards in State-run Cuban restaurants to be on par with those of the United States and Europe, you will be disappointed. Despite the preferential treatment tourists get when in Cuba, you still need to remember that Cuba is a very poor country. There are probably other highly complex reasons for the poor service and standards, such as: The socialist requirement of classlessness; the ingrained indoctrination that the needs of the society take precedent over the needs of the individual; the ban of free-enterprise coupled with total State ownership of all businesses which eliminates the requirement for many businesses to turn a profit; and the lack of incentives when one works a guaranteed, low-paying job. Pretty hefty arguments to explain why the waiter sucks.
*   You will have a better chance of finding good, down-home traditional Cuban cuisine at privately owned *paladares*—licensed eat-in establishments operating out of personal homes. Also, personalized attention and better service because the *paladares* only have one or two tables. Section 8 of this manual discusses *paladares* and other options for eating out in Cuba.
*   If you are sitting at a *divisa* (convertible peso) restaurant, particularly in a tourist area, and you are waiting for a Cuban friend to join you, when your Cuban friend does

show up, be prepared for the waiter to try to shoo your Cuban friend away. The protective waiter may think your Cuban friend is a street hustler harassing you.

TIPPING
- A Cuban man once told me that Cubans don't normally leave a tip when they eat out at restaurants and that foreigners shouldn't feel obligated to tip either, unless they really feel that the server provided them with something above and beyond his duties. This same man, however, rarely frequented convertible-peso establishments that cater to foreigners, so don't adhere to his rule of not tipping everywhere you go. Cuban servers who work in restaurants frequented by foreigners have come to expect some tip, no matter how small. Yet, they probably won't be as heartbroken as their European or American counterparts would be if you left nothing. Many Cuba travel guides recommend tipping waiters and waitresses ten-percent of the bill, but keep in mind that a ten-percent tip on a ten-dollar bill amounts to more than what the government pays the average worker for an entire day's work. The server would still be content if you only left fifty cents. Also, keep in mind that the tip you give the server is often pooled for all the employees of the restaurant, including the manager. If you want a specific server to get the tip, hand it to the server directly instead of leaving it on the table.
- Some State-owned restaurants add the gratuity to the bill, so check the numbers before you pay.
- People in other professions who might merit a tip include tour guides, taxi-drivers, security guards for watching your car or belongings, and people in the service and hospitality industry such as bartenders, housekeepers, delivery personnel, and porters.
- Instead of tipping housekeepers, gardeners, *casa particular* proprietors, personal chefs, and other staff in the hospitality business, consider giving them personal care or household items that most Cubans have great difficulty obtaining with their measly peso earnings. These items include shampoo, soap, toothpaste, perfume, cologne, nail polish, razors, cigarette lighters, sheets, towels, and sunglasses. Toys and clothes of any kind for the kids are worth their weight in gold.
- Whenever possible, tip in convertible pesos rather than in national pesos.

STANDING IN LINE
- All societies use queues because it's just common

sense. Different cultures sprinkle queue etiquette with their own flavors and variations on the theme. In Cuba, queue lines are essential because of the serious material shortages and because almost all products and services are controlled by a centralized government bureaucracy. Many visitors to Cuba will notice that human waiting lines in Cuba are far more prevalent in the daily lives of the Cuban people than in their own countries. (Unless they lived in pre-1990 U.S.S.R.) Along with the pervasiveness of long lines in a socialist country of severe shortages come the peculiarities and quirks of the Cuban brand of queue protocol. There are a few peculiarities that the uninitiated visitor needs to heed if she or he wants to avoid the embarrassment of an impromptu public lecture while curious or indignant bystanders look on.   Some of these peculiarities are discussed below.

•   You will often find queues at the better sit-down restaurants that accept the national peso. This is because there aren't that many of them that are any good. You'll have a tough time finding a national peso restaurant near any of the tourist areas in Havana or Varadero, but they are there.

•   Milk, like many commodities in Cuba, is in very short supply. Much of what Cuba produces is rationed for children under the age of seven. The rest is earmarked for the hotels and resorts to keep the tourists happy, and offered for sale at the convertible peso (*divisa*) shops and, therefore, out of reach for the average Cuban. The result is that there are a limited number of national peso ice-cream parlors in the country. Those that exist are run by the State. (The sale of homemade items containing milk and other rationed products by one-person private enterprises is forbidden, unless the entrepreneur can show receipts for milk purchased at the *divisa* shops.   This makes milk-products too expensive to make; no one would pay what it would cost for the entrepreneur to turn a profit.) As one can imagine, the State-run ice cream parlors—called Coppelias—are immensely popular and draw huge lines that can snake around an entire block.   (Ice cream is available for sale at *divisa* parlors, but you won't find any long lines there.) Tourists at Havana's Vedado Coppelia are usually not allowed to stand in line with the Cubans, but bribing the usher sometimes works. It's worth the wait—not for the ice cream but for the gain in insight into the lives of the Cuban people and socialism at work.

•   Bus stops: The lack of signs or posted schedules at bus stops will befuddle first-time riders on public buses and *camiónes*. If rote hasn't taught you where the stops are, you'll just have to ask around. More often than not, you know you're close to a stop when you see some people standing around.   People standing around at some seemingly haphazard location often make newcomers wonder what these people are doing.

When you approach a stop where others are waiting, you must call out "*Ultimo*" or "*Quien es el ultimo*?" ("Who is last?") so that you will know who gets to board the bus ahead of you. If you are currently the *ultimo* person at the stop, you need to indicate this to the next person who comes along.   Obviously, this protocol is in place in case there's not enough room on the next bus for everybody. Often, there isn't. Amazingly, the '*ultimo*' procedure works. If you forget who is ahead of you, other people standing around will remind you politely as you begin to board out of turn. As you will discover, the queues at bus stops are not actual lines of people standing behind one another. Instead, the people are scattered about on walls, boxes, leaning against a tree, or sitting on the grass. Queuing up at a bus stop can be an interesting lesson in cultural psychology. The personalities of the ever-expressive, ever-social Cuban people tend to emerge, and joke-telling and impromptu singing are not uncommon.

•   Some bus stops in rural areas have a booth nearby where you need to buy a ticket. You still need to know who is ahead of you and board in sequence in case there's no room on the next bus or *camión* that comes by.

•   You will often see people in burnt-yellow uniforms (called *amarillos*, meaning 'yellow one') at bus stops collecting fares for buses and other vehicles of public transportation. If an *amarillo* is at an area where people are hitchhiking, he or she will even monitor the order in which the hitchhikers get picked up.

•   Many attractions (zoo, museums, etc) have separate windows (and, therefore, different rates) for tourists and nationals. Nationals can purchase tickets at the convertible peso window if they desire, but foreigners can't purchase tickets at the national peso window, unless they can produce a *carnet de identidad* that verifies their Cuban nationality.

•   Other places where you can expect to see *colas* is at bread shops, foreign embassies, *bodegas*, newly-legalized electronic or appliance distribution centers (for cell phones, computer stores), and the national peso ticket windows at train stations and bus depots.   Sometimes, you'll see a line coming out of a building without any signs

or notices posted. This is called a "mystery line" and the only way to find out what they're handing out at the head of the line is to join it.
*   If someone is waiting for you to end your call at a public payphone you are using, don't hang up the receiver when you're done. Hand it to the waiting person so they can use the remaining time to make a call and save a few centavos.
*   Conversely, if someone hands you the receiver of a public payphone you are waiting to use, it's because they're offering you the use of the remaining minutes—not because they're trying to save you the effort of taking the receiver off the cradle.

AT THE HOSPITAL
*   In some large cities, there are 'international hospitals' with English-speaking doctors, surgeons, and nurses that cater to foreigners. You will have to pay in full, in cash, prior to treatment, but costs are far more affordable than those found in their own countries.
*   If you speak some Spanish, and don't mind waiting in line, you can visit any of the public hospitals or polyclinics that service the Cubans. First visits are usually free, and prescriptions—if available—are only pennies to the dollar.
*   If you do check yourself in to one of the public hospitals, be prepared to bring many of the things normally supplied in U.S. hospitals. This includes sheets, fans, and even food.
*   Emergency rooms at all hospitals are open 24 hours a day and are available to all foreigners. Most hotels and resorts have a first-aid nurse on duty.
*   Many pharmaceuticals, even over-the-counter ones comparable to products like Tylenol and Imodium, are either unavailable or in very short supply.
*   If you have a serious medical emergency, the Cuban doctors and/or State authorities may insist on evacuating you, at a major cost to you, to the U.S.

IN THE HOME
*   The offer of coffee to visitors is the national sign of welcome. If you are not offered coffee, you are probably imposing. If you do not offer coffee to visitors, they will feel unwelcome.
*   If you are renting a room in a private home, don't bring in any guests without first asking the owners.
*   Don't drink the tap water without boiling it first. Not even the Cuban people drink the tap water without boiling it

first. Make sure even the water used to make ice cubes is boiled. Don't eat uncooked greens or other vegetables washed in tap water. Watch out for homemade fruit drinks mixed with tap water.

• Yes, even electricity is rationed in Cuba. The power doesn't go out nightly, though. Just frequently enough to make it a nuisance, and never for entire days or nights. Outages aren't as common in Havana, Varadero, and other select spots, as in other areas of the country. If you're in a closed room on a hot day during an outage, you're in trouble. Try selecting accommodations that have windows for breeze. During outages at night, many Cubans will sleep on their balconies or porches. City dwellers who live in box-like tenements often have to wait out the outage in the street in front of their buildings. Out come the tables and chairs.

• Water is rationed too, cut off far more frequently than the power. Many dwellings have back-up tanks on the roof or some other raised spot in the home so that gravity will allow the water to flow. Others have large drums of water in the bathroom or on the balcony. When water is needed to cook or bathe, a cup or a pot is simply dipped into the barrel. Most homes in Cuba have an alternative to electrical stoves (usually a kerosene stove) so that water can be heated even when the power is out. There is usually a set schedule for water service: A few hours in the morning, and a few hours at night. The schedule may differ from one neighborhood to another, and can even depend on what side of the block one lives.

• In the smaller towns, be prepared for rudimentary bathing facilities. The facility might be in an outhouse, and it might be a bucket of water. No matter where you go, most private residences in Cuba will not have hot, running water.

• Cuban people NEVER bathe after they eat dinner. They think it is harmful to your health and may even kill you. Be prepared for a big debate with the people with whom you are staying if you try this.

• There are only two television channels in Cuba, both controlled by the government. In private homes, cable or satellite T.V. is illegal (but not at tourist hotels and resorts). Soaps are aired during prime time because they are the national highlight of television viewing.

• If you are invited to stay overnight, don't expect to have your own bed. I'll say this again: The Cuban people are a friendly and trusting bunch. I once shared a bed with *two* other people and three or four more in the same room.

ON THE ROAD
- Don't expect drivers to use turn signals. Many of the cars on Cuban roads are dilapidated. Except in the tourist industry, you'll rarely see a car that has working A/C.
- There is a serious lack of signage on the streets and roads in the country.
- Night driving is dangerous. Railroad tracks cut across the highway with little or no warning. Other things you won't be able to see while driving at night are potholes, resting livestock, bicyclists, and horse-drawn carts lacking taillights.
- In rural areas, the absence of cars causes many pedestrians, bicyclists, operators of farm equipment, and horse-driven carts to drop their caution and regard for speedy motorized traffic.

ADDRESSING PEOPLE
- Use the respectable '*usted*' (meaning 'you') instead of the informal '*tu*' (also meaning 'you') when addressing strangers. However, don't use the formal address if a Cuban person doesn't use it to address you.
- The Cuban people do not address each other with the patriotic term '*compañero*,' or '*compañera*' (comrade) as much as they used to. More often than not, you will hear them call each other 'amigo' or '*compadre.*' (Both mean 'friend.')
- Children often address strangers by family relations names such as 'aunt,' 'grandmom,' or 'brother.' This is yet another sign of the high value the Cuban people place on friends and neighbors.

PUNCTUALITY, RELIABILITY
- The Cuban habit of tardiness is probably an extension of a syndrome common in other struggling nations in Latin America. Most Cubans are not insincere or deceptive when they break their promises; in their hearts and minds they really do have a desire and every intention of coming through. The problem is that the fantasy of things going according to plan glosses over the reality of the challenges and obstacles that get in the way.
- Often when you ask a Cuban person for directions, rather than say 'I don't know,' or 'I'm not sure,' many will act like they do and send you on a wild goose chase. I don't know and I am not sure why they do that. Perhaps they want to demonstrate that they are helpful. Or perhaps they are exacting revenge on your country's hostile actions during the last fifty years.

IN THE NEIGHBORHOOD
- Don't go shirtless in public (the police will scold you), and don't walk around town in a bathing suit like the tourists do in Key West.
- You may find, in certain situations, that people will object to having their picture taken. It is against the law to photograph military or police buildings, military or police personnel, factories, State port facilities, airports, and many public bus or train stations.
- Don't start a shark-feeding frenzy by handing out gifts or donated items from the trunk of your rented car.
- Out of pride, or as a statement that friendship is more important than money, most newfound acquaintances will turn down offers of money for their help, even if they desperately need it. Offer the money several times so they can say you insisted.
- The Cuban people are extremely social. They maintain epoxy-like bonds with their friends, with their families, and with their neighbors. This intimate, communal sense of belonging and sharing carries over into chance meetings with people they don't even know. Bonding among strangers is not only quick, but instantaneous, because the presumption of guilt until proven innocent (typical among strangers in the U.S.) does not exist in the first place. All of a sudden, after asking a man at the train station to show you how to use the pay phone (only the one-peso coin with the star—not the one with Jose Marti's likeness—works, and wait for the screen to tell you to put the coin in, and don't dial the city code, and press this button first, and wait for the signal,) he wants to know where did you come from, who are you calling, where are you staying, do you need a ride, who are you going to see while you're here, and then he starts giving you opinions when none was solicited, like, "You travel with too much stuff," or "Your cap needs a wash." The abruptness of such personal questions and opinions from a total stranger seems intrusive and nosy to first-time visitors, particularly Americans who tend to be self-reliant, independent, individualistic, more demanding of privacy, and like lots of space. But that is just the Cuban way, driven by the necessity to stick together during tough times and exacerbated, perhaps, by the fact that you are the official enemy of the *Estado*, an American, a voyager from a distant land where your own government forbids you to be here, a place where the soda dispensers in fast-food stores are self-service, where people have two, three cars, and

computers, and cool video games, and where a new president is elected every four years.

WITH FRIENDS

- Be aware that the Cuban people you hang out with may be questioned, detained, or even harassed by an inspector, a State security agent, or the police. There are understandable and not so understandable reasons why this happens. For one, the authorities have orders from above to question anyone suspected of breaking a law. For more ingrained, ideological reasons, Revolution and communist diehards fear that contact with (free-thinking, capitalist) foreigners corrupts socialist ideals. Many diehards are also hypersensitive of any possible counterrevolutionary activity that threatens national security. Some police officers will detain a Cuban person talking to a foreigner if they suspect that the Cuban is harassing the foreigner for money or black market business transactions.

ENTERTAINMENT AND RECREATION

- Hanging out is the number one form of recreation and entertainment in Cuba. This is not just because it is free in a nation of poor, but because, as mentioned several times in this travel manual, the Cuban people by nature are very social creatures. The most popular destinations for hanging out are:
  - Street corners
  - Balconies
  - On the sidewalk in front of their buildings
  - In the street in front of their homes
  - On the front porch
  - In neighborhood parks
  - At the seawall
  - The beach
  - The main square of town
  - Peso cafés
  - Coppelia ice-cream parlors
  - Pedestrian promenades
- If you catch a baseball while in the stands at a major league game, it's uncool to keep it. Yes, the material shortage affects everybody. If you don't throw the ball back, there's a good chance a security officer will hunt you down and pry it from your hands.
- While on the subject of baseball, it's proper etiquette to applaud steals and homeruns made by a player on the opposing team.
- When seeking an autograph of a sports superstar, it

is not necessary to scream and push your way through a mob of fans. Sports superstars in Cuba are surprisingly accessible. You can stop in and see them at home, if you know where they live. They walk around their neighborhoods in flip-flops and T-shirts like everybody else. They hitchhike for rides on the highway, stand in line to pick up their rations at the *bodegas*, and board the crowded buses in the cities. World champion high jumper Javier Sotomayor likes to hang out at a certain beach bar in Santa Maria del Mar. The accessibility of Cuba's sports stars may have something to do with socialism. Everybody's equal, remember? Sports superstars make the same amount of money that all Cubans make (more or less), and so therefore must toil alongside the rest of the pack to make ends meet.

- Music: Not cool to sing songs of protest at concerts like Bob Dylan did. Also, if you dance freestyle to salsa or *merengue*, people will laugh at you.
- Movies: Not cool to make scathing exposés of presidents and other high-level government officials like Michael Moore does.
- Some discos and nightclubs only permit couples to enter, but often make exceptions to tourists. Also, the cover charges (and drink prices) are way out of reach for most Cubans. These realities, combined with the fact that Cuban women love to dance, cause long lines of date-seeking, single Cuban women to form at the club entrances. If you arrive unaccompanied at one of these clubs, expect to be solicited.

DATING AND SEX ATTITUDES
- Sexual attitudes in Cuba are far more relaxed than you will find in the U.S. One reason for this may be because most people don't have much money to spend on other forms of entertainment. And the government knows that if it interferes with the one thing people can do for free, a revolt would certainly follow.
- Although prostitution is illegal in Cuba, it is widely accepted within the social parameters as a trade. Cubans make a big distinction between prostitutes and the more respected *jineteras*—women who become temporary companions to tourists for pay.
- If you are sitting at a tourist café in Varadero or Old Havana, and a Cuban person of the opposite sex approaches you for a light for their cigarette, the person probably wants something else besides a light.
- The unfair double standard of *machismo*—where

it's more acceptable for men to have extramarital affairs but not acceptable for the women—is alive and well in Cuba.

- Since living quarters in most Cuban homes are generally crowded, with family members commonly sharing bedrooms if not beds, the government sanctions sex motels called *posadas* where couples can reserve cheap, no-frills rooms on an hourly basis.
- It's O.K. for the guys to wear Speedos on the beach, like the Italians do.
- Lycra-spandex body tops and bottoms are commonly worn on the streets by the ladies.
- Do not hold hands, kiss, or conduct other forms of intimacy with a member of the same sex. It's not against the law, but many Cuban people are still uncomfortable with it.

Somewhere in Cuba, somebody is writing a book about social rules and customs that are unique to the U.S. way of life. It is a book that, for the Cuban who reads it, is as full of oddities and hard-to-believe facts as the one you are reading now.

SECTION 13

MIKE'S TOP TEN AND BOTTOM TEN LISTS

1. **Top ten and bottom ten places to visit, by consensus.**
(Compiled by correlating the opinions of various guidebooks, visitors, newspaper and magazine articles, television reports, travel magazines, websites, and other sources.)

Top Ten

1. Habana Vieja. (Historic district in Havana.)
2. Valle de Viñales, Piñar del Rio.(Scenic valleys.)
3. Trinidad. (Colonial town.)
4. A *casa particular.*
5. Topes de Collantes,, Sierra Escambray. (Mountain hiking).
6. Remedios, and *parranda*. (Colonial town, and festival.)
7. Santiago de Cuba (and *Carnaval*).
8. Centro Habana (street life).
9. Scuba diving, Isle of Youth (Hotel Colony).
10. Guanabo, Playas del Este.

Bottom Ten

1. A Cuban prison.
2. A public hospital.
3. Pestering street hustlers in Habana Vieja and Santiago de Cuba.
4. Public rest stops on the main highway.
5. Moa and nickel smelters.
6. *Camello* bus ride in Havana during rush hour.
7. Villa Maspoton hunting "resort" in the Piñar del Rio province.
9. State-run, Cuban peso restaurants and motels.
10. Concrete dinosaur park in Valle de la Historia, Baconao.(Could be one of top ten best laugh.)

2. Top ten and bottom ten places to visit, according to the author's personal opinion.

Top Ten

1. Centro Habana (street life) and the Malecon.
2. Habana Vieja. (Historic distric in Havana.)
3. Staying with a family in a *casa particular*.
4. Valle de Viñales in the Piñar del Rio Province. (Scenic valleys.)
5. Cruising the cays and diving the "wall" off the Santa Clara province coast.
6. Guanabo or Santa Maria beaches at Playas del Este (Havana province).
7. A *paladar* (privately owned restaurant) with tables under some trees.
8. Trinidad. (Colonial town.)
9. *Carnaval* in Santiago de Cuba
10. Remedios, and the *parranda*. (Colonial town, festival.)

Bottom Ten

1. A Cuban prison.
2. A public hospital.
3. Pestering street hustlers in Habana Vieja and Santiago de Cuba.
4. State-run, Cuban peso restaurants and motels.
5. Public rest stops on the main highway.
6. Moa and nickel smelters.
7. Ciego de Avila, Placetas and other neglected, remote mid-sized cities.
8. The public bus terminals in neglected and remote mid-sized cities.
9. A *camello* bus ride in Havana during rush hour.
10. Worst beach (visited by author): Punta Gorda in Cienfuegos.

3. Top ten and bottom ten author personal experiences in Cuba.

Top Ten

1. Staying in a *casa particular* and getting to know the family and neighborhood.
2. Strolling Habana Vieja and sitting at an outdoor café.
3. Strolling Centro Habana (street life) and the Malecon.
4. Cruising the cays off the coast of the Santa Clara province (and diving the "wall").
5. Renting a beach house in Guanabo (Playas del Este).
6. Home-cooked meals in a private house.
7. Hiking the Valle de Viñales in the Piñar del Rio province.
8. Swimming with friends in a river with a small waterfall in the Santa Clara province.
9. Attending a cock-fight—not for the duels themselves, but for the activities surrounding the event and the social interaction.
10. *Carnaval* in Santiago de Cuba.

Bottom Ten

1. Witnessing a knife-fight between two men that ended in a death.
2. Getting kicked out of an illegal *casa particular* by MINIT housing authorities.
3. Being detained and interrogated by a MINIT immigration officer.
4. Becoming a victim of theft.
5. Body aches, fever, and diarrhea after drinking contaminated water.
6. Pestering *jineteros* and black market street hustlers in Habana Vieja, Vedado and other tourist areas.
7. Public rest stops on the main highway.
8. Staying in a Cuban peso "motel."
9. Showering in an outhouse.
10. Crooked MINIT customs officers.

4. Top Ten Scenic Drives in Cuba.

1. Viñales to Guane, via Piñar del Rio. (Piñar del Rio province.)
2. Circuito Norte: Mariel to Viñales. (Piñar del Rio province.)
3. Santa Clara to Trinidad, via Cienfuegos. (Santa Clara and Sancti Spiritus provinces.)
4. Marea del Portillo to Santiago de Cuba. (Granma and Santiago de Cuba provinces.)
5. Bartolome Maso to Marea del Portillo. (Granma province.)
6. Buena Ventura to Maneadero, Zapata Peninsula. (Matanzas province.)
7. Sagua de Tanamo to Baracoa. (Holguin and Guantanamo provinces.)
8. Holguin to Banes, via Guardalavaca. (Holguin province.)
9. Santiago de Cuba to Baconao. (Baconao Biosphere Reserve, Santiago de Cuba province.)
10. Caibarien to Punta Alegre, via Chambas. (Santa Clara, Sancti Spiritus, and Ciego de Avila provinces.)

5. Top Ten Beaches in Cuba.

1. Playa Sirena, Cayo Largo del Sur.
2. Playa Paraiso, Cayo Largo del Sur.
3. Cayo Sabinal, Camaguey province.
4. Playa Ancon, Sancti Spiritus province.
5. Playa Ensenachos, Cayo Ensenachos,
6. Playa Megano, Cayo Ensenachos,
7. Guanabo, Playas del Este, Havana
8. Playa Cayo Coco and Playa Cayo Guillermo, Ciego de Avila province
9. Playa Esmeralda, Guardalavaca, Holguin province
10. Varadero beaches, Varadero, Matanzas province

6. Top Ten Fidel Castro Historic Landmarks in Cuba.

1. Moncada Barracks, Santiago de Cuba, Santiago de Cuba province. Site of Castro's first offensive against Batista's army that signaled the beginning of the Cuban Revolution.
2. Palacio de la Justicia, Santiago de Cuba, Santiago de Cuba province. Where Castro and other captured members of his guerilla group were put on trial after the failed assault on the Moncada barracks.
3. Granma yacht landing site, Parque Nacional Desembarco del Granma, Granma province. (Yacht was used to ferry

Castro and his tiny army from Mexico to continue the revolutionary fight against the Batista army. The actual yacht can be viewed at the Museo de la Revolucion, in Habana Vieja, Havana.

4. Comandancia de la Plata. (Castro headquarters during the revolution, in mountains near Villa Santo Domingo)
5. Bay of Pigs, Playa Giron. (Where Castro successfully fought off a CIA-backed counterrevolutionary invasion.)
6. Entrance to Neocropolis Colon, Vedado. (Where Castro made his first formal announcement that the Cuban Revolucion was a socialist one.)
7. Plaza de la Revolucion, Vedado. (Famous fiery Castro speeches.)
8. Museo de la Plata, five kilometers from Las Cuevas, Granma province. (Castro's first battle victory against the Batista army.)
9. Presidio Modelo prison, four kilometers east of Nueva Gerona, Isla de la Juventud. (Castro and was imprisoned here after his failed assault on the Moncada barracks in Santiago de Cuba)
10. Hotel Tryp Habana Libre, Vedado, Havana. (First temporary headquarters after Castro seized power)

7. **Top Ten Hotels in Cuba.** (See Appendix 24, page 231 for addresses and telephone numbers)

1. Hotel Nacional, Vedado, Havana (for charm and atmosphere).
2. Hotel Melia Cohiba (best business/executive service hotel).
3. Hotel NH Parque Central, Habana Vieja, Havana (for luxury).
4. Sol Club Cayo Largo, Cayo largo del Sur (best beach resort).
5. Melia Habana, Miramar, Havana (for style and class).
6. Paradisos Rio de Oro, Guardalavaca, Holguin Province (for popularity).
7. Iberostar Varadero, Varadero, Matanzas Province (for partying fun, social life).
8. Hotel Santa Isabel, Habana Vieja, Havana (former palace, colonial charm).
9. Royal Hideaway Ensenachos, Cayo Ensenachos, Villa Clara province (for seclusion and natural beauty).
10. Hotel Tryp Habana Libre, Vedado, Havana (for history and facilities).

8. Top Ten Restaurants in Havana.

1. La Cocina Lilliam, Calle 48 # 1311 e/ 13-15, Miramar.
    (Small, privately owned paladar.)
2. El Aljibe, 7ma, e/24 y 26, Miramar (Outdoor setting)
3. La Guarida, Concordia #418, e/Gervasio y Escobar, Cenro
    Habana. (joint State and private paladar, featured in
    Miramax's *Strawberry and Chocolate*)
4. La Fermina, # 18107 5ta Ave. e/182 y 184, Miramar
5. Las Ruinas, Calle 100 y Cortina de la Presa, Parque Lenin
    (Fidel Castro's favorite)
6. Gringo Viejo, Calle 21 #454 e/E y F, Vedado
7. Restaurante 5ta y 16, 5ta Ave y 16, Miramar
8. Restaurante Mediterraneo at Hotel NH Parque Central, on
    Neptuno between Prado y Zulueta.
9. Rooftop Garden Restaurant, Hotel Sevilla, Trocadero #55,
    e/Prado y Zulueta.
10. El Abanico, Hotel Melia Cohiba, Paseo y 1ra, Vedado.

Best casual/fun/cheap places to eat: 1) Pizzeria el Farallon, Calle 22
#361 e/23 y 21, Vedado. (Best pizza, privately owned paladar).
2) Pan.Com, Calle 26 y 7ma, Miramar. (All kinds of sandwiches, and
omelets, burgers, tortillas)

9. Top Ten Traditional Cuban Dishes

1. Ropa Vieja. (Sautéed flank strips.)
2. Puerco Asado (roast, pulled pork.)
3. Arroz con Pollo. (Rice is boiled with the chicken.)
4. Cuban Mix Sandwich. (Ham, cheese, pork, salami, lettuce,
    tomato, mayonnaise, mustard, pickle.)
5. Picadillo (Cuban Sloppy Joe, often served in a tortilla wrap.)
6. Boliche. (Pot Roast.)
7. Whole roast suckling pig.
8. Corn Tamales.
9. Masa de Puerco fritas (Fried pork chunks.)
10. Stews: Ajiaco Cubano (Pork, beef, chicken, and vegetables.)
    and Caldo Gallego (Ham, pork, chorizo, white beans.)

10. Top Ten Traditional Cuban Side Dishes

1. Croquettas
2. Empanadas—stuffed meat or vegetable turnovers
3. Frituras de maiz—deep fried corn batter (like hushpuppies)
4. Frituras de malanga—(like a deep-fried, potato batter)
5. Congris—red kidney beans with rice
6. Tostones—fried mashed plaintains
7. Chicharitas—plaintain chips
8. Moros y Cristianos—black beans and rice
9. Homemade yucca crackers
10. Battered and deep-fried boiled egg

11. Top Ten Traditional Cuban Desserts. (O.K., top eleven=baker's top ten)

1. Flan
2. Rice Pudding, bread pudding
3. Shaved and flavored ice
4. Fried plaintains
5. Ke ke or queique--sponge cake with thick, fluffy icing
6. Puddings—natilla (vanilla) or coconut (coco quemado)
7. Coco rayado—shaved, fried coconut with syrup (sometimes made with cheese, too)
8. Turron (homemade—farmers often hawk these along the highway)
9. Churrizo—deep-fried doughnut balls
10. Guayaba marmalade with cheese
11. Mani molido or granizado—ground peanut or whole peanut candy bars

12. Top Ten Traditional Cuban Cocktails.

1. Mojito
2. Daquiri
3. Cuba Libre—with Havana Club rum
4. Aguardiente (cane brandy firewater)
5. Rum Punch
6. Sangria
7. Havana Cooler (Rum, mint, ginger ale or lemon soda)
8. Piña Colada (use coconut cream)
9. Cuban-brewed Hatuey beer
10. Cuban-brewed Mayabe beer

13. Top Ten Traditional Cuban Non-alcoholic Beverages.

1. Café Cubano (also known as cafécito)
2. Café con leche
3. Guarapo—fresh sugar cane juice
4. Batido—milkshake with fruit such as mango or guayaba
5. Fruit smoothies—I.e., mango, pineapple
6. Pru—Naturally-fermented, sweet drink from root vegetables, fruit, herbs and sugar
7. Malta—caramel-flavored, carbonated malt drink
8. Homemade lemonade
9. Fresh-squeezed orange juice mixed with pineapple juice
10. Ice-cold Toki drink—similar to Kool-Aid

14. Top Ten Café con Leche in Havana.

1. Lobby bar at Hotel NH Parque Central, Habana Vieja.
2. Lobby bar at Melia Cohiba, Vedado
3. Pool bar at Hotel Nacional, Vedado
4. Lobby bar at Hotel Seville, Habana Vieja
5. Lobby bar at Hotel Ambos Mundos, Habana Vieja.
6. Lobby bar at Hotel Tryp Habana Libre, Vedado
7. Restaurant at Hotel Santa Isabel, Habana Vieja
8. Castillo de Farnes (café-bar), Habana Vieja.
9. Sidewalk café at Hotel Inglaterra, Centro Habana
10. Restaurant bar at the Hotel Capri in Vedado

SECTION 14

SOME POPULAR (MOSTLY SUBVERSIVE) CUBAN JOKES

1. The tourist and the Cuban in a Havana park.
To take in the sights and rest his feet, a newly arrived tourist from France sits on a bench under the shade of a laurel tree at a city park in Havana. Also on the bench is a Cuban fellow who is gazing pensively into the distant blur of crumbling buildings and passing traffic. After a few minutes, the Frenchman turns to the Cuban and asks,

"So how are things in Cuba?"

The Cuban, lulled out of his daydream, glances at the tourist and shrugs his shoulders. "We can't complain," he says.

"Making do, eh?"

"No, we're not," the Cuban said, irritation squeezing his words. "I said we can't complain."

2. Fidel's car hits a pig.
Fidel was out with his driver, taking a spin through the countryside when suddenly—Bam!—they ran over a pig darting across the road.

"Ay, *Dios!*" Fidel's driver exclaimed, fully aware how much the poor farmers treasure their livestock. "What should we do?"

"Look for the owner, explain what happened, and pay him for the loss," Fidel instructed.

Six hours later, the driver, looking disheveled and flushed, met up with Fidel again.

"What took you so long?" Fidel asked.

"You'll never believe it, *Comandante*," the driver said. "The owner of the pig invited me to a scrumptious meal, his wife made me drink some excellent wine, and I made love—twice—with their beautiful daughter."

"*Cojones*," Fidel said. "What did you tell them?"

"Nothing," the driver replied. "All I said was 'I am the driver of

Fidel Castro and I ran over the pig.'"

3. Colloquial expressions.
Colloquial expressions in Cuba:

- Buses are known as "aspirin" because you only get one every four hours.

- Steak is called "Jesus Christ" because everyone talks about it but no one has ever seen it.

- A refrigerator is called a "coconut" because the only thing in it is water.

- ETECSA (the national telephone company) stands for *Estamos Tratando de Establecer Comunicacion Sin Apuro*. (We Are Trying to Establish Communication Without Hurrying.)

4. The embarrassing sound.
A bricklayer, a doctor, a priest, a poet, and a revolutionary were chatting during a game of dominoes at a table placed in the street when an embarrassing sound caught their attention and caused them to ask, "What was that?"

The bricklayer said, "That was just a fart."

"That was not just a fart," said the doctor. "That was gas that is produced in the intestines."

"If you will," the priest said. "That was not just a fart or gas that is produced in the intestines. That was the soul of a bean in penance."

Said the poet, "If you would allow me just a moment, because that was not just a fart, or gas that is produced in the intestines, or the soul of a bean in penance. That was the breath of nether cheeks in love."

The revolutionary pounded the table with a fist, causing the dominoes to jump. "Let me tell you something," he said. "That was not just a fart, or gas that is produced in the intestines, or the soul of a bean in penance, or the breath of nether cheeks in love. That was the cry of a stinker seeking freedom."

5. The portrait of George Bush.
A teacher showed her grade-school class a picture of George Bush and asked them, "Does anybody know who this is?"

The classroom remained totally silent.

"Alright," the teacher said. "I'll give you a clue. Because of this person, many of us go hungry."

"Ah," little Pepito said. "I didn't recognize him without his uniform and beard."

6. Bragging moms.
At a bus stop in Havana, four Catholic women are bragging about how important their grown kids have become.

"My son is a priest," the first lady says. "When he enters a room, everybody calls him 'father.'"

"My son is a bishop," the second lady says. "Wherever he goes, people call him 'Your Grace.'"

"I don't mean to make you feel bad," the third lady says. "But my son is a Cardinal. Wherever he goes, people call him 'Your Eminence.'" The first three ladies turn to hear what the fourth lady has to say. But the fourth lady just stares at her feet and says nothing.

"Well?" the first three ladies demand of the fourth.

"Well," the fourth lady begins. "My son is a stripper. He's 6' 4", with a body as hard as a rock, buns of steel, and wherever he goes all the girls say, 'Oh, God.'"

7. Toilet time.
An older man goes to see a doctor at a polyclinic. "Doctor," he says. "I need your help with a problem that I have. Every morning, like clockwork, I pee at six and poop at seven."

"So, what's your problem?" the doctor asks.

"The problem is," the old man laments, "I don't wake up until eight."

8. Zoo signs of the times.
During the best years of the Cuban Revolution, the signs on the cages at the zoos displayed the same warning found at all zoos around the world: "Don't Feed the Animals." Today, however, the signs read "Don't Eat the Animals' Food," an indication of the current difficulties the country is facing. But the current zoo signs are not as bad as the ones that were displayed during the severe economic crisis of the Special Period in the early Nineties: "Don't Eat the Animals."

9. Beauty and the drunk.
A drunken man returns home late and finds that his wife, who is very angry with him, has locked him out.

"C'mon," the man pleads. "Let me in." But his wife wouldn't have it. After fifteen minutes of fruitless effort, the man gets an idea.

"I've brought a gift for the most beautiful woman in the world," he coos.

Upon hearing this, the wife softens her stance and lets him in. The man doesn't even look at his wife as he passes her.

"Where's the gift?" the wife asks.

"Where's the most beautiful woman in the world?" the man replies.

10. Recycled loot.
Pick pocketing is so common on the crowded buses in Havana that when people get off the bus, they often discover that they've stolen their own wallet back.

11. Strange rewards.
At a beach in Guanabo, Fidel, who does not know how to swim, strays into water over his head and begins to drown. Three children swimming nearby pull him to safety.

"You saved me from certain death," Fidel tells the children. "Ask me for anything you want and I will make sure you get it."

"I'd like a doll that walks and talks," little Yanelis says.

"A doll that walks and talks it will be," Fidel responds.

"And I'd like a ten-speed bicycle," Tomasito says.

"A ten-speed bicycle you shall have," Fidel replies. "And what would you like?" he asks the third child, whose name is Pepito.

"I don't want anything," Pepito replies. "But thank you anyway."

But Fidel refused to let Pepito go until he chose something.

"Alright," Pepito said. "I'd like a coffin."

"A coffin?" Fidel said, somewhat taken aback. "What do you want a coffin for?"

"Because when my father finds out I saved your life, he's going to kill me."

SECTION 15

USEFUL SPANISH WORDS AND PHRASES

1. **Common phrases—miscellaneous**
   A little *Un poco*
   A lot *Mucho*
   Big *Grande*
   Difficult *Dificil*
   Hello *Hola*
   He left *Se fue*
   How do you say *Como se dice*
   Easy *Facil*
   Goodbye *Adios*
   Yes *Si*
   No *No*
   Please *Por favor*
   Thank you *Gracias*
   You are welcome *De nada*
   Excuse me *Perdon* or *Disculpe*
   I am sorry (forgive me) *Lo siento/Disculpeme*
   How are you? *¿Como estas?*
   I am fine, thanks *Estoy bien, gracias*
   What is your name? *¿Como se llama?*
   My name is *Me llamo*
   Where are you from? *¿De donde eres?*
   I am from *Yo soy de*
   I don't understand *No entiendo*
   I need *Yo necesito*
   I want *Yo quiero*
   Do you speak English? *¿Habla Ingles?*
   Happy birthday *Feliz cumpleaños*
   Here is/are *Aquí está/están*
   Hello *Hola*
   Good morning *Buenos días*
   Good afternoon *Buenas tardes*
   Good night/Good evening. *Buenas noches*
   Very well, thanks. *Muy bien gracias*

Can you help me? *¿Me puede ayudar?*
I don't know. *No lo sé.*
Leave me alone. *Déjeme en paz.*
Less *Menos*
More *Mas*
Not very good *No muy bueno*
Please write it down. *Por favor, escríbalo.*
Quick *Raqpido*
Right Away *Enseguida*
Slow *Despacio*
Small *Pequeño*
Soon *Pronto*
There *Alli*
When? *¿Cuándo?*
Where *Donde*
Why? *¿Por qué?*
Who? *¿Quién?*
Which? *¿Cuál?*
How much is it? *¿Cuánto cuesta?*
How many? *¿Cuántos?*
What's that? *¿Qué es eso?*
I'd like. *Me gustaría*
I want. *Quiero.*
I don't like it. *No me gusta.*
OK/Agreed. *OK/De acuerdo.*
That's fine. *Está bien.*
Very bad *Muy mal*

2. **Articles, Prepositions, Pronouns, Conjunctions**
   And *Y*
   After *Despues*
   Already *Ya*
   At *A*
   Before *Antes*
   For *Para*
   From *De/Desde*
   He *El*
   I *Yo*
   It *El/La/Lo/Le/Ello/Ella/Esto/Esta*
   In *En*
   Of *De*
   She *Ella*
   This *Esto*
   To *A*
   We/US *Nosotros*
   You (plural) *Ustedes*

You (singular) *Tu/Usted*
With *Con*
Without *Sin*

3. Family Relations
Aunt *Tia*
Brother *Hermano*
Cousin *Primo* (male) *Prima* (female)
Daughter *Hija*
Father *Padre*
Father-in-law *Suegro*
Godfather *Padrino*
Godmother *Padrina*
Grandfather *Abuelo*
Grandmother *Abuela*
Granddaughter *Nieta*
Grandson *Nieto*
Husband *Esposo*
Mother *Madre*
Mother-in-law *Suegra*
Sister *Hermana*
Son *Hijo*
Uncle *Tio*
Wife *Esposa*

4. Bank and Post Office
Airmail *Correo Aereo*
Letter *Carta*
Package *Paquete*
Post office *Correos*
Registered *Mail Certificado*
Stamps *Sellos*
Postcard *Postal*

5. Transportation/Getting Around
Airplane *Avion*
Airport *Aeropuerto*
Bicycle *Bicicleta*
Car *Auto/Maquina*
Motorcycle *Motocicleta/Moto*
Boat *Barco/Buque*
Taxi *Taxi*
Truck *Camión*
Bus *Autobus/Gua Gua/Ominibus*

Train *Tren*
Ticket *Boleto*
Hitchhike *Hacer botella*
What time does the... leave/arrive? *¿A que hora sale/llega el...?*
Where is...? *¿Donde esta...?*
The bus stop *La parada de autobus*
The train station *La estacion de tren*
I would like a ticket *Quisiera un billete*
One way *De solo ida*
Return *De ida y vuelta*
I want to go to...*Quiero ir a...*

6. Directions
Can you show me (on the map)? *¿Me puede indicar (en el mapa)?*
Go straight ahead *Vaya todo recto/derecho*
Turn left *Gire a la izquierda*
Turn right *Gire a la derecha*
At the traffic lights *En el semaforo*
At the next corner *En la proxima esquina*
I am looking for...*Estoy buscando...*
Bank/embassy/post office *banco/embajada de/correos*
Floor *Piso*
Tourist office *Oficina de turismo*
Down *Abajo*
Up *Arriba*
Where? *¿Dónde?don-deh*
Where is a cheap hotel? *¿Donde hay un hotel barato?*

7. Accommodations
Air conditioning *Aire condicionado*
Blankets *Mantas*
Do you have any rooms available? *¿Tiene habitaciones libres?*
Double *Doble*
Fan *Ventilador*
Hotel *Hotel*
Is breakfast included? *¿Esta incluido el desayuno?*
Key *Llave*
May I see it? *Puedo verla?*
Per night *Por noche*
Per person *Por persona*
Pillow *Almohada*
Private *Privado*

Reception *Carpeta*
Single *Sencillo/Para Uno*
Shared bath *Baño compartido*
Sheets *Sabanas*
Youth hostel *Albergue juvenil*

8. Geography

Avenue *Avenida*
Bay *Bahia*
Beach *Playa*
Between *Entre*
Block *Bloque*
Bridge *Puente*
Cay *Cayo*
City *Ciudad*
Corner *Esquina*
Cove *Enseñada*
East *Este*
Highway *Carretera*
Hill *Loma/Cerro*
Kilometer *Kilometro*
Lake *Lago*
Lagoon *Laguna*
Marsh *Estero*
Mile *Milla*
Mountain *Montaña*
Mountain Range *Cordillera*
National Park *Parque National*
North *Norte*
Pass *Paso*
Park *Parque*
Point *Punta*
Reef *Arecife*
River *Rio*
Resevoir *Embalse*
Road *Camino*
South *Sur*
Street *Calle*
Swamp *Cienaga*
Town *Pueblo*
Waterfall *Salto/Cascada*
West *Oeste*

9. Food and Drink

Apple *Manzana*

Avocado *Aguacate*
Bacon *Tocino*
Banana *Banano/Platano dulce*
Banana Chips *Chicharitas*
Fried Squashed Banana *Tostones*
Beef *Res*
Beer *Cerveza*
Beans *Frijoles*
Black beans *Frijoles negros*
Black Beans and Rice *Moros y Cristianos*
Boiled *Hervido*
Bread *Pan*
Breakfast *Desayuno*
Butter *Mantequilla*
Carrot *Zanahoria*
Cassava *Yucca*
Cabbage *Col*
Carbonated water *Agua carbonada/Agua con gas*
Caramel Pudding *Flan/Natilla*
Cheese *Queso*
Chicken *Pollo*
Chickpeas *Garbanzos*
Cucumber *Pepino*
Coffee *Café*
Corn *Maiz*
Crab *Cangrejo*
Cream *Crema*
Dinner *Cena*
Drink *Beber/Tomar*
Eat *Comer*
Egg *Huevo*
Fish *Pescado*
Fried *Frito*
French *Fries Papas fritas*
Fruit *Fruta*
Garlic *Ajo*
Grapefruit *Toronja*
Guava *Guayaba*
Ham *Jamon*
Hamburger *Hamburgesa*
Hot Dogs *Perros Calientes*
Ice cream *Helado*
Jam *Mermelada*
Juice *Jugo*
Lamb *Cordero*
Lemon *Limón*
Lettuce *Lechuga*

Lobster *Langosta*
Lunch *Almuerzo*
Manioc *Yucca*
Mashed potatoes *Pure de Papas*
Meat Stew *Ajiaco*
Meat *Carne*
Milk *Leche*
Milkshake *Batido*
Mincemeat *Picadillo*
Omelets *Tortilla*
Onion *Cebolla*
Orange *Naranja*
Oysters *Ociónes*
Papaya *Fruta Bomba*
Peas *Guisantes*
Pear *Pera*
Pepper *Pimienta*
Pig *Cochino*
Pineapple *Pina*
Plantain *Platano burro or platano macho* (two types)
Potatoes *Papas*
Pork *Puerco/Cerdo*
Roasted *Asado*
Roast Beef *Rosbif/Puerco Asado*
Rum *Ron*
Salad *Ensalada*
Salt *Sal*
Sandwich *Bocadillo*
Sausage *Chorizo* (hard)/*Salchicha* (soft)
Scrambled eggs *Revoltillo*
Seafood *Mariscos*
Shrimp *Camarones*
Soup *Sopa*
Spinach *Espinaca*
Stew *Caldo*
Strawberry *Fresa*
Suckling Pig *Lechón*
Sugar *Azucar*
Sweet Potato *Boniato*
Taro *Malanga*
Tea *Te*
Toasted *Tostada*
Tomato *Tomate*
Rice *Arroz*
Veal *Ternera*
Vegetarian *Vegetariano*
Vegetables *Vegetales/Legumbres*

Water *Agua*
Water without gas *Agua sin gas*
Wine *Vino*

10. Money
Dollars *Dólares*
Euros *Euros*
Convertible pesos *Pesos convertibles*
The Bill *La Cuenta*
Cheap *Barato*
Expensive *Caro*
How much *Cuanto*
Money *Dinero*
National currency *Moneda nacional*
Too much *Demasiado*
What is the exchange rate? *Como es el cambio?*

11. House Things
Bathroom *Baño*
Bed *Cama*
Bedroom *Dormitorio*
Cold water *Agua fria*
Hot water *Agua cliente*
Kitchen *Cocina*
Room *Cuarto*
Shampoo *Champu*
Shower *Ducha*
Soap *Jabon*
Toilet *Baños*
Toilet paper *Papel sanitario*
Towel *Toalla*

12. Clothing/Dress
Jacket *Chaqueta*
Pants *Pantalones*
Rain jacket *Capa de Agua*
Sandals *Chancletas*
Shirt *Camisa*
Shoes *Zapatos*
Shorts *Chors*
Socks *Medias*
Sweater *Sueter*
T-shirt *Pullover*
Underwear (males) *Calcetines*

Underwear (females) *Blumers*

13. Utensils/Dishware/Eating Out
Bowl *Tazon*
Cup Taza
Fork *Tenedor*
Frying pan *Sarten*
Glass *Vaso*
Knife *Cuchillo*
Menu *Carta*
Napkin *Servilleta*
Plate *Plato*
Pot *Olla*
Spoon *Cucharra*
Server *Camarero*

14. Days of the Week
Monday *Lunes*
Tuesday *Martes*
Wednesday *Miercoles*
Thursday *Jueves*
Friday *Viernes*
Saturday *Sabado*
Sunday *Domingo*

15. Months of the Year
January *Enero*
February *Febrero*
March *Marzo*
April *Abril*
May *Mayo*
June *Junio*
July *Julio*
August *Agosto*
September *Septiembre*
October *Octubre*
November *Noviembre*
December *Diciembre*

16. Time and numbers
In the morning *En la mañana*
Last night *Anoche*
The day before *El dia antes*

Last year *El año pasado*
Last week *La semana pasada*
Today *Hoy*
Tonight *Esta noche*
Tomorrow *Mañana*
Yesterday *Ayer*
What time is it? *¿Que hora es?*
0 *cero*
1 *uno,una*
2 *dos*
3 *tres*
4 *cuatro*
5 *cinco*
6 *seis*
7 *siete*
8 *ocho*
9 *nueve*
10 *diez*
20 *veinte*
30 *treinta*
40 *cuarenta*
50 *cincuenta*
100 *cien/ciento*
1000 *mil*
10000 *diez mil*
one million *un millon*

17. Medical

Antibiotic *Antibiótico*
Antiseptic *Antiseptico*
Aspirin *Aspirina*
Condoms *Condones/preservativos*
Diarrhea *Diarrea*
Drugstore *Farmacia*
Medicine *Medicamento*
Nausea *Nausea*
Pain *Dolór*
Pill *Pastilla*
Stomachache *Dolór de estomago*
Cream *Crema*
Help *Socorro*
I need help *Necesito ayuda*
I am ill *Estoy enfermo*
Call a doctor *Llame a un doctor*
Call the police *Llame a la policia*
Vomiting *Vomitando*

18. How to Speak Cuban

The language spoken in Cuba is classic Spanish (Castilian), but like natives in every country, the Cuban people have invented or adopted a few handy words of their own. These are listed below. The Cubans pronounce their words with an accent and speech pattern that is unique. Words are strung together and spoken in rapid-fire staccato. To make matters worse for those with an untrained ear, most consonants and many syllables at the end of each word are dropped, and the 's,' is frequently abandoned entirely. *Para que* ('for what') becomes *pa'que*, *hasta la vista* ('see you later') becomes *ha'ta la vi'ta*, and *por alla* ('over there') becomes pa'ya. The origin of some words and much of the Cuban pronunciation can be traced to the Canary Islands, a Spanish territory that saw massive migrations to Cuba in the 19th and early 20th century. I acquired my Spanish pronunciation growing up in Spain and when I am in Cuba I always get compliments on how clean and proper my accent sounds. I also get called *Gallego* a lot. (*Gallego* means Galician, a person from the Galician province in Spain.)

Acere Close friend
Amarillo Fare collector for hitchhikers
Babalawo Santeria priest
Barabaro Neat/Cool/Nice/Sharp
Barbacoa A loft built above a room for additional space
Baro Dollars
Blumers Ladies panties
Bohio Thatched hut
Bollo Vagina
Bómbo (U.S. visa lottery)
Botella hitchhike (*Botella* means 'bottle')
Caballito Motorcycle police
Camello Conjoined public bus
Candela Bad situation, or broke
Carro car
Chavitos Convertible pesos
Chivata/Chivaton Snitch
Chors Shorts
Chopin Convertible peso shop
Cola Queue
Colectivo Shared taxi *Coche* Horse-drawn shuttle (wagon)
Como anda How is it going (*Anda* means 'walk.')
Congri Rice with red beans
Coño Holy crap (similar), sometimes abbreviated to *ño*
Embori Informer
Esta en talla This is excellent
Esta en llamas This is terrible (Llamas means 'flame')

Fajar To fight
Filin romantic music with feeling
Fula U.S. dollars
Fulano What's-his-(or her)-name
Gua-gua Bus
Guano Money (guano means 'palm leaf')
Guapo hustler-type person
Guarapo Fresh-squeezed sugarcane juice
Gusano Derogatory term for defector, counterrevolutionary
Jaba Plastic grocery bag
Jeva Woman
Jinetera female black market street hustler
Jinetero male black market street hustler
Jon ron Home run
La Yuma U.S.A
Maquina '50s American car
Marinovia Live-in girlfriend
Me quedan pintadas They look great on me
Moros y Cristianos Black beans and rice
Nailon Plastic grocery bag (From 'nylon')
Ojala If only, or Hopefully
Overol Dungarees
Paladar Small, privately owned restaurant
Pan Gloria ('Glory bread') White Cuban bread loaf
Pan del Diablo ('Devil's bread) Poor quality ration rolls
Parada bus stop
Pinga Penis
Pitusa Jeans
Platano burro a type of plaintain
Ponchero Tube puncture repair person
Pulover T-shirt
Que bola What's up
Queic Cake
Saco Suit
Sueter Sweater
Tenis Sneakers
Verde U.S. dollar
Yin Jeans

END NOTES

SECTION ONE
[1] "It shall be unlawful for any person in the United States, except with the license of the President, granted to such person…to trade or attempt to trade with…any person, with knowledge or reasonable cause to believe that such other person is an enemy or ally of enemy." (Trading with the Enemy Act of 1917, also called the War Powers Act, invoked by President Kennedy in 1962 and codified by the Cuban Assets Control Regulations in 1963.) Besides the Trading With the Enemy Act, the U.S. embargo laws against Cuba consist of two other Acts (and a multitude of amendments): The Democracy Act (Torricelli Law) (1992), and The Cuban Liberty and Solidarity Act (Helms-Burton Law) (1996). For overviews or copies of these laws, contact the Office of Foreign Assets Control, U.S. Department of the Treasury at 1500 Pennsylvania Ave NW, Annex Building, 2nd Floor, Washington, D.C. 20220 (telephone 202-622-2529), or visit the U.S. Treasury website at www.treas.gov/OFAC (click on "sanctions"). The embargo laws are frequently amended or changed and have waiver clauses; in June of 2004, sanctions were tightened even further and the enforcement of the embargo laws were stepped up after President Bush created a task force called the Commission for Assistance to a Free Cuba. The restrictions even forbid U.S. citizens to spend money in other countries if that money will end up in Cuba or in the hands of a Cuban national. This means buying a plane ticket from an airline or agency from a foreign company for Cuba travel is prohibited because some of the proceeds are used to pay airport and other fees in Cuba.
[2] The maximum individual fine is $250,000 and the maximum corporate fine is $1,000,000.
[3] Presently, non-U.S. citizens may freely travel to Cuba from other countries and spend money in Cuba. But they must be aware of a

stipulation (currently waived, and traditionally waived for six-month periods) of the Torricelli Law and Helms-Burton Act that bars them from returning to the U.S. or doing business in the U.S.

[4] The address is: Licensing Division, Office of Foreign Assets Control, U.S. Department of the Treasury at 1500 Pennsylvania Ave NW, Annex Building, 2nd Floor, Washington, D.C. 20220. Telephone (202) 622-2480. You can also visit the U.S. Treasury website at www.treas.gov/OFAC (click on "sanctions").

[5] Appendix 1 on page 164 lists the categories of travel that are permitted.

[6] Also known as the 'maximum per diem rate' for Havana, Cuba. This per diem rate often changes; for current rates, check the Department of State Standardized Regulations supplement to section 925, "Maximum Travel Per Diem Allowances for Foreign Areas." This supplement can be found on the Internet at www.state,gov/m/a/als/prdm or you can contact the Government Printing Office, Superintendent of Documents, P.O. Box 371945, Pittsburgh, PA 15250-7954.

[7] Only one exception to this rule permits you to bring back "informational material," such as publications, films, posters, phonograph records, photographs, tapes, CDs, and certain artworks (regulation number 515.332).

[8] Office of Foreign Assets Control. This is a department of the U.S. Treasury that administers and codifies all U.S. embargo laws.

[9] Warning: If you tell the Cuban immigration officer you are a journalist or visiting for business purposes, you risk being assessed a fee for a special visa.

[10] The conference or meeting can only be organized by an entity not based in Cuba or the United States and which regularly organizes conferences and meetings in other countries. See Appendix 1 on page 164 for more information about qualifying for a license to travel to Cuba under this category.

[11] For an updated list, you can also dial a fax-on-demand service at 202-622-0077 and request document number 1207.

[12] Sometimes the Cuban immigration officers place an almost indiscernible mark, usually a tiny square or part of a square, in the back pages of U.S. passports. The mark may appear innocuous, but the U.S. authorities are very familiar with this mark and will find it if they are looking for it. The marks, however, will not tell the U.S. immigration officers WHEN you went to Cuba.

[13] An immigration or customs agent at the U.S. checkpoint will provide you with this form. The flight attendants on the arriving planes often pass these around to the passengers before the plane lands. Refer to Appendix 5 on page 181 for a sample of one.

SECTION TWO

[14] Lying to a government agent is a federal crime. The consequences may be more severe than committing the civil offense of spending money in Cuba.

[15] Contact the Center's Cuba Travel Project Coordinator. The CCR address is 666 Broadway, 7th Floor, N.Y., N.Y. 10012.

[16] Miami Herald article by Frances Robles, November 5, 2008.

[17] Cuban Interest Office, 2639 16th St. NW, Washington D.C., 20009 tel 202-797-8609/797-8610

[18] Ibid.

[19] For a list of immigration offices in Cuba see the appendix on page 192.

[20] Cuban Interest Office, 2639 16th St. NW, Washington D.C., 20009 tel 202-797-8609/797-8610

[21] Section 16, Chapter 106, War Powers Act of 1917, which is currently invoked.

[22] Customs and Border Patrol telephone numbers and locations for Florida, Puerto Rico, and the U.S. Virgin Islands are listed in Appendix 14 on page 194.

[23] You will need to provide the name, date of birth, citizenship, and passport numbers of all persons aboard as well as the boat registration number.

[24] There is also a Local Boater Program enrollment option that enables qualified applicants to report their arrival telephonically in lieu of a face-to-face interview. This requires advance filing.

SECTION THREE

[25] I.e., the ongoing flight of professionals from the country and an inefficient and cumbersome socialist economic model of a centralized (state-owned and operated) system of production and distribution (typical in socialist countries).

[26]Cuban Assets Control Regulations, 31 CFR amended paragraph (f) of 515.560.

SECTION EIGHT

[27] Eradicated diseases include malaria, typhoid, diphtheria, tetanus, polio, and hepatitis A.

[28] Cuban hospitals will accept credit card payments, but not if the credit card is drawn on a U.S. bank.

SECTION NINE

[29] These very words were lifted from a consular information sheet distributed by the U.S. State Department's Bureau of Consular Affairs. The president, officials of the Defense Department, as well as many members of congress voice the same opinion.

[30] "American" hereafter refers to citizens of the U.S., and not citizens of South America, Central America or Canada.

[31] A stipulation in the Criminal Codes of Cuba nullifies the rights and freedoms guaranteed in the Constitution if they are contrary to "the people's decision to build socialism and communism."

[32] Article #144 of the Criminal Code of Cuba

[33] Law #80 *Reaffirming Cuban Dignity and Sovereignty* (December 1996).

[34] Article 53, Cuban Constitution states that "Press, radio, television, cinema and other mass media are state or social property and can never be private property."

[35] Article 72, Criminal Code of Cuba (Law 62)

[36] Article 10 and 62 of the 1992 Cuban Constitution.

[37] Law 88 (Law for the Protection of Cuban National Independence and Economy)

[38] Law # 62, Criminal Code of Cuba

[39] (Cuban Constitution, Article 64)

[40] (Cuban Constitution, Article 10 and 62)

BLANK PAGE FOR NOTES

APPENDICES

APPENDIX 1
(from page 13 and 156)

OVERVIEW OF ACTIVITIES FOR WHICH CUBA TRAVEL-RELATED TRANSACTIONS ARE GENERALLY LICENSED OR MAY BE SPECIFICALLY LICENSED BY THE OFFICE OF FOREIGN ASSETS CONTROL

The numbers in the parenthesis refer to the pertaining section of the regulations, known as the Cuban Assets Control Regulations, found in the U.S. Federal Code of Regulations (title 31).

I. Persons Visiting Members of their Immediate Family in Cuba (§§515.560(a)(1) & 515.561)
Specific license consideration for visiting a member of the person's immediate family who is a national of Cuba every three years and for visiting a member of the person's immediate family who is not a national of Cuba in certain exigent circumstances.

II. Official business of the U.S. and foreign governments and certain intergovernmental organizations (§§ 515.560(a)(2) & 515.562)
Authorized by general license for officials of the U.S. Government, any foreign government, and certain intergovernmental organization of which the United States is a member who are traveling on official business.

III. Journalistic activity (§§ 515.560(a)(3) & 515.563)
Authorized by general license for journalists regularly employed by a news reporting organization and for persons regularly employed as supporting broadcast or technical personnel.

Specific license consideration for free-lance journalists.

IV. Professional research and meetings (§§ 515.560(a)(4) & 515.564)
Authorized by general license for full-time professionals attending meetings or conferences or conducting professional research in their professional areas. Research requires a full work schedule of noncommercial, academic research that has a substantial likelihood of public dissemination and is in the traveler's professional area. Meetings or conferences must be organized by an international professional organization, institution, or association headquartered outside the United States that regularly sponsors meetings or conferences in other countries. If a meeting or conference is organized by an organization headquartered in the

United States, that organization must have a specific license from OFAC to organize the meeting or conference. The meetings or conferences may not be for the purpose of promoting tourism in Cuba or other commercial activities involving Cuba that are not licensable under current U.S. policy and may not be intended primarily for the purpose of fostering production of any biotechnological products.

Specific license consideration for other professional research and attendance at professional meetings when the general license criteria above do not apply.

V. Educational activities (§§ 515.560(a)(5) & 515.565)

Specific license consideration for an accredited U.S. undergraduate or graduate degree-granting academic institution authorizing the institution, its students enrolled in an undergraduate or graduate degree program at the institution, and its full-time permanent employees to engage in transactions incident to:

(1) participation in a structured educational program as part of a course offered at the licensed institution, provided the program constitutes a full term of study and no shorter than 10 weeks in duration in Cuba;

(2) noncommercial academic research in Cuba specifically related to Cuba for the purpose of obtaining a graduate degree;

(3) participation in a formal course of study at a Cuban academic institution, provided the formal course of study in Cuba will be accepted for credit toward the student's undergraduate or graduate degree at the licensed institution and provided that the course of study is no shorter than 10 weeks in duration;

(4) teaching at a Cuban academic institution by an individual regularly employed in a teaching capacity at the licensed institution, provided the teaching activities are related to an academic program at the Cuban institution and the duration of the teaching will be no shorter than 10 weeks;

(5) sponsorship, including the payment of a stipend or salary, of a Cuban scholar to teach or engage in other scholarly activity at the licensed institution; or

(6) the organization of and preparation for activities described in (1)-(5) above by a full-time permanent employee of the licensed institution.

Specific license consideration for individual students to engage in educational activities described in (2)-(3) above but that do not take place pursuant to a license issued to an academic institution.

VI. Religious activities (§§ 515.560(a)(6) & 515.566)
Specific license consideration for a religious organization located in the United States authorizing the organization and individuals and groups affiliated with it, to engage in a full-time program of religious activities in Cuba under the auspices of the organization.

Specific license consideration for religious activities engaged in by individuals that do not take place pursuant to a license issued to a religious organization.

VII. Public performances, athletic and other competitions, and exhibitions (§§ 515.560(a)(7) & 515.567)
Specific license consideration for athletic competition by amateur or semi-professional athletes or teams selected by the relevant U.S. federation and traveling to participate in athletic competition held in Cuba under the auspices of the relevant international sports federation when the competition is open for attendance, and in relevant situations participation, by the Cuban public.

Specific license consideration of participation in a public performance, other athletic competition, non-athletic competition, or exhibition in Cuba by participants in such activities, provided that the event is open for attendance, and
in relevant situations participation, by the Cuban public and all U.S. profits from the event after costs are donated to an independent nongovernmental organization in Cuba or a U.S.-based charity that benefits the Cuban people.

VIII. Support for the Cuban people (§§ 515.560(a)(8) & 515.574)
Specific license consideration of activities intended to provide support for the Cuban people including but not limited to:

1) activities of recognized human rights organizations;
2) activities of independent organizations designed to promote a rapid, peaceful transition to democracy; and
3) activities of individuals and nongovernmental organizations that promote independent activity intended to strengthen civil society in Cuba.

IX. Humanitarian projects (§§ 515.560(a)(9) & 515.575)

Specific license consideration of humanitarian projects in or related to Cuba designed to directly benefit the Cuban people, including but not limited to: medical and health-related projects; construction projects intended to benefit legitimately independent civil society groups; environmental projects; projects involving formal or non-formal educational training, within Cuba or off-island, on topics including civil education, journalism, advocacy and organizing, adult literacy, and vocational skills; community-based grass roots projects; projects suitable to the development of small-scale private enterprise; projects that are related to agricultural and rural development that promote independent activity; and projects to meet basic human needs.

X. Activities of private foundations or research or educational institutes (§§ 515.560(a)(10) & 515.576)

Specific license consideration of activities by private foundations or research or educational institutes that have an established interest in international relations to collect information related to Cuba for noncommercial purposes.

XI. Exportation, importation, or transmission of information or informational materials (§§ 515.560(a)(11) & 515.545)

Specific license consideration of travel-related transactions for purposes related to the exportation, importation, or transmission of information or informational materials as defined in § 515.332.

XII. Certain export transactions that may be considered for authorization under existing Department of Commerce regulations with respect to Cuba or engaged in by U.S.-owned or controlled foreign firms (§§ 515.560(a)(12), 515.533 & 515.559)

Exports from the United States and reexports of 100% U.S.-origin items: Specific license consideration of travel-related transactions and other transactions that are directly incident to the marketing, sales negotiation, accompanied delivery, or
servicing of exports and re-exports that appear consistent with the export licensing policy of the Department of Commerce, including but not limited to the commercial export sale of agricultural commodities and the donation of goods to meet basic human needs.

Exports from foreign countries of certain foreign-produced merchandise: Specific license consideration of travel-related transactions and other transactions that are directly incident to marketing, sales negotiation, accompanied delivery, or servicing of medicine or medical supplies, or donated food, from a third country to Cuba, or of telecommunications equipment from a third country to Cuba, when the equipment is determined to be necessary for efficient and adequate telecommunications service between the United States and Cuba.

APPENDIX 2
(from page 13)

APPLICATION GUIDELINES AND RECOMMENDED LETTER FORMAT WHEN APPLYING FOR A TRAVEL LICENSE FROM THE OFFICE OF FOREIGN ASSETS AFFAIRS

How to Apply for a Specific License

In most cases, applications for specific licenses should be made in writing to OFAC in letter format not less than forty-five (45) days but no more than six (6) months prior to the proposed date of departure to Cuba. The processing of applications by the OFAC-Miami office for specific licenses to visit immediate family (both Cuban nationals and non-Cuban nationals) may be expedited by using the format suggested later in this document.

The contents of the letter application should be structured in a manner that adequately addresses all the applicable criteria for that category. To facilitate review, applications may be typed in an outline format with a header citing the category of travel and addressing each application criterion and other relevant information. In most circumstances, the receipt of an application will automatically generate an acknowledgment letter, assigning a case number that should be referenced in all subsequent oral and written communication with OFAC concerning the application. You may also use your case number to obtain the status of your application by contacting the OFAC Licensing Division's automated voice response system at (202) 622-2480.

Persons specifically licensed must keep records that must be furnished to OFAC or other law enforcement officials (e.g., Bureau of Customs and Border Protection) upon demand for a period of five years after the travel transactions take place. See 31 CFR 501.601 and 501.602.

Most applications to engage in travel-related transactions involving Cuba are processed by OFAC's main office in Washington, DC, with the notable exception of applications to visit immediate family members in Cuba, which are processed by OFAC's Miami Office.

Requests of Extensions or Renewals of Specific Licenses

When applying for an extension or renewal of a license, be sure to reference the license number in your application. You must also include an explanation why an extension or renewal is necessary, a detailed report setting forth a record of all activities undertaken pursuant to the original license, and append a complete copy of the license to the submission.

Recommended Letter Format

> Note: The recommended letter format that follows is for applicants attempting to qualify for the private foundations/educational research institutes category of travel. For other category-specific guidelines, visit the U.S. Treasury website at www.treas.gov/OFAC or contact OFAC at the address listed above.

You may request a specific license on behalf of your private foundation or educational or research institute authorizing transactions incident to activities intended to provide support for the Specific license consideration of activities by private foundations or research or educational institutes that have an established interest in international relations to collect information related to Cuba for noncommercial purposes (31 CFR § 515.576).

Application Criteria for a specific license under § 515.576:

1. Identify your organization. Provide the name and address of your organization and include the name and phone number of the organization's contact responsible for the application. Provide information that illustrates how your organization qualifies as a private foundation, research institute, or educational institute.

2. Established interest in international relations. Provide a description, including supporting documentation, of your organization's established interest in international relations. You may include a mission statement, charter, by-laws, or other literature describing typical activities the organization engages in.

3. Identify the category of travel. State that your organization requests a specific license pursuant to § 515.576 of the Regulations to collect information related to Cuba for noncommercial purposes.

4. Identify project. Describe the specific international relations

project your organization is working on that necessitates the collection of information in Cuba, the methods that will be used for collecting that information, how your organization will record that information, and whether and how the information collected will be publicly disseminated. Provide a declaration that the information collected related to Cuba will be used for non-commercial purposes. If your organization seeks authorization to engage in travel-related transactions for multiple trips to Cuba for the same project, explain why multiple trips are necessary. State the projected time frame for completion of the project.

5. Certification of full-time schedule. Certify that the proposed information collection activities will constitute a full-time schedule for all the participants that could not be completed in a shorter period of time.

6. Extensions & renewals. When applying for extensions or renewals of licenses, be sure to reference the license number in your application. You must also include the following:
    (a) an explanation why an extension or renewal is necessary;
          (b) a detailed report setting forth a record of all activities
    undertaken pursuant to the original license; and
          (c) a complete copy of the license.

7. Signature. Your signature is your certification that the statements in your application are true and accurate.

Examples of licensable criteria for private foundations and educational research institutes:

Example 1: A private research foundation with a 10-year history of producing essays on international relation issues wishes to send a team made up of its full-time employees to Cuba to collect information relevant to a current study of the relationship that countries in the Western Hemisphere have with Russia. This current project as well as the information collected in Cuba will not be used for any commercial purpose.

Example 2: The same research foundation described in the first example wishes to hire temporarily and send to Cuba a college professor who is not an employee of the foundation, to collect information for the same project.

Examples of criteria that is not licensable for private foundations and educational research institutes:

Example 1: A museum of fine arts wishes to send its board of directors to Cuba to collect information relevant to an upcoming display of artworks of Cuban artists at the museum. The fact that the museum has displayed works of international artists on numerous occasions in its history does not demonstrate that the museum has an established interest in international relations. In addition, the display of artworks of Cuban artists would not be viewed as an international relations project. Authorization may be available, however, under § 515.545, regarding the importation of informational materials. (See: Application Guidelines, X. EXPORTATION/IMPORTATION OF INFORMATION AND INFORMATIONAL MATERIALS – 31 CFR § 515.545.)

Example 2: An interest group that organizes information gathering trips to Cuba for individuals who are not full-time employees or paid consultants of the organization wants to take a delegation to Cuba to learn about the country's current conditions. This fact-finding mission to allow prominent citizens to be educated about Cuba so they can participate in the public debate concerning the U.S. embargo against Cuba is not eligible for a license.

Mailing Address

Applications for specific licenses under this category should be submitted to:

Licensing Division
Office of Foreign Assets Control
U.S. Department of the Treasury
1500 Pennsylvania Avenue, N.W.
Washington, D.C. 20220
Tel. 202/622-2480

Text of Regulatory Provision for § 515.576:

"§ 515.576 Activities of private foundations or research or educational institutes.

Specific licenses may be issued on a case-by-case basis authorizing the travel-related transactions set forth in § 515.560(c) and such additional transactions as are directly incident to activities by private foundations or research or educational institutes that have an established interest in international relations to collect information related to Cuba for noncommercial purposes, not otherwise covered by the general license for professional research contained in § 515.564 or more properly issued under § 515.575, relating to humanitarian projects. Specific licenses may be issued pursuant to this section authorizing transactions for multiple trips to Cuba for the same project over an extended period of time."

OFAC Internet website at www.treas.gov/ofac (Sanctions Programs & Country Summaries—Cuba, Guidelines and Information)

APPENDIX 3
(from page 15 and page 19)

LIST OF OFAC-AUTHORIZED PROVIDERS OF AIR, TRAVEL, AND REMITTANCE FORWARDING SERVICES TO CUBA

This list identifies only a few of the OFAC-authorized Carrier Service Providers, Travel Service Providers, and Remittance Forwarders. For a complete list, visit the U.S. Department of the Treasury website at www.treas.gov/OFAC. Click on "sanctions," "Cuba sanctions," then "Authorized Travel, Carrier, and Remittance Forwarding Service Providers. For a regularly updated list, you can also dial a fax-on-demand service at (202) 622-0077 and request document number 1207. For additional information, you can contact OFAC at their Miami office (786-845-2828) or call the Cuba Embargo Hotline at (786) 845-2829.

Legend: All d/b/a are underlined. **CSP**: Carrier Service Provider. **TSP**: Travel Service Provider. **RF**: Remittance Forwarder. The numbers in parenthesis following the company name is the OFAC Service Provider code.

A Mi Cuba Travel Express (001) TSP, RF (305) 447-0886
Mr. Juan C. Martinez
4874 NW 7 ST
Miami FL 33126

A B C Charters (002) CSP, TSP (305) 263-6555
Also d/b/a A Better Choice Travel
Ms. Maria S. Brieva
1125 SW 87 Ave
Miami FL 33174

Academic Travel Abroad (003) TSP (202) 785-9000
Mr. David T. Parry
1920 N ST NW #200
Washington DC 20036-1601

Ada Wong (004) TSP
747 10th Ave
New York, NY 10019

Agencia 12 y 23 (005) TSP, RF (813) 414-9510
Mr. Jose Mendoza
5027 North Lois Ave
Tampa FL 33614

Agencia Costa Azul (006) TSP, RF (407) 208-9354
Ms. Cecilia C. Benito
392 Briar Bay Circle
Orlando FL 32825

Agencia Cristiana (146) TSP, RF
Also Religious & Family Travel Services

Agencia Via Cuba (007) TSP, RF (323) 587-0611
Ms. Estrella Santos
3009 E Florence Ave
Huntington Park CA 90255

AHI International (008) TSP (847) 384-4500
Mr. Richard D. Small
6400 Shafer CT
Rosemont IL 60018

Celimar Travel of Hialeah(038) TSP, RF
Also Celimar Travel

Celimar Travel Services (039) TSP (305) 228-6161
Ms. Celia De Los Angeles Leon
9831 SW 40 ST
Miami FL 33165

Chalk's International Airlines (040) CSP (305) 373-1120
Capt. Jim Wagner
750 SW 34 ST
Fort Lauderdale FL 33315

Chichy's Envios (041) TSP, RF (305) 827-3585
Mr. Andres Peña
5358 W 12 Ave
Hialeah FL 33012

Cielomar Travel (042) TSP, RF (562) 698-7800
Ms. Niurys Elverson
12110 Slauson Ave #3
Santa Fe Springs CA 90670

Cojimar Express Services (043) TSP, RF (305) 512-9233
Mr. Mario B Romero
5370 Palm Ave # 3
Hialeah FL 33012

Common Ground Education (044) TSP (617) 661-7653
& Travel Services
Ms. Merriam S Ansara
359 Main ST, Unit 2A
Easthampton MA 01027

Continental Airlines (045) CSP, TSP
Mr. David Grizzle
1600 Smith ST
Houston TX 77002

Costa Cuba (047) TSP, RF (305) 559-7585
Ms. Viviany Gonzalez
9732 SW 40 ST
Miami FL 33165

Costa del Sol Travel Agency (048) TSP, RF (201) 867-7013
Mr. Paul Falcon
4111 Park Ave
Union City NJ 07087

Education Travel Alliance (072) TSP (617) 938-7660
Mr. Michael I. Eizenberg
41 Longfellow Road
Wellesley, MA 02481

Español Accounting Service (073) TSP, RF (773) 278-6688
Mr. Orlando Sierra
2644 N Milwaukee Ave
Chicago IL 60647

Exportaciones Cubanacan (074) TSP, RF (305) 649-3210
Mr. Jose S Mesa
2319 NW 7 ST 10682 Coral Way
Miami FL 33125 Miami FL 33165

Falcon Air Express (075) CSP, TSP (305) 592-5672
Mr. Emilio Dirube
9500 NW 41 ST
Miami FL 33178

Falcon-SAA Travel (076) TSP, RF (305) 250-7330
Ms. Marta R. de Vera
1900 SW 22 ST #403
Miami FL 33145

FED USA (154) TSP, RF
Also Sol del Caribe

Flor Caribe (077) TSP, RF (813) 875-3021
Rev. Jose Rangel
2526 W Tampa Bay Blvd. #B 8226 W Walter Ave 801 Madrid #3
Tampa FL 33607 Tampa FL 33615 Coral Gables FL 33134
6233 14 ST W #B
Bradenton FL 34207

Floridita Travel Services (078) TSP, RF (305) 557-4535
Mr. Enrique Baltar
2050 W 56 ST #20
Hialeah FL 33016

Frederick Poe Travel Service (079) TSP (501) 376-4171
Also d/b/a Poe Travel
Ms. Margaret F. Kemp
915 Cumberland ST
Little Rock AR 72203

M & D Immigration Consultants (108) TSP (305) 362-0398
Ms. Daisy Angulo
11300 NW 87 CT #152
Hialeah Gardens FL 33018

M & G Professional Services (109) TSP (305) 556-7380
Ms. Marisela G. Melcon
10111 W Okeechobee Rd
Hialeah Gardens FL 33016

Machi Community Services (110) CSP, TSP, RF (305) 442-8022
Ms. Maria S. Brieva
5791 NW 7 ST 1125 SW 87 Ave
Miami FL 33126 Miami FL 33134

Macol Corporation (111) TSP (201) 867-2844
Also d/b/a Peerless Travel Services
Ms. Olga Machado
5601 Bergenline Ave
West New York NJ 07093

Mambi International Group (112) TSP, RF (305) 223-8470
Mr. Santiago R. Castro
7795 W Flagler ST #39
Miami FL 33144

Manuel Garcia (113) TSP (305) 263-9647
Also d/b/a Amor Travel
Mr. Manuel Garcia
8520 NW 1 Terrace
Miami FL 33126

Marazul Charters (114) CSP, TSP, RF (305) 559-3616
Mr. Francisco G. Aruca
771 NW 37 Ave 8324 SW 40 ST 5358 W 16 Ave 4100 Park Ave
Miami FL 33125 Miami FL 33155 Hialeah FL 33012 Weehawken
NJ 07086

Margo Travel (115) CSP, TSP (212) 944-1333
Ms. Margo Grant
130 West 42 ST #1904
New York NY 10036

Maria Del Carmen Sicard (116) TSP (323) 569-7147
Also d/b/a Marimar Travel & Tours
Ms. Maria Del Carmen Sicard
3325 Tweedy Blvd
South Gate CA 90280

T M I Travel Management (168) TSP (208)765 1111
Ms. Rhonda Sand
105 N First ST #200
Coeur d'Alene ID 83814

Taino of Tampa (162) TSP, RF (813) 876-7080
Ms. Martha Cainas
3243 West Columbus DR
Tampa FL 33607

Tainos Travel (163) TSP (561) 248-6564
Mr. Francisco F. Vega
425 Colonial Rd 2559 N Dixie Hwy
West Palm Beach FL 33405 Lake Worth FL 33460

Tampa Envios (164) TSP, RF (813) 873-0533
Mr. Armando Ramirez
2919 W Columbus DR 4453 W Hillsborough Ave
Tampa FL 33607 Tampa FL 33614

Taxplus & Accounting (165) TSP (305) 828-7227
Ms. Ana Gonzalez
4445 W 16 Ave # 406
Hialeah FL 33012

Tellez's Tour & Travel Agency (166) TSP, RF (305) 556-4680
Ms. Caridad Carriles
1986 W 60 ST
Hialeah FL 33012

Tico Card Company (167) CSP, TSP (954) 493-8426
Also d/b/a Tico Travel
Mr. Robert M Hodel
161 E Commercial Blvd 151 E Commercial Blvd
Fort Lauderdale FL 33334 Fort Lauderdale FL 33334

Tico Travel (167) CSP, TSP
Also Tico Card Company

Toda Cuba Travel & Envios (169) TSP (305) 631-1818
Mr. Rolando Suarez
1880 W Flagler ST
Miami FL 33135

APPENDIX 4
(From page 15)

OFAC-LICENSED, SPECIAL INTEREST TOUR OPERATORS ORGANIZING CULTURAL, EDUCATIONAL, AND HUMANITARIAN-THEMED TRIPS TO CUBA FROM THE U.S.

Center for Cuban Studies
124 West 23rd Street
New York, NY 10011
Tel: (212) 242-0559
Website:
www.cubaupdate.org

Marazul Charters, Inc.
Main Office:
100 Park Avenue
Weehawken, NJ 07086
Tel: (201) 319-8970
Website:
www.marazulcharters.com

Miami Offices:
•8328 SW 40th Street
 Miami, FL 33155
 Tel: (305) 485-1203 or
     (800) 993-9667

•771 NW 37 Ave
Miami, FL 33125

•5358 W 16 Avenue
Hialeah, FL 33012

Global Exchange
2017 Mission Street, #303
San Francisco, CA 94110
Tel: (415) 255-7498
Website:

www.globalexchange.org

Pastors for Peace
402 West 145th Street
New York, NY 10031
Tel: (212) 926-5757
Website: www.ifconews.org

Venceremos Brigade
P.O. Box 5202
Englewood, NJ 07631
Tel: (212) 560-4360
Website:
www.venceremosbrigade.org
(Note: Arranges unlicensed trips)

Last Frontier Expeditions
4900 NW Cherry Street
Vancouver, WA 98663
Tel: (360) 597-3455
Website:
www.hemingwaytoursandsafaris.com

Island Travel and Tours
2111 Wisconsin Avenue NW,
Suite 319
Washington, DC 20007
Tel: (202) 342-3171
Website:
www.islandtraveltours.com

APPENDIX 5
(from page 156)
SAMPLE OF U.S. CUSTOMS DECLARATION FORM

U.S. Customs and
Border Protection

Customs Declaration
19CFR 122.27, 148.12, 148.13, 148.110, 148.111, 1498; CFR 5316

FORM APPROVED
OMB NO. 1651-0009

Each arriving traveler or responsible family member must provide the following
Information (only ONE written declaration per family is required):

1.   Family **Name** _____

        First (Given) _____ Middle _____

2.   **Birth date**   Day _____ Month _____ Year _____

3.   Number of **Family members** traveling with you _____

        (a) U.S. Street **Address** (hotel name/destination) _____

        _____

        (b) City _____ (c) State _____

5.   **Passport issued by** (country) _____

6.   **Passport number** _____

7.   Country of **Residence** _____

8.   **Countries visited** on this _____

        trip prior to U.S. arrival

9.   **Airline/Flight No**. or **Vessel Name** _____

10.   The primary purpose of this trip is business   Yes ____ No ____

11.   I am (We are) bringing
       (a) fruits, vegetables, plants, seeds, food, insects: Yes ____ No ____

       (b) meats, animals, animal/wildlife products: Yes ____ No ____

       (c) disease agents, cell cultures, snails: Yes ____ No ____

       (d) soil or have been on a farm/ranch/pasture: Yes ____ No ____

12.   I have (We have) been in close proximity of
       (such as touching or handling) **livestock**:   Yes ____ No ____

13.   I am (We are) carrying **currency or monetary**
       instruments over $10,000 U.S. or foreign equivalent: Yes ____ No ____

14.   I have (We have) **commercial merchandise:**
       (articles for sale, samples used for soliciting orders,   Yes ____ No ____
       or goods that are not considered personal effects)

15.   **Residents** – the **total value of all goods**, including commercial
       merchandise I/we have purchased or acquired abroad, (Including gifts
       for someone else, but not items mailed to the U.S.) and am/are bringing
       to the U.S. is: $ _____

       Visitors – the **total value of all articles** that will remain in the U.S.,
       including commercial merchandise is: $ _____

Read the instructions on the back of this form. Space is provided to list all the
Items you must declare.

**I HAVE READ THE IMPORTANT INFORMATION ON THE REVERSE SIDE OF
THIS FORM AND HAVE MADE A TRUTHFUL DECLARATION.**

X _____
    (Signature)   Date (day/month/year)

For Official Use Only

CBP Form 6059B (01/04)

APPENDIX 6
(from page 16)

FORM LETTER IN RESPONSE TO OFAC's "Requirement to Furnish Information" LETTER

[DATE]

U.S. Department of the Treasury
Office of Foreign Assets Control (OFAC)
Attn: Mr./Ms. _____
1500 Pennsylvania Avenue, N.W. (Annex)
Washington, D.C. 20220
FAX: 202 622-0447

Re: **[INSERT YOUR NAME]** (FAC #CU-**[INSERT "CU" NUMBER FROM OFAC LETTER TO YOU]**)

Dear Mr./Ms. _____:

This letter is in response to your "Requirement to Furnish Information" letter to me, dated **[INSERT DATE OF OFAC LETTER TO YOU]** and received by me **[INSERT DATE YOU ACTUALLY RECEIVED THE LETTER]**. For the reasons stated below, I respectfully decline to respond.

OFAC's regulations of transactions incidental to travel, and OFAC's demand for information pursuant to such regulations are a violation of the rights of U.S. citizens to travel abroad, to seek information through foreign travel relevant to public issues, and to exchange information and views with foreign persons, all as guaranteed by the First and Fifth Amendments to the Constitution of the United States.

Furthermore, OFAC's regulations regarding transactions incidental to travel, and OFAC's demand for information pursuant to such regulations constitute discriminatory enforcement of the laws on the basis of national origin and political viewpoint, in violation of the First and Fifth Amendments to the Constitution of the United States. The imposition of any penalties is also discriminatory. Such conduct is arbitrary and capricious and in violation of the Administrative Procedure Act. In this respect, it is noted that substantial numbers of Cuban-Americans and others travel to Cuba with the knowledge of OFAC, in apparent violation of the Cuban Assets Control Regulations, but without consequence.

Furthermore, with respect to any further communication, I assert my privilege against self-incrimination under the Fifth Amendment to the Constitution of the United States.

Sincerely,

APPENDIX 7
(from page 16)

FORM LETTER IN REPLY TO OFAC's "Pre-penalty Notice"

[DATE]

Chief of Civil Penalties
Office of Foreign Assets Control
U.S. Treasury Department
1500 Pennsylvania Avenue, NW.
Washington DC 20220

Re: **Response to Pre-penalty Notice**
        **FAC No. CU-[INSERT "CU" NUMBER FROM LETTER REC'D
        FROM OFAC]**
        [INSERT YOUR NAME]
        **[Either print this letter on stationery or add other lines here with
        address & phone.]**

Dear Chief of Civil Penalties:

This letter is in response to the above-referenced Pre-penalty Notice dated
[INSERT DATE OF PREPENALTY NOTICE], which was postmarked on
[INSERT DATE OF POSTMARK ON ENVELOPE] and received on
[INSERT DATE NOTICE RECEIVED].

I assert my Fifth Amendment privilege against self-incrimination. I specifically
reserve my right to amend or supplement this response, or to raise at a later time
facts and arguments here omitted. In addition, I invoke my right to a hearing in
connection with this matter. Without waiving any of my rights, I offer the
following affirmative defenses:

1.   The Office of Foreign Assets Control's ("OFAC") action, including the
       proposed penalty, is arbitrary and capricious, and fails to set forth the
       basis upon which said penalty or the amount thereof is based;

2.   OFAC's action, including the penalty proposed, violates my due process
       rights;

OFAC's action, including the penalty proposed, is a violation of my rights to travel
abroad, to seek information through foreign travel relevant to public issues,

(continued)

3. and to exchange information and views with foreign persons, all as guaranteed by the First and Fifth Amendments to the Constitution of the United States;

4. OFAC's action, including the penalty proposed, constitutes discriminatory enforcement of the laws on the bases of race, color, national origin, political viewpoint and association, in violation of the laws and the Constitution of the United States, including the First and Fifth Amendments, and is arbitrary and capricious (in this respect, it is noted that substantial numbers of Cuban-Americans and others travel to Cuba with the knowledge of OFAC, in apparent violation of the Cuban Assets Control Regulations, but without consequence);

5. The Cuban Assets Control Regulations discriminate based on national origin by allowing Cuban-Americans broader license to travel to Cuba than persons of different ethnic and national origin, and are not narrowly tailored to meet a compelling government interest, in violation of the Equal Protection Clause;

6. OFAC's proposed penalty violates my rights under the Excessive Fines Clause of the Eighth Amendment;

7. OFAC's action, including the penalty proposed, is invalid because it relies on a presumption that compels me to give evidence against myself in violation of the privilege against self-incrimination under the Fifth Amendment to the Constitution of the United States; and

8. OFAC is precluded from asserting the claims set forth in the Notice by reason of the prejudice to me and to the detriment thereof, all of which has resulted from the agency's failure to pursue said claim in a timely fashion.

I hereby request that OFAC voluntarily dismiss this matter in the interest of justice.

Signature and date:_____

APPENDIX 8
(from page 22 and page 55)

TRAVEL AGENCIES OUTSIDE THE U.S.

MEXICO

Havanatur Merida
Calle 60 #448
E/ 49 y 51, Dpto 113
Colonial Centro
Merida

Cubana Tours
Baja California 255
Edificio B, Despacho 103
Colonia, Hipodromo
Condesa, Mexico D.F.
Tel: 574-4921

Cubamar
Eje Lazaro Cardenas No. 623
Colonia Portales
03300 Mexico, DF
Tel: (52) (5) 601-1302
Fax: (52) (5) 604-6215

Viajes Sol y Son
Temistocles No. 246
Colonia Polanco
11550 Mexico, DF
Tel: (52) (5) 250-6355
Fax: (52) (5) 255-0835

Cuba Travel Corporation
(Roberto Paneque)
Tel: (52) 98.80-8160
         (52) 98.80-8184
Fax: (52) 98.48-0175

Viajes Divermex (Cuban company)
Avenida Coba #5
Centro Comercial Plaza
America
Cancun, Quintana Roo
Mexico CP 77500
Tel: (9988) 884-5005
Website:
www.divermex.com

BAHAMAS

Havanatur Bahamas
P.O. Box N-10246
Nassau, Bahamas
Tel: (242) 393-5281
through 5284
Fax: (242) 356-2773

CANADA
Cubanacan Tours
1255 Universite,Suite 211
Montreal, Quebec
H3B 3B2
Tel: 861-4444

A. Nash Travel, Inc.
865 McLaughlin Road,
Unit 2B
Mississauga, Ontario
L5R 1B8 Canada
E-mail:
www.nashtravel.com
Tel: (905) 755-0647,
         (800) 818-2004 x 221
Fax: (905) 755-0729

Alba Tours
790 Arrow Rd
Weston, Ontario
M9M 2Y5
Tel: (416) 746-2488
Fax: (416) 746-0397

Canadian Holidays
191 The West Mall
16th Floor
Etobicoke, Ontario
M9C 5K8
Tel: (416) 746-2488
Fax: 9416) 620-9267

Signature Vacations
111 Avenue Rd.
Suite 500
Toronto, Ontario
M5R 318
Tel: (416) 967-1112
Fax: (416) 967-3862

JAMAICA

Caribbean Vacations
69 Gloucester Avenue
Montego Bay
Tel: (809) 952-5013

Intercaribe
1112` Ardenne Rd.
Kingston 10, Jamaica
Tel: (809) 929-7865

SPAIN

Guama S.A.
Paseo de La Habana 28
28036, Madrid
Tel: (34) (1) 411-2048
Fax: (34) (1) 564-3918

UNITED KINGDOM

Havanatur UK
Interchange House
27 Stafford Rd.
Croydon, Surrey
CRO 4NG
Te: (44) (181) 681-3613
Fax: (44) (181) 760-0031

Progressive Tours
12 Porchester Place
Marble Arch, London
W2 2BS
Tel: (44) (171) 262-1676

APPENDIX 9
(from page 24)

FERRY INFORMATION BAHAMAS-FLORIDA

For ferry schedules and fares:

Discovery Cruise Lines
1775 NW 70th Ave
Miami FL 33126

1-800-259-1579, 1-800-866-8687
Website: www.discoverycruise.com

Bahamas Florida Express
1-866-313-3779
Website: www.ferrybahamas.com

Note: As of December '08, the ferries listed above only travel between Port Everglades in Florida and Grand Bahama Island in the Bahamas. To travel between Nassau (where the airport is) and Grand Bahama you need to charter a small plane or hop on an inter-island ferry. Contact the Bahamas Port Authority (242-393-1064) for the inter-island "mail boat" schedule. The *Fiesta Mail* boat departs Nassau to Grand Bahama on Mondays and Wednesdays at 5:00 p.m. It costs fifty-seven dollars one way and the sail time is eight hours.

You can also contact one of the many private Bahamas charter cruises that operate out of the Port Everglades/Fort Lauderdale. They might have space available on their return to the U.S.

Many cruise ships stop in Nassau, but their booking policies will normally not allow you to board for individual legs of the cruise.

If you've got time on your hands and are feeling adventurous, check out the international marinas in Nassau, Bimini, and Freeport for pleasure boats from the U.S. returning home. An extra body sharing helm duties might appeal to one of the captains.

If you do return to the U.S. by boat, you will have to be added to the passenger list of the vessel (the captain of the boat will arrange this) and officially clear out (along with the rest of the passengers and crew) with Bahamas immigration and customs.

APPENDIX 10
(from page 24)

HOW TO GET A PASSPORT CARD

Who can apply for one?
U.S. citizens and naturalized citizens of the U.S. The requirements for qualifying for a passport card are exactly the same as the requirements for qualifying for a regular passport (book).

What documents do I need when I apply?
First time adult and minor applicants under the age of 16 will need to submit a completed Form DS-11 "Application for a U.S. Passport", two photos, evidence of citizenship, the application fee, and an execution fee. Adult applicants with fully- valid passports can apply for the passport card by mail by submitting Form DS-82 "Application for a U.S. Passport by Mail," two photos, a fully valid passport issued within the last fifteen years, and the passport card application fee.

Where can I apply for the card?
Many U.S. post offices, county clerks of courts, public libraries and other state, county, township, and municipal government offices are authorized to accept passport and passport card applications. You can search for a facility nearest you on the State Department's website at www.travel.state.gov/passport.

How much does it cost?
Twenty dollars if you have a fully-valid passport issued within the last fifteen years. If you are a first-time adult applicant, or if you are applying for a lost or stolen passport, there is an additional "execution" fee of twenty-five dollars. Children under the age of sixteen pay less for the execution fee.

How long does it take to receive a passport?
About the same time it takes for a regular passport book—four to six weeks.

For how long a period is the passport card valid?
Ten years for adults, five years for minors under the age of sixteen.

For more information about passport cards, log on to the U.S. State Department's website at www.travel.state.gov/passport.

APPENDIX 11
(from page 24)

CHECKLIST FOR GETTING THROUGH THE U.S., CUBA, AND THIRD COUNTRY IMMIGRATION AND CUSTOMS CHECKPOINTS

(Note: U.S. citizens and residents are pre-cleared by the U.S. immigration and customs authorities at certain foreign airports—such as Nassau, Toronto, Montreal, and in the Dominican Republic and Jamaica—rather than on the U.S. mainland):

Third (springboard) Country to Cuba:

1. Plane lands in third country (ie., Mexico or the Bahamas). Fill out landing card given to you by the flight attendant or pick one up at the entrance to the "international/foreign arrivals" immigration checkpoint.
2. Stand in line at the immigration checkpoint and wait to be called by the immigration officer. Hand him or her your passport and landing card. Do not tell the officer you are planning to travel on to Cuba. Have on hand the address of a place where you could conceivably stay in the third country.
3. Collect your passport and visa or landing card from the immigration officer and proceed to the baggage claim area.
4. Pick up your bags and head to the customs checkpoint. They might or might not search your baggage.
5. Proceed to the foreign airline ticket counter at which you will purchase your ticket to Cuba or where you will check-in if you have a reservation on the flight. Check any baggage here as well. As mentioned in Section 2 (question number four), if you are flying to Cuba from Mexico, make sure you obtain TWO Mexican tourist cards: one for your arrival in Mexico from the U.S. and one for your arrival in Mexico from Cuba. Without these tourist cards, the Cuban immigration officer might not let you in. The airline or travel agency that sold you the tickets can tell you how to obtain these Mexican tourist cards. Pay in cash for all of your Cuba flights. Do not use your credit card, as that will leave a paper trail.
6. Proceed to the gate.
7. Board the plane to Cuba.
8. After getting off the plane in Cuba, make your way to the Cuban immigration checkpoint. There are separate lines for foreigners and Cuban nationals.

9. Present the immigration officer with your passport and tourist card (and visa, if you have one). Be prepared to give the address of the place where you are staying.
10. Pass through the door.
11. Pass through a metal detector with your carry-ons.
12. If you are going to declare any items, go to customs window (pay customs fees if necessary).
13. Proceed to baggage claim and pick up your checked baggage.
14. Pass through the customs checkpoint with your bags. You may or may not have your bags searched. Quite often, foreigners' bags are not searched but Cuban nationals' bags are. Items clearly not yours may be charged a 100 percent importation fee. See Section 3, Question number three for a list of things you are not allowed to bring into Cuba.
15. After passing through the customs checkpoint, you will arrive at the airport lobby.

Cuba to Third (springboard) Country:

1. Check in at ticket counter, check your bags.
2. Purchase Departure Tax Stamps at a separate window.
3. Return to the ticket counter with your Departure Tax Stamps. (You do not have to go to the end of the line again.)
4. Pass through the metal detectors and into the airport lobby near your boarding gate.
5. Board plane

Third (springboard) Country to U.S.:

1. Plane lands in third country. Proceed to immigration checkpoint.
2. Fill out the Arrival/Declaration card.
3. Present passport and Arrival/Declaration card to springboard country immigration. Remember to ask the springboard country immigration officer not to stamp your passport.
4. Pick up your baggage at the baggage claim carousel.
5. Pass through customs checkpoint with your bags into airport main terminal airport lobby.
6. Remove all Cuba-related baggage tags from your bags.
7. Discard all evidence related to your stay in Cuba, including all receipts, airline tickets, telephone numbers and addresses, travel documents, Cuban money, baggage tags, or products purchased in Cuba.

8. Go to the airline ticket counter to check in and check your bags.   Obtain a U.S. Customs and Declaration card from the ticketing agent or at the entrance to the immigration and customs checkpoint.

9. Proceed to the U.S. immigration and customs pre-clearance checkpoint, if there is one. (Otherwise, go through the detectors to the waiting area near your boarding gate.) Wait in line at the U.S. immigration checkpoint. Hand over your passport and the customs and declaration form to the officer.

10. Pass through the U.S. customs pre-clearance checkpoint, if there is one. If there is a U.S. customs pre-clearance checkpoint, you will probably have to go through a second customs checkpoint manned by officers of the foreign country you are departing.

11. Proceed to the waiting area near your boarding gate.

12. Board plane.

13. If you pre-cleared with U.S. immigration and customs officers before your flight, you will not have to go through U.S. immigration and customs checkpoints when you arrive in the U.S. If you were not pre-cleared before boarding your flight, proceed to the respective immigration and customs checkpoints when you arrive in the States.

14. Go to the baggage claim carousel to pick up your bags.

15. Buy a milkshake and a hamburger at the nearest McDonald's to remind yourself you are home.

APPENDIX 12
(from page 53 and page 157)

IMMIGRATION OFFICES IN CUBA

CAMAGUEY
Calle 3ra #156, e/ 8 y 10
Reparto Vista Hermosa

CIEGO DE AVILA
Independencia Este #14
Tel: (33) 22-3625

CIENFUEGOS
Avenida 48, e/ 29 y 31
Tel: (43) 52-4437
Cienfuegos

GUANTANAMO
Calle 1 Oeste between 14
and
15 Norte
Guantanamo

HAVANA
Miramar
Calle 20
Between Avenida 3 and
Avenida 5
Miramar, Havana
Tel (7) 58-5100

Vedado
Calle Factor y Final
(Tulipas and Plaza de la
Revoulcion)
Nuevo Vedado

LAS TUNAS
Avenida Camilo
Cienfuegos
(one km north of the train
station)

MATANZAS
Varadero
Calle 39 y 1ra, e/ 38 y 39
Tel: (45) 61-3494
Varadero

SANCTI SPIRITUS
Trinidad
Perseverancia,
esq Paseo Agramonte
Trinidad

SANTA CLARA
Avenida Sandino, corner
Sextra
(three blocks east of
Estadio Sandino)
Santa Clara

SANTIAGO DE CUBA
Calle 13 between
Carretera de Carey
and 14
Tel (022) 64-1983
Vedado, Havana

ISLA DE LA JUVENTUD
• Calle 35, esq 34
  Nueva Gerona

• Airport
  El Pueblo
  Cayo Largo
  Tel: (45) 24-8244

APPENDIX 13
(from page 26)

REQUESTING VESSEL CLEARANCE FROM THE U.S. COAST GUARD TO DEPART A MARITIME SECURITY ZONE

Fax your completed application for clearance and all other required information to (305) 415-6925 (Seventh Coast Guard District in Miami, Florida). To speak with someone about any questions you may have about your application, call (305) 415-6920. You can request that an application form "to travel to Cuban territorial seas" be e-mailed to you.

1) If you are using an individual specific license from OFAC to travel to Cuba, you must include with your application:

- A copy of the OFAC license.
- The completed application form.
- A copy of your vessel export license or temporary sojourn license from the U.S. Department of Commerce's Bureau of Industry and Security (BIS).
- The names of the vessel's owner, master, officers, operator, persons-in-charge, or crewmembers.

2) If you are using a specific OFAC license issued to an institution, you must include all of the above plus a copy of the license and/or letter indicating the specific license number and bearing the signature of an authorized representative of the licensee.

3) If you are traveling to Cuba under the general license provisions, you must explain in detail why you qualify for the general license, plus:

- The completed application form.
- A copy of your vessel export license or temporary sojourn license from the U.S. Department of Commerce's Bureau of Industry and Security (BIS).
- The names of the vessel's owner, master, officers, operator, persons-in-charge, or crewmembers.

APPENDIX 14
(from page 157)

U.S. CUSTOMS AND BORDER PATROL OFFICES

Note: Since most boaters returning to the U.S. from Cuba will be calling on a Florida port, only the Florida or Caribbean CBP reporting locations are listed below.   For other CBP reporting locations in the U.S., visit the CBP Web site at www.cbp.gov or call the CBP headquarters in Washington, D.C.

CBP reporting locations in South Florida:

Key West
Monday through Friday 8AM – 4PM
301 Simonton Street, Suite 201
Key West, Florida
(305) 296-5411

Port of Miami
7 days a week 6AM - 10PM
903 South America Way
Terminal H
Miami, Florida
(305) 536-4758

Tamiami Executive Airport
7 days a week 11AM – 7PM
14720 SW 128th Street
Miami, Florida
(305) 969-7511

Opa Locka Airport
7 days a week 9AM – 9PM
4371 NW 150th Street
Opa Locka, Florida
(305) 687-5475

Port Everglades
7 days a week 5AM – Midnight
1800 Eller Drive, Suite 110Ft. Lauderdale, Florida
(954) 761-2000

Ft. Lauderdale General Aviation Facility
7 days a week 24 hours a day
1050 Lee Wagner Blvd
Ft. Lauderdale,
Florida
(954) 356-7946

Ft. Lauderdale Executive Airport
7 days a week 9AM – 9PM
5575 NW 15 Street
Ft. Lauderdale, Florida
(954) 356-7412

West Palm Beach
Monday through Friday 8AM – 4PM
1 East 11th Street
Riviera Beach, Florida
(561) 848-6922

Palm Beach International Airport
7 Days a week 8AM – 8PM
Bldg. 1612 South Perimeter Road
West Palm Beach, Florida
(561) 233-1083

Ft. Pierce, St. Lucie County Intl. Airport
7 days a week 10AM – 6PM
2990 Curtis King Blvd
Ft. Pierce, Florida
(772) 461-1733

CBP reporting locations in North/Central Florida:

Port Canaveral
120 George King Blvd.
Cape Canaveral, FL 32920
(321) 783-2066 ext. 2

Daytona Beach Intl Airport
720 Coral Sea Ave
Daytona Beach, FL 32114
(386) 248-8043

Fernandina Beach
403 N. 3rd St
Fernandina Beach, FL 32034
(904) 261-6154

Ft. Myers
SW Florida Intl Airport
11000 Terminal Access Rd
Ft. Myers, Fl 33913
(239) 561-6205

Orlando
9076 Binnacle Way
Orlando, Florida 32827
(407) 825-4360

Jacksonville
2831 Talleyrand Ave.
Jacksonville, FL 32206
(904) 360-5020

Manatee
300 Tampa Bay Way
Palmetto, FL 34221
(813) 634-1369

Melbourne
One Air Terminal Parkway
Melbourne, FL 32901
(321) 674-5796

Panama City
5209 W. Highway 98
Panama City, FL 32401
(850) 785-4688

Pensacola
600 University Office Blvd
Pensacola, Fl 32504
(850) 476-0117

Sarasota
6048 Airport Circle
Sarasota, FL 34243
(941) 359-5040

CBP reporting locations in Puerto Rico:
During other than regular business hours (5:00pm-8:00am) call
787)253-4533 or (787) 253-4538

Port of Fajardo
Perto Real Municipal Pier
I front of the Customhouse
787) 863-0950
(787) 863-0102

Vieques Station
Mosquito Pier
(787) 741-8366
Alternate: 787-863-0950

Culebra Station
Dewey Dock Ensenada Honda
(787) 742-3531
Alternate: 787-863-0950

Port of Ponce
Ponce Pier
Ponce Yatch Club
(787) 841-3130
(787) 841-3131

Port of Mayagüez
Mayagüez Public Pier
(787) 831-3342
(787) 831-3343

Port of San Juan
CBP Boathouse Facility (Next to San Juan Bay Marina)
(787) 729-6600

CBP reporting locations in United States Virgin Islands

Port of St. Thomas
Customs and Border Protection
Edward W. Blyden Terminal
Veterans Drive
(340) 774-6755

During other than regular business hours (5:00pm-8:00am) call
(340) 774-4554

Port of St. Croix
Customs and Border Protection
Gallows Bay Marine Facility
(340) 773-1011

During other than regular business hours (5:00pm-8:00am) call
(340) 773-1490

Port of St. John
Customs and Border Protection
Cruz Bay, St. John VI
(340) 776-6741

During other than regular business hours (5:00pm-8:00am) call
(340) 773-1490

APPENDIX 15
(from page 34)

CAR RENTAL AGENCIES IN CUBA

(Note: All of the car rental agencies listed below have branch offices at the Jose Marti airport in Havana.)

Cubacar
Avenida 5ta and Calle 84
Miramar, Havana
Tel: (07) 24-2718
Website: www.cuba.tc
Note: Cubacar has nine branch offices in Havana (at major hotels) and two in Playas del Este, as well as in other major cities in Cuba.

Cubamar Campertour
Calle 3ra, esq Malecon
Havana
Tel: (07) 833-7558
Website: www.cubacamper@enet.cu
Note: Rents Mercedes and Ford motorhomes that sleep six people and include toilet, shower, kitchen, and refrigerator.

Havanautos
Avenida 5ta and Calle 84
Miramar, Havana
Tel: (07) 835-3142 or (07) 203-9825
Fax: (07) 203-9652
Website: www.havanautos.com
Note: Havanautos has the largest number of branch offices throughout the country including at many Servicupet gas stations.

Micar
Calle 13 #562
Vedado, Havana
Tel: (07) 833-0202
Fax: (07) 833-0301
Website: www.micarrenta.cu

(Car rental agencies in Cuba--continued)

Panautos
Linea and Malecon
Vedado, Havana
Tel: (07)5-3255
Website: www.cuba.cu/turismo/panatrans/panautos

Rex Limousine Service
Tel: (07) 683-0303
Fax: (07) 273-9167
Website: www.rex-rentacar.com
Note: Rex Limousine Service is a Danish-Cuban joint venture
and the only car rental agency in Cuba that accepts a U.S.-
issued Mastercard. Also rents a VW mini-van.

Via Rent-a-Car
Avenida del Puerto
Edificio La Marina, 3rd Floor
Old Havana
Tel: (07) 66-6777
Website: www.cuba.tc/Gaviota/GaviotaCarRental

APPENDIX 16
(from page 43)

INTER-CITY TRAIN SCHEDULE

Note: Not all of the departure times listed below are daily, and many of the departures to less traveled destinations are subject to frequent change. Always confirm departure times with the local station. The telephone number for the main FerroCuba office in Old Havana (Calle Arsenal, between Cienfuegos and Apontes) is (7) 861-4259. Their website is ferrotur@ceniai.cuz. In Havana, trains depart from either the La Coubre station on Avenida del Puerto in Old Havana or at the nearby Estacion Central at Egidio and Arsenal. Those using convertible pesos to buy tickets normally must obtain them at the La Coubre station.

Havana—Santiago de Cuba	5:35 p.m. (#31), 6:20 a.m. (#43), 3:15p.m.(#11), 6:05p.m. (#1 specl.)
Havana—Bayamo	10:30 a.m. (#13)
Havana—Holguin	7 p.m. (#15)
Havana—Sancti Spiritus	6 a.m. (#17)
Havana—Cienfuegos	7:30 a.m. (#19), 6:45 p.m. (#37)
Havana—Pinar del Rio	2 p.m. (#39), 10:35 p.m. (#21)
Sta. Clara—Santiago de Cuba	7:45 a.m. (#47)
Pinar del Rio—Havana	5:10 a.m. (#40), 8:45 a.m. (#22)
Holguin—Guantanamo	2:55 p.m. (#89)
Guantanamo—Holguin	5:30 a.m. (#88)
Santiago de Cuba—Sta. Clara	4:35 a.m. (#46)
Santiago de Cuba—Havana	6 a.m. (#2 specl.), 10:30a.m. (#44), 8:25 p.m. (#12), 11:10 p.m. (#32)
Sant. de Cuba—Guantanamo	5:30 a.m. (#11)
Guantanamo—Havana	6:45 p.m. (#12)
Bayamo—Havana	7:40 p.m. (#14)
Holguin—Havana	6:15 p.m. (#16)
Cienfuegos—Havana	7 a.m. (#20), 2 p.m. (#38)
Sancti Spiritus—Havana	9 p.m. (#18)
Havana—Camaguey	2 p.m. (#33)
Camaguey—Havana	6:35 p.m. (#34)
Havana—Moron	4:45 p.m. (#35)
Moron—Havana	5:40 a.m. (#36)

APPENDIX 17
(from page 42)

VIA AZUL INTER-CITY BUS SCHEDULE

Note: Some cities have more than one bus terminal. Via Azul buses normally depart from interprovincial bus terminals. Confirm all bus departure and arrival terminals with the local Via Azul ticket office. The Via Azul main office in Havana is (7) 881-1413, and the Via Azul website is www.viazul.cu.

Havana—Playas del Este	8:40 a.m., 2:20 p.m. daily
Playas del Este—Havana	10:30 a.m., 4:40 p.m. daily
Havana—Guardalavaca	8:30 p.m. Mon., Wed., Fri.
Guardalavaca—Havana	7:50 p.m.,Tue., Thurs., Sat.
Havana—Matanzas—Varadero Airport—Varadero	8 a.m., 12 pm., 6 p.m. daily
Varadero—Varadero Airport— Matanzas—Havana	8 a.m., 4 p.m., 6 p.m. daily
Havana—Pinar del Rio—Vinales	9 a.m., 2 p.m. daily
Vinales—Pinar del Rio—Havana	8 a.m., 2 p.m. daily
Havana—Entronque de Jaguey— Cienfuegos—Trinidad	8:15 a.m., 1 p.m. daily
Trinidad—Cienfuegos—Entronque De Jaguey—Havana	7:45 a.m., 3:15 p.m. daily
Havana—Entronque de Jaguey— Santa Clara--Sancti Spiritus— Cienfuegos—Camaguey— Las Tunas—Holguin—Bayamo— Santiago de Cuba	9:30 a.m., 3 p.m., 6:15 p.m. (daily)

(Via Azul Inter-city bus schedule—continued)

Santiago de Cuba—Bayamo—
  Holguin—Las Tunas—Camaguey—
  Cienfuegos—Sancti Spiritus—
  Santa Clara—Entronque de   9 a.m., 3:15 p.m., 6 p.m.
  Jaguey—Havana   (daily)

Trinidad—Sancti Spiritus—Ciego
  De Avila—Camaguey—Las
  Tunas—Holguin—Bayamo—
  Santiago de Cuba   8:15 a.m. daily

Santiago de Cuba—Bayamo—
  Holguin—Las Tunas—
  Camaguey—Ciego de Avila—
  Sancti Spiritus—Trinidad   7:30 p.m. daily

Santiago de Cuba—El Cristo—
  La Maya—Guantanamo—
  San Antonio—Imias—Baracoa   7:45 a.m. daily

Baracoa—Imias—San Antonio—
  Guantanamo—La Maya—
  El Cristo—
  Santiago de Cuba   2:15 p.m. daily

Varadero—Entronque de Jaguey—
  Santa Clara—Sancti Spiritus—
  Trinidad   7:30 a.m. daily

Trinidad—Sancti Spiritus—
  Santa Clara—Entronque de
  Jaguey—Varadero   2:45 p.m. daily

APPENDIX 18
(From page 43)

CUBAN DOMESTIC TOUR OPERATORS

Note: Many hotels have tourist information desks that can arrange or book tours of their own or through the operators listed below.

Agencia San Cristobal
Oficios #110
e/Lamparilla y Amargura
Habana Vieja, Havana
Tel (07) 860-9585
E-mail:
reserves@sancrist.get.tur.cu
Note: Habana Vieja tours

Cubamar Viajes
Avenida 3ra
e/12 y Malecon
Havana
Tel: (07) 832-1116,
   (07) 833-2523
Website:
www.cubamarviajes.cu
Note: Specializes in nature
and scuba diving trips

Cubanacan Viajes
Calle 23 #156 e/ O y P
Vedado, Havana
Tel: (07) 833-4090
Website: www.cubanacan.cu

Cubatur
Calle 23, esq L
Vedado, Havana
Tel: (07) 833-3569
Website: www.cubatur.cu

EcoTur, S.A.
Avenida Independencia #116,
esq Santa Catalina,
Cerro, Havana

Tel: (07) 41-0306
Fax: (07) 53-9909
E-mail:
ecoturhabana@miraqmar.co.
  cu
Note: Specializes in nature
and ecotourism tours

Gaviota Tours
Avenida 49 #3620
Reparto Kohly, Havana
Tel: (07) 204-7683
Fax: (07) 204-9470
Website:
  www.gaviota-grupo.com

Havanatur
Calle 1 e/2 y O
Edificio Sierra Maestra
Miramar, Havana
Tel (07)204-7541
Website: www.havanatur.cu

Calle 23, esq Avenida M
Vedado, Havana
Tel (07) 755-4082
Website: www.havanatur.cu

Avenida 3ra, e/33 y 34
Miramar, Havana
Tel: (07) 66-7027, (07) 204-0993
Fax: (07) 66-7027, (07) 204-1760
Website: www.havanatur.cu

APPENDIX 19
(From page 44)

DOMESTIC TRAVEL AGENCIES

Note: The agencies listed below sometimes have branch offices or representatives working from desks or offices in major hotels.

Asistur
Prado 254,
Habana Vieja, Havana
Tel: (07) 62-5519, ()7) 63-8284, (07) 33-8527
Fax, (07) 33-8087.
Note: A reservations office, tourist information office, and a visitor assistance office to help visitors resolve problems and emergencies they may encounter during their stay.

Caribe Sol
Calle 2 #17 e/ Avenida 1 y 2
Miramar, Havana
Tel: (07) 33-2161

Cubatur
Calle F No. 157 between Calle 9 and Calzada
Vedado, Havana
Tel: (07) 33-4155, (07) 33-3529.
Note: Specializes in group and private tours.

Cuba Linda
Tel: (07) 553-686;
Fax: (07) 553-980.
Website:
www.cubalinda.com.
Note: Travel agency operated by former CIA agent Phillip Agee.

Havanatur

Calle 1 e/2 y O
Edificio Sierra Maestra
Miramar, Havana
Tel (07)204-7541
Website: www.havanatur.cu

Calle 23, esq Avenida M
Vedado, Havana
Tel (07) 755-4082
Website: www.havanatur.cu

Avenida 3ra, e/33 y 34
Miramar, Havana
Tel: (07) 66-7027, (07) 204-0993
Fax: (07) 66-7027, (07) 204-1760
Website: www.havanatur.cu

Hola Sun
Calle 2 #17, e/ Avenida 1 y 2
Miramar
Tel: (07) 33-2273, (07) 33-2877

Infotur
Avenida Obispo, e/Bernaza y Villegas
Habana Vieja, Havana
Tel: (07) 863-4586

(Also at the cruise terminal on Avenida del Puerto and at Jose Marti airport.)
Note: Sells maps, guides, and books and can help you rent a car or find lodging

APPENDIX 20
(From page 45)

DOMESTIC AIRLINES IN CUBA

Aero Caribbean
Calle 23 #64
Vedado, Havana
Tel: (7) 879-7524
Fax: (7) 336-5016
Website: www.aero-caribbean.com
Note: Offers affordable inter-city fares between Havana, Holguin, Santiago de Cuba, Baracoa, Varadero and other cities

Aerogaviota
Avenida 47 #2814, e/ 28 y 34
Reparto Kohly, Havana
Tel: (07) 203-0668
Fax: (07) 204-2621
Website: www.aerogaviota.com
Note: Small carrier that offers charter flights on 39- and 45-seat planes and 18-seat helicopters.

Aerotaxi
Calle 27 #102, e/ M y N
Vedado, Havana
Tel: (07) 836-4064
Website: aerotaxi@ensa.avianet.cu
Note: Another small carrier that charters small planes and executive jets. For only thirty CUC, Aerotaxi offers seats on a large bi-plane from Vinales in Pinar del Rio to Nueva Gerona on Isla de Juventud.

Cubana de Aviacion
Calle 23, e/ O y P
Vedado, Havana
Tel: (7) 834-4449
Webste: www.cubana.cu
Note: The largest airline offering flights to major cities.

APPENDIX 21
(From page 45)

BICYCLE RENTALS IN HAVANA

Edificio Metropolitano
San Juan de Dios, esq Aguacate
Habana Vieja, Havana
Tel; (07) 860-8532

El Orbe
Monserrat #304, e/O'Reilly y San Juan de Dios
Habana Vieja, Havana
Tel: (07) 860-2617, (07) 860-8532

Cubalinda
Calle E #158
Piso 4-A, esq 9na
Vedado, Havana
Tel: (07) 264-9034
Website: www.cubalinda.com

APPENDIX 22
(from page 50)

UNIVERSITY/SCHOOL DORMITORIES

The following is a short list of dormitory housing known to rent to non-students depending on availability.   More dormitory-style accommodations are available to visiting students, teachers, and education administrators through state agencies such as the Ministerio de Educacion (MINED) and the Ministerio de Salud Publica (MINSAP).

City of Havana

Residencia Academica
Convento de Santa Clara
Cuba #610
E/Luz y Sol
Tel: (7) 861-3335
E-mail:
reaca@cencrem.cult.cu

25 CUC per person
or 35 CUC per suite

Trinidad

Casa de la Amistad
Instituto Cubano de la
Amistad
Zerquera, esq Frank Pais
Tel: (419) 3824
E-mail: amistur@ceniai.inf.cu

15 CUC per room, one or two
beds

City of Las Tunas

Hotel Caribe, Universitur,
S.A.
Lorenzo Ortiz, e/ Aguera y
Heredia
Tel: (31) 44262

City of Holguin

Hotel Tour Arcada,
Universitur, S.A.
Manduley, e/8 y 10
Tel: (24) 46 28 23

City of Santiago de Cuba

Hotel Bitiri, Universitur, S.A.
Calles L y 7
Reparto Vista Alegre
Tel: (22) 64 20 47

8 CUC single, 10 CUC double

APPENDIX 23
(from page 52)

CASAS PARTICULARES

Note: This is a listing of potential accommodations in private homes to help travelers to Cuba find lodging. The *casas particulares* in this list are not necessarily the recommendations of the author or publisher. Rates, conditions and availability may change. Author nor publisher do not accept any responsibility for any financial or material losses incurred as a result of making accommodation arrangements with any of the *casas particulares* listed. Rates are for one room (not per person) per day, unless specified. Cuban law limits 2 occupants per room (not including children.)

CITY OF HAVANA

Centro Habana

Casa Candida y Pedro
San Rafael # 403, bajos
E/ Manrique y Campanario
Tel: (7) 867-8902
Cell (7) 05268-4527
E-mail: candidacobas@yahoo.es
Near Chinatown, 10 minute walk from Prado
15-20 CUC, 2 rooms, one with private bath
Friendly, trustworthy, and helpful

Zoraya Marquez Borrego
Aguila 103 Apto. 3, entre Colon y Trocadero
Tel: (7) 861-5185
A/C; Near Malecon and Prado;

Triny Vital
Aguila 118 bajos, entre Colón y Trocadero
Tel: (7) 867-9132
Apartment w/2 bedrooms, sleeps 5

Elicio Fernández
Aguila 314 Apto 405, entre Neptuno y Concordia
Tel: (7) 861-7447
Two rooms w/shared bath, rooftop view, elevator

Maria Cuba Alarcón
Aguila 353, 1ro. Piso, entre Neptuno y San Miguel
Tel: (7) 863-9258
A/C

Esther Cardoso
Aguila 367, entre Neptuno y San Miguel
Tel: (7) 862-0401
Lots of foliage, 2 rooms w/2 double beds
Caridad Harris
Aguila 617, entre Reina y Dragones
Tel: (7) 863-3693
Modern, each room has two double beds.

Dulce María González
Amistad 220, entre Neptuno y San Miguel
Tel: (7) 863-2506
Colonial flavor, high ceilings, quiet.

Raudelina Rodríguez
Amistad 302 esq San Rafael
Tel: (7) 862-6181
E-Mail: raudelinarod@hotmail.com

Marina Oriol
Amistad 556, Apto. 5, 3er piso, entre Monte y Estrella
Tel: (7) 867-3125
Near Capitolio, well-maintained.

Anita
Animas 404, esquina Galiano
Tel: (7) 863-8992
Ten minutes from Malecon, helpful and friendly host.

Campanario #212 e/Concordia y Virtudes
E-mail: AlquilerCasaHabana@yahoo.com
25 CUC
Has three bedrooms avail, one with private bath
Balcony w/ ocean view

Blanco Street
111 Blanco between Ánimas and Trocadero
Tel: 7 8634033
E-mail: rbarroso@infomed.sld.cu
Private bath, A/C, fridge
One single bed and one double bed

Vedado

Jorge Luis Duany Ribas
#917 @ 13 Street between 8 & 6.
Phone : (537) 833-5697
E-mail : CBL917@hotmail.com
25 CUC
2 double bed,
    Private Bathroom with hot and cold water,
    Air conditioning,

Villa Babi.
Calle 27 # 965 entre 6 y 8.
Phone: (537)-830-6373
Fax: (537)-830-2094
E-mail: villababi@aol.com
A bohemia flavor; antiques, artwork.

Residencia Del Bosque
Ave. del Bosque No.152
e/ Ave. ZoolÃ³gico y 36
Tel: +53 7 8813670

Independent Apartment on Linea
Linea No:1156 Apto D
between 16 y 18
Phone: (53) 878 2923
E-mail: montrealoscar@yahoo.com.au
Independent apartment w/ 2 rooms
Has a telephone

Nelson y Aurora
Calle 15 No. 962 apto. 5 e/ 8 y 10
Teléfono: (57) 38659
Fax:(7) 311420
25-30 CUC per room

Casa Vicki
Calle F No. 508 Between 23 and 21
Independent apartment with ocean view
TV, telephone, 30 CUC per room

Oreste y Maria
Calle 12 #155 apart. 21
entre Calzada y Linea

Teléfono: (57) 8303290
E-mail: booking@havanacasaparticular.com

"La Superabuela" (Lola)
Calle I #355, Apt.1, 2do piso, e/17 y 19
Telephone: (537) 832-3033 in Havana.
E-mail: la_superabuela@hotmail.com
Double bedrooms, TV and VCR.
25-30 CUC per night

Twenty-fifth and G
Calle 25 No. 571, esq. a G
Floor 8 Apto. 811
Tel: (7) 37613, (7) 302920
Elevators, single or double rooms, TV
Comfort and privacy

Habana Vieja

Rafael y Martha
Aguacate 480, entre Brasil y Muralla
Tel: (7) 867-5005, 867-9101
Clean, privacy

Orlando y Liset
Aguacate 509, Apto 301, entre Sol y Muralla
Tel: (7) 867-5766

Elvia Olivares
Aguacate 509, Apto 402, entre Sol y Muralla
Tel: (7) 867-5974
E-Mail: elviaoli@yahoo.es

Fefita y Luis
Aguacate 509, Apto 403, entre Sol y Muralla
Tel: (7) 867-6433, 861-3210
E-Mail: fefitayluis@yahoo.es
Modern, clean. A/C, TV, VCR

Jesús y María
Aguacate 518, entre Sol y Muralla
Tel: (7) 861-1378
E-Mail: jesusmaria2003@yahoo.com
Website: www.cubacasas.particuba.info
Room or small apartment; renovated, balcony

Elsa y Julio Roque
Consulado 162, Apto 2, entre Colon y Trocadero
Tel: (7) 861-8027
TV, A/C, separate entrance

Carcel (Capdevila)#156 Apto3
entre Prado y San Lazaro

Yamelis and Federico
25-35 CUC per room
Two rooms
A/C, telephone safe box. stereo,
Balcony with a street view

Casa Gudelia
Prado #20 Apto.6A piso 6
entre San Lazaro y Carcel
30 to 35 CUC
Terrace overlooking the Morro and the sea
Elevator, A/C

Playas del Este—Guanabo

Casa de Dona Carmen
Calle 5ta C #49808 /498 y 500
5 min walk from beach
Tel: (7) 96 433, (7) 96 3463
E-mail: frykaren1@hotmail.com
Apartment with separate entrance, double BR
A/C, TV, fully-equipped kitchen
25-30 CUC per room

Casa de Julio y Mileydis
Calle 468 #512
E/ 5ta y 7ma
Tel: (7) 96 01 00
Garden area, A/C

Casa Trujillo
Ave Quebec #55
E/ 478 y 482
Tel: (7) 96 33 25
30-35 CUC, large bedroom, A/C

Casa Alberto y Nelsa
Calle 500 #5008
E/ Ave 5 y 7

Casa Armada
Ave A #50025
E/ Calle 500 y la playa

CAMAGUEY PROVINCE

Camaguey

Casa Andres y Martha
Prolongacion de Fernando de Zayas
Apto 8 e/ 1ra y 2da paralela
Rpto La Vigia
Tel: (32) 28-4087

Casa Manuel
Independencia #251, altos
E/Hermanos Aguero y Gomez
Tel: (32) 29 46 06
2 very large rooms with high ceilings
Overlooks the Plazuela Maceo
15-20 CUC

Casa Lucy y Ivan
Calle Alegria #23
E/ Agramonte y Montera
Tel: (32) 83701
Colonial ambiance, antique furnishings

Casa Caridad
Oscar Primelles #310
E/ Bartolome Maso y Padre Alallo
Tel: (32) 91554
2 large rooms w/private bath, A/C
Very friendly and helpful hosts

Hostal Hiram y Marlene
San Ramon #216
E/Santa Rita y San Martin
Tel: (32) 29 83 09
2 rooms w/private bath, A/C

Colonial house, garden
20 CUC

CIEGO DE AVILA PROVINCE

Ciego de Avila

Casa de Aleida Castro
Calle 3 #16
E/Independencia y Joaquin de Aguero
Tel: (33) 22 83 55
'50s style décor, rooftop terrace
2 rooms w/private bath, A/C
20-30 CUC

Casa Jose
Calle A #384
E/ 6ta y 7ma

Casa de Bilkis
Chicho Valdes #76
E/Maceo y H. Castillo
Tel: (33) 22 46 09
2 rooms w/private bath, separate entrances
Own telephones, fridge

Moron

Casa Carmen
General Peraza #38
E/ Ave Felipe Poey y Carlos Manuel de Cespedes
Tel: (33) 54181
2 rooms, A/C, antique furnishing

Casa Juan Perez
Castillo, #189
E/ San Jose y Serafin Sanchez
Tel: (33) 53823
Near the center, 2 rooms w/ private bath, A/C

CIENFUEGOS PROVINCE

Cienfuegos

Casa Bertha
Calle 43 #3402
E/ Ave 34 y 36
Tel: (25) 19926
E-Mail: berta@correosonline.co.cu
3 rooms, all w/ private bath
Quiet neighborhhod, very clean

Casa Elias y Mary
Calle 57 #4813
Tel: (432) 52 28 07
Near public swimming pool

Casa Pineiro
Calle 41 #1402
E/ 14 y 16
Tel: (432) 3808

Casa Colonial
Calle Camilo Cienfuegos #213
E/ Francisco Cadahia y Jose Marti
Tel: (41) 94140
Rooms w/ private bath, A/C

Finca los Colorados
Carretera de Psascaballo KM 18
Playa Rancho Luna
Tel: (43) 54 80 44
Fax: (43) 51 32 65
E-mail: fincaloscolorados
@casapineiro.com
Villa-style home, well-furnished
Private bath, outdoor dining area

GRANMA PROVINCE

Bayamo

Casa Lydia y Manuel
Calle Marmol #323

E/ Figueredo y Lora
Tel: (23) 42 31 75
Near the center
Clean room, A/C, private bath

Casa de Yisel
Saco #16
E/Cespedes y Maximo Gomez
Tel: (23) 42 49 73
1 room w/ private bath, A/C
Colonial home, patio

Casa Jose Luis
Calle Saco #275
E/Pio Rosado y Capotico
Tel: (23) 53028

Villa Coral
Calle Ruben Noregas #22
E/Casique Guama y Jose Antonio Saco
Tel: (23) 42 31 65
2 rooms, private bath, A/C

Manzanillo

Casa Adrian y Tonia
Martires de Vietnam #49
Esq Calle de la Caridad
Tel: (23) 53028
1 room w/private bath, A/C
Balcony overlooking steps to
Monumento Celia Sanchez; roof terrace
20-25 CUC

Casa Yory
Pedro Figueredo #121
E/Luz Caballero y Martirez de Vietnam
Tel: (23) 52127
2 rooms w/shared bath, A/C
25 CUC

GUANTANAMO PROVINCE

Baracoa
Casa Tony
Calle Republica #8
Tel: (21) 42751

Casa Nalvis y Efer
Calle Jose Marti # 147
Tel: (21) 43715
Quaint, clean, secure

Casa Marlin
Calle Ciro Frias #1`8
E/ Calle Marti y Maceo
Rooms w/private bath , A/C
Very clean

Casa El Mirador
Maceo 386
E/24 de Febrero y 10 de Octubre
Tel: (21) 42647
E-mail: jodn@toa.gtm.sld.cu
2 rooms w/private bath, A/C
Colonial home, high ceilings, balcony

Casa Ana
Calle Clixto Garcia #162
E/Ave Cespedes y Coroneles Galano
Tel: (21) 42754
2 rooms w/private bath, clean

Guantanamo

Casa Lissett
Pedro A. Perez #661
E/ Jesus de Sol y Prado

HAVANA PROVINCE

Cojimar

Casa Hostal Marlins
Calee Real #128A

E/Santo Domingo y Chacon
Tel: (7)65 32 61
Independent apartment w/kitchenette
20-25 CUC

Casa Arsenio
Calle 27 #98
E/Maceo y Los Pinos
Tel: (7) 65 29 62
2nd floor apartment w/kitchen
20 CUC

HOLGUIN PROVINCE

Holguin

Casa Mechy y Francisco
Calle Peralta #28
E/ Cables y Angel Guerra
Tel: (24) 46 36 55
Clean; tree-lined street
Villa Celia
Pepe Torres #75 Bajos
E/ Arias y Agramonte
Tel: (24) 42 45 81
Room w/ 2 beds, private bath
5 minute walk from center of town

Villa Liba
Maceo #46
Esq 18 Reparto El Llano
Tel: (24) 42 38 23
E-mail: villaliba@yahoo.es
2 rooms w/private bath, A/C
Well-maintained, '50s style home
25 CUC

Casa Luis
Calle Cervantes #205
E/ Arias y Agramonte
Tel: (24) 22062
5 blocks from center
private entrance, A/C

Casa Juan Figueiras
Calle Narciso Lopez #81
E/ Agramonte y Garayalde
Tel: (24) 24585
2 rooms w/private bath, private entrance

Gibara

Villa Caney
Sartorio #36
E/Peralta y Luz Caballero
Tel: (24) 34552
2 rooms w/private bath, A/C
Colonial home, garden, thatched restaurant

Casa de los Hermanos
Cespedes #13
E/Peralta y Luz Caballero
Tel: (24) 34542
2 rooms w/private bath,
Colonial home, rear patio

ISLA DE LA JUVENTUD MUNICIPALITY

Nueva Gerona

Casa Elena
Calle 54 #4500
E/ Ave 45 y 47
Tel: ($6) 332-3992
E-mail: henry44@web.correosdecuba.cu
1 room, rear patio, A/C
10 minute walk from center

Villa Pena
Calle 10 #3710
E/ Ave 37 y 39
Tyel: (46) 332-2345
E-mail: magui@ahao.iju.sld.cu
2 rooms, A/C, private bath
center of town

Casa Rafael
Calle 32 #4701-A

E/47 y49
Tel: (46) 32 31 67
2 rooms but whole house available
private bath

Villa Ninita
Calle 32 #4110
E/41 y 43
Tel: (46) 32 12 55
E-mail: zerep@web.correosdecuba.cu
2 rooms, A/C, private baths
one room has a kitchen w/fridge

LAS TUNAS PROVINCE

Las Tunas

Casa Rodrigo y Yosi
Coronel Reyes #41
Esq Gonzalo de Quesada
Tel: (31) 48760, 41153
1 large, clean room, A/C

Casa de Enrique y Giennys
Villamar # 30A
E/Aguero y Guardia
Tel: (31) 45596
1 room w/private bath, A/C
Radio, fridge
15-25 CUC

Casa Yacqueline
Ave Frank Paios # 37
E/ Fernando Suarez y Maximo Gomez
Reparto Velazquez

Hospedaje Dona Nelly
Lucas Ortiz #111
E/Gonzalo de Quesada y Coronel Fonseca
Tel: (31) 42526
1 room w/private bath, A/C
Colonial home, patio
15-20 CUC

MATANZAS PROVINCE

Matanzas

La Villa Sonada
Santa Teresa # 6701
Esq Santa Isabel
Tel: (45) 42 27 61

Casa Jorge y Nadia
Calle Paraiso #25406
E/ Levante y Descanso
La Playa
Tel: (45) 29 25 64

Casa de Roberto y Margarita
Calle79 #27608
E/276 y 280
Tel: (45) 24 25 77
At center, colonial house,
2 large rooms, courtyard

Casa de Evelio e Isel
Calle 79 #28201
E/282 y 288
Tel: (45) 24 30 90
Website: www.cubacasas.net
1 room with A/C, fridge, TV, private bath

Cardenas

Hostal El Italiano
Playa Larga #61
Tel: (52) 1879

Casa Ricardo
Palma #520
E/ Coronel Verdugo y Industria
Cell: (53) (7) 2701284

Playa Larga

Villa Juana
Tel: (45) 98 73 08

E-mail: caribesolpz@yahoo.es
1 room, private bath and fridge, A/C

Casa de Enrique Rivas
Tel: (45) 98 71 78
1 room w/private bath, A/C

Playa Giron

Casa de Gelasio y Lourde
Tel: (45) 98 41 46
1 room w/ private bath, fridge
20 CUC

Hostal Silvia
Tel: (45) 98 42 49
2 rooms w/private bath, clean
20 CUC

Varadero

The government does not permit
casas particulares in Varadero

PINAR DEL RIO PROVINCE

Vinales

Casa Graciela y Carlos
Rafael Trejo # 116
E/ Celso Maragoto y Sergio Dopico
Quiet street, private bathroom, fantastic cooks

Villa Nene
Calle Adela Azcuy #35
Tel: (8) 79 33 14

Villa Isabelita
Camilo Cienfuegos #1B
Tel: (8) 79 32 67
1 room w/ two double beds
Near plaza, A/C, private bath

Villa Nelson
Camilo Cienfuegos #4
Tel: (8) 79 32 68
15-20 CUC 1 room, A/C near plaza

Casa de Oscar
Adela Azcuy #43
Tel: (8) 79 33 81
2 rooms, 1 w/private bath

Pinar del Rio

Casa Tanya y Rodrigo
Calle Colon # 167
E/Mariana Grajales y Labra
Tel: (82) 375-3359, 375-3875
2 large rooms, one w/ private bath

Villa Blanca
Rafael Morales #233
Esq Horriman
Tel: (82) 75 20 12
1 room, private bath and entrance
20 CUC, A/C

Casa de Rene
Calle Union #13
E/ Capitan San Luis y Carmen
Reparto Villamil
Tel: (82) 75 51 96
2 rooms, A/C, private entrances
balcony, own fridge

Casa Adela Cruz
Gerardo Medina #67
Tel: (82) 75 31 33
Colonial house with various rooms
Private bath, patio, garden
15-20 CUC

Puerto Esperanza

Casa de Teras
Calle 4ta #7

Tel: (8) 79 38 03
15 CUC 2 rooms, comfy and clean

Casa Leolila
Calle Hermanos Caballeros #41
Tel: (8) 93843
15-20 CUC, 2 rooms

SANCTI SPIRITUS PROVINCE

Sancti Spiritus

Casa Tomas Dias
Maximo Gomez #9
E/ Plaza Serafin Sanchez y Ave Honorato
Tel: (41) 27626
Room in a cottage w/private bath

Casa Anais y Cayucxo
Calle Piro Guinart #254
E/ Gomez Toro y Ruben Villena
Tel: (41) 23462
2 rooms, A/C w/ private bath
Colonial mansion, center of town

Hostal Los Espejos
Socorro #56
E/Cespedes y Marti
Tel: (41) 26262
2 rooms in colonial home
Private bath, TV, fridge
15-20 CUC per room

Casa de Maria teresa
Adolfo del Castillo #33
E/Ave de los Martires y Valdina
Tel: (41) 24733
2 rooms, A/C, private bath,
Own fridge 15-20 CUC

Trinidad

Casa Mercedes
Calle Jose Mart #330

E/ Simon Bolivar y Francisco Javier
Zerquera
Tel: (419) 3350

Hostal Coatzacoalcos
Camilo Ciebfuegos #213
E/ Francisco Cadahia y Jose Marti
Tel: (419) 4140
3 rooms, old mansion, A/C

Casa Sara Sanjua
Simon Bolivar #266
E/Frank Pais y Marti
Tel: (419) 3997
2 rooms w/A/C, fridge, private bath
Colonial home, furnished w/antiques

Hostal Bastida
Maceo #537
E/ Simon Bolivar y Piro Guinart
Tel: (419) 6686
Colonial elegance, historical center

Casa Isobel y N. Gil
Calle Gustavo Izquierdo #28
E/ Ave Colon y Francisco Javier Zerquera
Tel: (419) 3229
Large room, private bath

VILLA CLARA PROVINCE

Caibarien

Casa Eladio
Ave 35 #1016B
E/ Calle 10 y 12
(33) 64253
2 rooms, A/C, comfy beds

Santa Clara

Casa Simon
Jose Roberto Simon Cardenas
7ma No. 619 E/ 6TA Y 8RA

Reparto Universitario
Tel: (422) 27 55 54
E-mail: hostalsimon@yahoo.es

Casa Ernesto
Calle Cuba #227 (altos)
entre Sindico y Pastora
Tel: (422) 27 35 01
daily rates: $20 cuc

Leoncio Vidal #1
Primer piso
Entre parque y Maceo
Tel: (422) 21 74 44
E-mail: hostalpark@yahoo.com

Francisco and Adeleida Reguera
Calle N #4,
e/ Reparto Sueno y Avenida Cespedes
(No telephone)

Martha Artiles Alemán
Marta Abreu no. 56
e/ Villuendas y Zayas
Tel: (422) 05008
20-25 CUC

Orlando Garcia Rodriguez
Rolando Pardo N°7
entre parque y Maceo
Tel: (422) 26761
10-15 CUC
A/C

Consuelo Ramos Rodriguez
Independencia #265 Apto 1
entre Union y San Isidro
10-15 CUC
A/C

Casa Maria
e/ Maceo y Luis Estevez
Santa Clara
(No telephone)
 A/C

Fefita y Pedrin
Placido 63A
e/ Marti y Bolivar
(No telephone)
A/C

Maria Sanchez
Calle Maceo #6
Cespedes y Buenviaje
(No telephone)

Mauricio hostal
Calle Martha Abreu #58(altos)
entre Zayas y Villuendas
(No telephone)
20 CUC
A/C

Omelio Moreno Lorenzo
San cristobal no.4
e/Cuba y Colon
42 2-3967
20 CUC
A/C

Casa Francisco
Francisco Moreno Mata
Calle 2, 119
e/ 5ta y 7ma, Rpto. Escambray
Santa Clara, Villa Clara, Cuba
Tel: 42 - 273273
20 CUC
Quiet residential area

Remedios

Casona Cuerto
Alejandro del Rio #72
Esq Enrique Malaret
Tel: (42) 39 53 50
E-mail: amartelys@capiro.vcl.sld.cu
18th-century home furnished w/antiques
2 rooms w/private bath, A/C
Courtyard, terrace. 20-25 CUC

Casa de Jorge Rivero
Brigadier Gonzalez #29
Tel: (42) 39 63 10
2 blocks from the plaza
2 rooms, 1 with separate entrance
Private bath, fridge 15-25 CUC

SANTIAGO DE CUBA PROVINCE

Santiago de Cuba

Casa Jose Manuel
San Agustin #419
E/ San Francisco y San Geronimo
Tel: (22) 62 91 60

Casa Maria de la Cruz
Rey Pelayo #83
E/ El Reloj y Calvario
Tel: (22) 62 87 78
City center

Casa de Abel y Milagros
Jaguey #164
E/Padre Pico y Corona
Tel: (22) 65 93 20
Website: www.realcubaonline.com
Large rooms with private bath, A/C
Neocolonial home, downtown
25 CUC

Casa Doris
Calle Corona #608
E/ Ave Heredia y Aguilera
Tel: (22) 62 21 61
Large room in colonial building
Private bath, A/C
Room has table, chairs, fridge

Casa Ana Delia
Calle B Masso #172,
E/ Corona y Padre Pico, 2ndo piso
Tel: (22) 6511 91
Room w/private bath, A/C

Playa Verraco

Casa de Enrique y Rosa
Carretyera de Baconao Km 17.5
Communidad Artistica Los Mamoncillas
Tel: (22) 35 62 05
1 room w/private bath, A/C
Spacious, own fridge
20 CUC

Siboney

Casa de Ovidio Gonzalez Sabaido
Ave Serrano y Calle del Barco
Tel: (22) 39340
2 rooms w/private bath, also a
two-bedroom apartment available

Casa de Maria Elena Gonzalez
Obelisco #10
Tel: (22) 39200
2 rooms, 1 w/terrace
Modern, three-story house
Stone patio, swimming pool
20 CUC

APPENDIX 24

RESORTS AND HOTELS IN CUBA
(From page 55)

Note: Not a complete listing. Except for the hotels in the budget and super low budget category, the hotels in this list were selected based on a consensus of favorites culled from various guidebooks and websites. Websites such as www.havanatur.com, www.cubanacan.cu, www.grancaribe.cu, www.islazul.cu, (all Cuban enterprises), www.cubalinda.com, and www.cuba-junky.com (two reputable private Cuba travel websites) offer in-depth details about each property (including photos and rates).

Key: **S** = Super high-class and service, 300 to 500 CUC per night
   H = High-class and service, 150 to 300 CUC per night
   M = Medium price and service, 80 to 150 CUC per night
   B = Budget, 25 to 80 CUC per night
 SLB = Super low-budget, less than 25 CUC per night
       Resorts indicated in parenthesis— (Resort)

CITY OF HAVANA

Habana Vieja

Hotel Armadores de
Santander (M)
Luz #4
Esq San Pedro
Tel: (7) 862-8000

Hotel Ambos Mundos (M)
Obispo #153
E/San Ignacio y Mercaderes
Tel: (7) 860-9530

Hotel Caribbean (B)
Prado #164
E/Colon y Refugio
Tel: (7) 860-8241

NH Parque Central (H) (S)
277 rooms
Neptuno, esquina Prado y

Zulueta
Tel: (7) 866-6627

Hotel Santa Isabel
Calle Baratillo #9
E/O'Reilly y Narcisco Lopez
Tel: (7) 860-8201

Hotel Saratoga (H) (S)
Paseo del Prado #603
Esq Dragones
Tel: (7) 868-1000

Hostal Valencia (B)
Oficios #53 e/ Obrapia y
Lamparilla
Tel: (7) 857-1037

Centro Habana

Hotel Islazul Lido (L)
Consulado, esq Animas
Tel: (7) 867-1102

Hotel Lincoln (L)
Ave de Italia #164
Esq Virtudes
Tel: (7) 862-8061

Vedado

Melia Cohiba (H)
Paseo, esq 1ra
Tel: (7) 833-3636

Hotel Nacional (M)
Calle O y 21
Tel: (7) 873-3564

Hotel Presidente (M)
Calzada #110
Esq Ave de los Presidentes
Tel: (7) 55 18 01

Hotel Tryp Habana Libre (H)
Calle L
E/23 y 25
Tel: (7) 834-6100

Hotel Vedado (L)
Calle O #244
E/23 y 25
Tel: (7) 836-4072

Hotel Victoria (L)
Calle 19 #101
Esq M
Tel: (7) 833-3510

Miramar

Hotel Comodoro (M)
Ave 1ra y Calle 84
Tel: (7) 204-2551

Marina Hemingway (L) (M)
Ave 5ta y Calle 248
Sante Fe
Tel: (7) 204-7628

Hotel Kohly (L)
Ave 49 y 36A
Reparto Kohly, Playa
Tel: (7) 204-0240

Hotel Melia Habana (H) (S)
Ave 3ra e/76 y 80
Tel: (7) 204-8500

Hotel Occidental Miramar (M)
Ave 5ta e/ 72 y 76
Tel: (7) 204-3584

CAMAGUEY PROVINCE

Camaguey

Hotel Camaguey (L)
Carretera Central Km 4.5
Tel: (32) 87267

Hotel Colon (L)
Republica #472
E/San Jose y San Martin
Tel: (32) 28 33 68

Gran Hotel (L)
Calle Maceo #64
E/Gomez y Agramonte
Tel: (32) 29 23 14

Hotel Plaza (SLB)
Van Horne #1
E/Republica y Avellaneda
Tel: (32) 28 24 13

Playa Santa Lucia

Club Amigo Mayanabo (L)
(Resort)
Playa Santa Lucia
Tel: (32) 36 51 76

Club Amigo Caracol (M)
Playa Santa Lucia
Tel: (32) 36 51 58

Gran Club Santa Lucia (L)
Playa Santa Lucia
Tel: (32) 36 51 53

Hotel Brisas Santa Lucia (M)
Playa Santa Lucia
Tel: (32) 33 63 17

CIEGO DE AVILA
PROVINCE

Cayo Coco

Hotel Blau Colonial (M)
(Resort)
Playa Larga
Tel: (33) 30 13 11

Villa Gaviota (M)
Playa Larga
Tel: (33) 30 21 80

Motel Jardin Los Cocos (L)
Via Azul, Punta Almacigo
Tel: (33) 30 91 21

Hotel Tryp Cayo Coco (H)
(Resort)
Playa LargaTel: (33) 30 13 00

Melia Cayo Coco (H)
(Resort)
Playa Larga
Tel: (33) 30 11 80

Sol Cayo Coco
(Resort)
Playa Larga
Tel: (33) 30 12 80

Cayo Guillermo

Villa Cojimar (M)
(Resort)
Playa el Paso

Tel: (33) 30 17 12

Iberostar Daiquiri (M) (H)
(Resort)
Playa el Paso
Tel: (33) 30 15 60

Melia Cayo Guillermo (H)
(Resort)
Playa el Paso
Tel: (33) 30 16 85

Sol Cayo Guillermo (H)
(Resort)
Playa el Paso
Tel: (33) 30 17 60

Ciego de Avila

Hotel Ciego de Avila (SLB)
(L)
Carretera Ceballos
Tel: (33) 22 80 13

Hotel Santiago-Havana (SLB)
(L)
Independencia y
Honorario del Castillo
Tel: (33) 22 57 03

Moron

Hotel Carrusel Moron (L)
Ave Tarafa
Tel: (335) 50 22 30

La Casona de Moron (SLB)
Cristobal Colon #41
Tel: (335) 50 22 36

CIENFUEGOS PROVINCE

Cienfuegos

Hotel El Union (L)
Calle 31, esq 54
Tel: (41) 91204

Hotel Faro de Luna (L)
Carretera de Pasacaballos
Km 18
Tel: (43) 54 80 62

Hotel Pasacaballo (M)
Carretera Rancho Luna
Tel: (49) 66013

Hotel Rancho Luna (L)
Carretera de Rancho Luna
Km 18
Tel: (43) 55 14 84

GRANMA PROVINCE

Bayamo

Hotel Royalton (SLB)
Maceo #53
Tel: (23) 42 47 92

Hotel Teligrafo ((SLB)
Saco #108
E/Garcia y Marmol
Tel: (23) 42 55 10

Dos Rios

Villa el Yarey (L)
Loma Yarey, Jiguani
Tel: (42) 7684

Manzanillo

Hotel Guacanayabo (L)
Circunvalacion Camilo
Cienfuegos
Tel: (23) 4012

Marea del Portillo

Club Amigo Farallon del
Caribe (L)
Playa Marea del Portillo
Tel: (23) 59 71 03

Club Amigo Marea del Portillo
(L)
(Resort)
Playa Marea del Portillo
Tel: (23) 59 71 03

Niquero

Hotel Niquero
Calle principal
Tel: (23) 59 23 67

Parque Nacional Pico Turquino

Villa Santo Domingo (L)
Centro de Visitantes
Santo Domingo
Tel: (59) 56 56 13

HAVANA PROVINCE

Cojimar

Hotel Islazul Panamericano
(L)
Calle A y Ave Central
Tel: (7) 95 10 21

Playas del Este

Blau Horizontes Club Arenal
(M)
Lago de Boca Ciega
Ave 1ra
E/Santa Maria del Mar y Boca
Ciega
Tel: (7) 97 12 72
Web: www.bla-hotels.com

Hotel Gran Via (SLB)
Ave 5ta e/ 502 y 504
Guanabo
Tel: (7) 96 43 00

Hotel Horizontes (L)
Ave de las Terrazas
E/5 y 7
Santa Maria del Mar
Tel: (7) 97 13 71

Villas Marina Tarara (M)
Calle 9na, esq 14
Villa Tarara
Santa Maria del Mar
Tel: (7) 97 14 62

San Antonio de los Banos

Hotel Las Yagrumas (L)
Calle 40 y Final Autopista
Tel: 650) 38 44 60

Santa Cruz del Norte

SuperClubs Breezes Jibacoa
(M) (H)
(Resort) 250 rooms
Via Blanca Km 60
Arroyo Bermejo Beach
Tel: (692) 85122
Web:
www.superclubscuba.com

Occidental
Royal Hideaway Ensenachos
Cayo Ensenachos ( ) 506
rooms
Santa Maria Clara

GUANTANAMO PROVINCE

Baracoa

Hotel El Castillo (L)
Calle Calixto Garcia
Tel: (21) 42125

Hostal La Habanera (L)
Maceo #68
Esq Frank Pais

Tel: (21) 45273

Hotel La Rusa (L)
Maximo Gomez #161
Tel: (21) 42337

City of Guantanamo

Hotel Guantanamo (L)
Calle 13
E/Ahogado y Oeste
Tel: (21) 38 10 15

Parque Nacional
Alejandro Humboldt

Villa Maguana (L)
Bahia de Taco
Tel: (21) 45165

HOLGUIN PROVINCE

Guardalavaca

Club Amigo Guardalavaca (L)
(M)
(Resort)
Playa Las Brisas
Tel: (24) 30180

Brisas Guardalavaca (M)
(Resort)
Playa Las Brisas
Tel: (24) 30218

Occidental
Grand Playa Turquesa (H)
Playa Yaraguanal
Tel: (24) 39545

Paradisus Rio de Oro (H)
(Resort)
Carretera Guardalavaca
Playa Esmeralda
Tel: (24) 30090

Hotel Playa Costa Verde (M)
(H)
Playa Pesquero
Tel: (24) 30530

Villas Cabanas (L)
Playa Las Brisas
Tel: (24) 30314

City of Holguin

Hotel Pernik (L)
Ave Dimitrov
Tel: (24) 48 10 11

Villa El Bosque (L)
Ave Dimitrov
Tel: (24) 48 10 12

Mirador de Mayabe

Villa Mirador de Mayabe (L)
Mirador de Mayabe
Tel: (24) 42 21 60

Moa

Hotel Miraflores (SLB)
Ave Amistad
Tel: (24) 66332

ISLA DE JUVENTUD

Nueva Gerona

Hotel Rancho El Tesoro ((L)
Carretera La Fe Km 2.5
Nueva Gerona
Tel: (46) 32 30 55

Villa Isla de la Juventud (L)
Carretera La Fe Km 1.5
Nueva Gerona
Tel: (46) 32 32 90

Ensenada de Siguanera

Hotel Colony (L)
Carretera de Siguanera Km
41
Tel: (46) 39 81 81

Cayo Largo

Barcelo Cayo Largo Resort
(M)
(Resort)
e/Playa Lindamar y Playa
Blanca
Tel: (45) 24 80 80

Club Coral (M)
(Resort)
Eden Village
Playa Lindamar
Tel: (45) 24 81 11

Sol Club Cayo Largo (H)
(Resort)
Playa Paraiso Km 15
Tel: (42) 24 82 60

Sol Pelicano (H)
(Resort)
Playa Lindamar Km 15
Tel: (42) 54 83 33

Villas Marinera (L)
Carretera final oeste
El Pueblo
Tel: (42) 24 83 85

LAS TUNAS PROVINCE

Las Tunas

Hotel Las Tunas (SLB) (L)
Avenida 2 de Diciembre
Tel: (31) 43336

Puerto Padre

Villa Covarrubias (M)
Playa Las Bocas

MATANZAS PROVINCE

Jaguey Grande

Motel Batey Don Pedro (L)
Autopista Km 142
Tel: (45) 91 28 25

Playa Larga

Playa Larga Hotel (L)
Playa Larga
Tel: (45) 97225

Villas Playa Larga (L)
Playa Larga
Tel: (45) 98 72 94

Playa Giron

Hotel Playa Giron (L)
Playa Giron
Tel: (45) 94118

Laguna del Tesoro

Villas Guama (L)
Laguna del Tesoro
Tel: (45) 95515

Matanzas

Canimao Hotel (L)
Carretera de Varadero Km
3.5
Tel: (52) 61 01 14

Hotel Velasco (L)
Calle Milanes
Plaza Libertad
Tel: (52) 54074

Valle de Yumuri

Horizontes Casa del Valle (M)
Carretera de Chirino Km 2
Tel: (52) 54584

Varadero

Barcelo Marina Palace (H)
Punta Hicacos, final
Tel: (45) 66 99 66

Club Amigo Tropical (M)
(Resort)
Ave 1ra e/21 y 22
Tel: (45) 61 39 15

Club Barlovento (H)
(Resort)
Ave 1ra e/10 y 12
Tel: (45) 66 71 40

Hotel Ledo (L)
Ave de la Playa
E/43 y 44
Tel: (45) 61 32 06

Iberostar Varadero (H)
(Resort)386 rooms
Crta Las Morlas km 16
Punta Hicacos
Tel: (45) 66999

Mercure Cuatro Palmas (M)
Ave 1ra e/61 y 62
Tel: (45) 66 81 01

Mansion Xanadu (H)
Carretera Las Morlas
Tel: (45) 66 77 50

Villa La Mar (L)
Ave 3ra e/28 y 30
Tel: (45) 61 39 10

PINAR DEL RIO PROVINCE

Cayo Levisa

Villa Cayo Levisa (L)
Cayo Levisa (Boat departs from
Palma Rubia on the mainland)
Tel: (8) 66 60 75

Playa Maria La Gorda

Hotel Maria La Gorda (L)
Cabo Corrientes
Tel: (82) 77 81 31

Pinar del Rio

Hotel Aguas Claras (SLB)
Carretera de Vinales Km 7.5
Tel: (8) 77 84 26

Hotel Pinar del Rio (L)
Marti y final autopista
Tel: (82) 75 50 70

Hotel Vuelta Abajo (L)
Marti #103
Esq Rafael Morales
Tel: (82) 75 93 87

San Diego de los Banos

Hotel el Mirador (L)
Calle 23 final
Tel: (82) 77 83 38

Vinales

Hotel La Hermita (L)
Carretera de la Ermita Km 2
Tel: (8) 79 60 81

Hotel Las Jazmines (L)
Carretera de Vinales Km 25
Tel: (8) 79 62 05

SANCTI SPIRITUS PROVINCE

Embalse Zaza

Hotel Zasa ((L)
Embalse Zaza, norte
Tel: (41) 27015

Parque Nacional Caguanas

Villa San Jose del Lago ((L)
Mayijagua, este
Tel: (41) 56290

Playa Ancon

Hotel Ancon (M)
(Resort)
Playa Ancon
Tel: (419) 6120

Hotel Costa Sur (M)
Playa Ancon
Tel: (419) 6174

Brisas Trinidad del Mar (M)
Playa Ancon
Tel: (419) 6565

Parque Topes de Collantes

Kurhotel Escambray (L)
Topes de Collantes
Tel: (42) 54 01 17

Hotel Los Helechos (L)
Topes de Collantes
Tel: (42) 54 03 30

Sancti Spiritus

Hostal del Rio (L)
Calle Honorato del Castillo #12
Tel: (41) 28 58 88

Hotel Plaza (L)
Calle Independencia #1
Parque Central
Tel: (41) 27102

Trinidad

Iberostar Grand Hotel (H)
Calle Jose Marti y Lino Perez
Parque Cespedes
Tel:

Hotel La Ronda (L)
Calle Marti #239
Tel: (419) 4011

Hotel Horizontes Las Cuevas
(L)
Calle General Lino Perez,
final
Tel: (419) 6161

SANTA CLARA PROVINCE

Cayo Santa Maria

Hotel Sol Cayo Santa Maria
(H) (Resort)
Tel: (42) 35 15 00

Melia Cayo Santa Melia
(H) (S) (Resort)
Tel: (42) 35 02 00

Royal Hideaway Ensenachos
(H) (S) (Resort)
Tel:

Remedios

Hotel Mascotte (L)
Calle Maximo Gomez
Tel: (42) 39 54 67

Santa Clara

Carrusel La Granjita (L)
Carretera Malez Km 2.5
Tel: (422) 28192

Hotel Los Caneyes (L)
Ave de los Eucaliptos esq
Circunvalacion de Santa
Clara
Tel: (422) 21 81 40

Hotel Santa Clara Libre (L)
Parque Vidal
Tel: (422) 20 75 48

Embalse Hanabanilla

Hotel Hanabanilla (SLB)
Tel: (42) 20 23 99

SANTIAGO DE CUBA
PROVINCE

City of Santiago de Cuba

Hotel Casa Granda (M)
Heredia #201
E/ Lacret y Hartman
Tel: (22) 68 66 00

Hotel Las Americas (L)
Ave de las Americas
Esq General Cebreco
Tel: (22) 64 20 11

Hotel Libertad (L)
Aguilera #658
Tel: (22) 62 83 60

Hotel Melia Santiago de Cuba
(M)
Ave de las Amercas
Esq M
Tel: (22) 68 71 70

Hotel San Juan (L)
Ave Siboney y Calle 13
Tel: (22) 68 72 00

Chivirico

Brisas Los Galeones (M)
(Resort)
Carretera de Chivirico Km 60
Tel: (22) 62 61 60

Brisas Sierra Mar (L)
Carretera de Chivirico Km 60
Tel: (22) 62 91 10

El Cobre

Hospedaje El Cobre (SLB)
Basilica de Nuestra Senora
del Cobre
Hotel Costa Marena
Carretera de Baconao Km 38.5
Playa Larga
Tel: (22) 35 61 26

Tel: (22) 36246
El Salton

Hotel Horizontes El Salton (L)
Carretera Puerto Rico a File
III Frente
Tel: (225) 6326

Laguna Baconao

Club Amigo Carisol
Carretera de Baconao
Playa Cazonal
Tel: (22) 35 61 15

Club Amigo los Corales
Carretera de Baconao
Playa Cazonal
Tel: (22) 53 61 22

APPENDIX 25
(From page 55)

CAMPISMO POPULAR OFFICES IN CUBA—BY PROVINCE

Note: For more information about camping in Cuba, contact Empresa Nacional de Campismo Popular at (7) 831-3645 (Calle 13 #857 in Vedado, Havana) or a tour operator (such as Cubamar) listed in Appendix 18 (page 194) and Appendix 19 (page 195). Some campgrounds, particularly those on the beaches, may be off-limits to foreigners.

PROVINCE OF CAMAGUEY

Recepción - Ave.Libertad No.208 La Caridad
         Monte Oscu
Camagüey286824

A.A.Mola Camagüey380709

Ave.Libertad No.208 La Caridad Camagüey221462

Ave.Libertad No.208 La Caridad Camagüey221463

B.Ventas - J.Vega Camagüey297299

Base Batalla de Saratoga - Carr.Cubanacán

Camagüey399428

Base Las Clavellinas - Jimaguayú Camagüey285800

Base Las Palmas - Maceo No.11 Camagüey674745

Base Monte Oscuro - Cdad.Pueblo Nuevo

Camagüey871036

Base Monte Oscuro – Camagüey813001

Base Punta de Ganado – Camagüey336448
Dirección - Ave.Libertad No.108 La Caridad Camagüey292641

Dirección - Ave.Libertad No.208 La Caridad Camagüey298837

Económico - Ave.Libertad No.208 La Caridad Camagüey286823

General - Ave.Libertad No.208 La Caridad Camagüey285896

Las Palmas – Maceo No.11 Camagüey674881

Pta.de Ganado Camagüey336289
Reservaciones – Ave.Libertad No.208 La

Caridad
Camagüey296855
Reservaciones –
Pdte.Gómez
Camagüey515501

Taller - Cam.Jagüey
Marquesado
Camagüey272492

Unidad de Abastecimiento -
Cam.Jagüey Marquesado
Camagüey271179

PROVINCE OF CIEGO DE AVILA

Base de Campismo
Boquerón - Boquerón Ciego
de Ávila69318

Base Los Naranjos -
LosNaranjos
Ciego de Ávila536700
Campismo - Cayo Coco
Ciego de Punta Alegre -
Maceo Final Ciego de
Ávila66412

Recepción - Carr.Central
No.111
Ciego de Ávila222501

Unidad de Transporte -
Ml.Gómez Ciego de
Ávila203428

PROVINCE OF CIENFUEGOS

Campismo Jagua - Base de
Campismo La CEN
Cienfuegos512312
63 No.7201 P.Griffo
Cienfuegos550284

Campismo Jagua – Base
de Campismo La CEN
Cienfuegos512313

Campismo Jagua – Base
de Campismo La CEN
Cienfuegos512314

Dirección - 37 No.5405
Cienfuegos519345

Dirección - 63 No.km1
P.Griffo
Cienfuegos516692

Reservaciones – 37
Cienfuegos519423

GRANMA

Abastecimiento –
Car.Manzanillo La
Hacienda
Granma426668

Administración –
Gral.García No.456
Granma427824

Administración –
Gral.García No.465
Granma422450

Base de Campismo El
Chapuzón –
Car.Manzanillo El
Chapuzón Granma421466

Base de Campismo El
Chapuzón - Car.Manzanillo
El Chapuzón
Granma422499

Base de Campismo La
Sierrita - Sierrita De

Nagua Granma326

Base de Campismo La
Sierrita - V.Grande
Granma565584

Base de Campismo Las
Coloradas - Las Coloradas
Niquero Granma901126

Base de Campismo Los
Cantiles - Santa Rita
Jiguaní Granma424862

Campismo El Salto - El Salto
Granma572351

Centro de Información -
Gral.García No.456
Granma424883

Dirección - Gral.García
No.456 Granma421875

Dirección - Gral.García
No.456 Granma427814

Recepción - Gral.García
No.456 Granma422283

Recepción - Gral.García
No.456 Granma424807

Recepción - Gral.García
No.456 Granma427698

Reservaciones - Ave.Masó
Granma565679

Reservaciones - Gral.García
No.112 Granma424200

Reservaciones - Villuendas
No.102 Granma573662

Transporte - Car.Manzanillo
La Hacienda

Granma422104

**PROVINCE OF
GUANTANAMO**

Base de Transporte – 8
Oeste
Guantánamo327447

Dirección - B.Masó No.809
Guantánamo326552

Dirección – Cajobabo
Cajobabo
Guantánamo880304

Pizarra - B.Masó
Guantánamo355957

Reservaciones –
F.Crombet No.408
Guantánamo327356

Reservaciones - J.Martí
No.225
Guantánamo642776

PROVINCE OF HOLGUIN

400 ROSAS – Gral
Marrero Holguín802309

Aseguramiento –
Camin.del Infierno
Holguín421585

Base de Transporte –
Camin.del Infierno
Holguín421588

Centro Juvenil Recreativo
Siboney - Libertad
No.189 Holguín425715

Dirección - Gibara
Holguín421586

Dirección - Miró No.183
Holguín423523

Pizarra - Miró No.183
Holguín421519

Pizarra - Miró No.183
Holguín421520

Pizarra - Miró No.183
Holguín462492

Reservaciones - Mártires
No.85 Holguín422881

ISLA DE LA JUVENTUD

Carr.Bibijagua Km 9
Bibijagua Isla de la Juventud
325323

Dirección - Carr.Bibijagua Km
9 Bibijagua Isla
de la Juventud 325266

Dirección - Carr.Bibijagua Km
9 Bibijagua Isla
de la Juventud 325313

RESERVACIONES - 37
No.2201 Nueva Gerona Isla
de la Juventud 324517

CITY OF HAVANA

Comercial - Calzada Vdo.
Ciudad de La
Habana8368525

Economía - 13 Vdo. Ciudad
de La Habana8323874

Almacén - Calzada Vdo.

Ciudad de La
Habana8368524

Dirección - 13 No.857 Vdo
Ciudad de La
Habana8309044

Dirección - 13 No.857 Vdo
Ciudad de La
Habana8338595

Dirección - Diaría
Hab.Vieja
Ciudad de La Habana
8660244

Dirección Provincial - 13
No.857 Vdo. Ciudad de
La Habana8367064

La Habana Vieja - O'Reilly
No.307 Hab.Vieja
Ciudad de La
Habana8630653

La Habana Vieja - O´Reilly
No.307 Hab.Vieja
Ciudad de La
Habana8636400

Oficina de Reservaciones
Edif.A-56 Zona 1
Alamar Ciudad de La
Habana7630241

Oficinas de Reservaciones
60 No.29A02 Playa
Ciudad de La
Habana2096666

Oficinas de Reservaciones
Ave. 31 Playa Ciudad
de La Habana2062636

Oficinas de Reservaciones
Calzada Vdo. Ciudad
de La Habana8322634

Oficinas de Reservaciones
Czda.de Güines
No.19517 Rosalía Ciudad
de La Habana6916835

Oficinas de Reservaciones -
Edif.A-56 Zona 1
Alamar Ciudad de La
Habana7630231

Oficinas de Reservaciones -
Edif.A-56 Zona 1
Alamar Ciudad de La
Habana7630333

Operaciones - 13 No.857
Vdo. Ciudad de La
Habana8312492

Operaciones - 13 No.857
Vdo. Ciudad de La
Habana8313645

Pizarra - 13 No.857 Vdo.
Ciudad de La
Habana8310080

Reservaciones Cotorro - 103
A.Hatuey Ciudad de
La Habana6823788

Subdirección de Operaciones
- 13 No.857 Vdo.
Ciudad de La
Habana8310083

Subdirección de Operaciones
- 13 No.857 Vdo.
Ciudad de La
Habana8310084

Tco. de Pizarra - 13 No.857
Vdo. Ciudad de La
Habana8310081

PROVINCE OF LA HABANA

Base de Transporte –
Carr.Rincón-Bejucal La
Habana681973

Campismo Escaleras de
Jaruco - Carr.Tapaste La
Habana873266

Carpeta - Carr.
Panamericana El Salado
La Habana378293

Dirección - Carr.
Panamericana El Salado

Habana378288

Dirección - Versalles
No.10701
Res.Almendares
Ciudad de La
Habana2601154

Economía - Carr.
Panamericana El Salado
La Habana378134

Economía - Norte Mnao.
Ciudad de La
Habana2611223

El Abra - Campismo El
Abra La Habana295258

Garita - Carr.
Panamericana El Salado
La Habana378292

Personal - Versalles
No.10701
Res.Almendares
Ciudad de La
Habana2652369

Recepción -
Carr.Panamericana Playa
Salado La
Habana378171

Recepción -
Carr.Panamericana Playa
Salado La
Habana378192

Recepción - Versalles
No.10701 Res.Almendares
Ciudad de La
Habana2605162

Reservaciones - 33 No.4206
La Habana363004

Reservaciones - 69 No.8210
La Habana525333

Subdirección - Versalles
No.10701 Res.Almendares
Ciudad de La
Habana2652368

JIBACOA (BEACH)—EAST OF HAVANA

Campismo Los Cocos - Los
Cocos Jibacoa Playa La
Habana295105

DirecciÃ³n - Jibacoa Playa La
Habana295120

DirecciÃ³n - Jibacoa Playa La
Habana295314

DirecciÃ³n - Jibacoa Playa La
Habana295351

Pizarra - Jibacoa Playa La
Habana295300

Pizarra - Jibacoa Playa La

Habana295302

Pizarra - Jubacoa Playa
La Habana295301

Planta de Bombeo –
Central No.6 La
Habana204300

SubdirecciÃ³n General –
Jibacoa Playa La
Habana295356

PROVINCE OF LAS TUNAS

Abastecimiento y
Transporte - Sendero Las
Tunas346107

Base Corella - Corella Las
Tunas515447

Base de Campismo Las
Tunas696666

Base Guayabal - 1ra.
Guayabal Las
Tunas696312

Base Guayabal - 1ra.
Guayabal Las
Tunas696461

Base RÃo Jobabo - San
Antonio Los Sitios
Las Tunas627504

Campismo Aguada de
VÃ¡zquez - La Aguada
Las Tunas549881

Cerro de CaisimÃº - Cerro
de CaisimÃº Las
Tunas371307

DirecciÃ³n - Carr.Central

Oeste La Victoria Las
Tunas371337

Los Pinos Las Tunas221923
Pizarra - Carr.Central Oeste
Las Tunas344884

Reservaciones - A.Guardia
No.17 Las Tunas347001

SubdirecciÃ³n de EconomÃa
- Sendero Las
Tunas346800

Vice DirecciÃ³n de
ExplotaciÃ³n - Carr.Central
Oeste La Victoria Las
Tunas371336

PROVINCE OF MATANZAS

Base de Transporte - 135 I
Iglesias Matanzas282823

DirecciÃ³n - 14
Matanzas614501
DirecciÃ³n - 14
Matanzas668855

DirecciÃ³n - Playa Larga
Matanzas915621

DirecciÃ³n - Sta.Cristina
Versalles
Matanzas244628

EconomÃa - Sta.Cristina
Versalles
Matanzas267181

Pizarra - Sta.Cristina
Versalles
Matanzas243951

Puesto de Mando –
Sta.Cristina

Matanzas260494
RÃo Mar - Medio
Matanzas265894

PROVINCE OF PINAR
DEL RIO

Base de Transporte –
Ave.Borrego No.km 3Â½
Hnos.Cruz Pinar del
RÃo762152

Campismo Copey – El
Copey Pinar del
RÃo648398

Campismo Cueva Los
Portales - El Abra Pinar
del RÃo636749

Campismo Dos Hermanas
Carr.El Moncada Pinar del
RÃo793223

Campismo El Taburete
El Taburete Pinar del
RÃo578670

Campismo La Caridad -
Carr.Soroa No.km 10Â½
Pinar del RÃo598487

Campismo Las Canas -
Las Canas Pinar del
RÃo794137

Campismo Pajarito -
P.Pajarito Pinar del
RÃo732864

Campismo Salto Los
Portales - Carr.L.Lazo
No.km
69 Pinar del RÃo497347

DirecciÃ³n - A.Maceo
No.113 Pinar del
RÃo727369

DirecciÃ³n - A.Maceo No.113
Pinar del RÃo752677

DirecciÃ³n - P.S.Pedro Pinar
del RÃo669296

EconomÃa - A.Maceo
No.113 Pinar del
RÃo752883

EconomÃa - A.Maceo
No.113 Pinar del
RÃo778003

La Altura - Fca.La Altura
Pinar del RÃo668470

RecepciÃ³n - A.Maceo
No.113 Pinar del
RÃo754657

RecepciÃ³n - P.S.Pedro Pinar
del RÃo669251

Reservaciones - I.Rubio
No.20 Pinar del
RÃo755316

VILLA INTERNACIONAL
AGUAS CLARAS -
Carr.ViÃ±ales
No.km 7 Pinar del
RÃo778427

**PROVINCE OF SANCTI
SPIRITUS**
Abastecimiento - Carr.Divep
ColÃ³n Sancti
SpÃritus335249

C.M.Fajardo Olivos 2 Sancti
SpÃritus327406

DirecciÃ³n –
Independencia No.201
Sancti SpÃritus326618

DirecciÃ³n –
Independencia No.201
Sancti Spiritus326631

EconomÃa - Carr.Divep
ColÃ³n Sancti
SpÃritus335250

El Pedrero Sancti
SpÃritus540507

InformÃ¡tica –
Independencia No.201
Sancti SpÃritus325401

Pizarra – Independencia
No.201 Sancti
Spiritus329082

Pizarra - Independencia
No.201 Sancti
SpÃritus329083

Pizarra - Independencia
No.201 Sancti
Spiritus334851

Pizarra - Independencia
No.201 Sancti
SpÃritus334852

Pizarra - Independencia
No.201 Sancti
SpÃritus336691

Poza Azul Sancti
SpÃritus899239

Vice-DirecciÃ³n
ExpotaciÃ³n y Desarrollo -
IndependenciaNo.201
Sancti SpÃritus334977

PROVINCE OF SANTIAGO DE CUBA

9 No.17 Santiago de
Cuba625072

Campismo Rio La Mula -
GuamÃ¡ Santiago de
Cuba326262

Carpeta - Carr.De CaletÃ³n
Km 30 No.s/n Santiago
de Cuba326126

Carr.Baconao Sigua Santiago
de Cuba356280

M.Arriba Santiago de
Cuba425797

Oficina de Reservaciones -
Jaguey Santiago de
Cuba653639

Pizarra - 9 No.173 Sta
Barbara Santiago de
Cuba625019

Seguridad - Microdistrito 1a
A.Sta.MarÃ-a
Santiago de Cuba671981

PROVINCE OF VILLA CLARA

Ave.9 de Abril No.8 Villa
 Clara207845

Base Rio Seibabo - RÃ-o
 Seibabo Villa Clara49832

Carpeta - Playa Ganuza
Villa Clara680206

DirecciÃ³n - Ave.9 de Abril
No.7 Villa
Clara206452

DirecciÃ³n - Playa Ganuza
Villa Clara680205

Inversiones - S.Miguel
No.7 Villa Clara222863

Reservaciones - Maceo
Villa Clara211569

Reservaciones - Maceo
No.315 Villa Clara204905

Sierra Morena – Playa
Sierra Morena Villa
Clara680200

Sierra Morena - S.Morena
S.Morena Villa
Clara680405

SubdirecciÃ³n de
Inversiones - S.Miguel
No.7
Villa Clara224731

Unidad Aseguramiento –
Desvio Caracatey Chichi
PadrÃ³n Villa Clara292177

Vice DirecciÃ³n
EconomÃ-a - S.Miguel
No.7 Villa Clara286460

APPENDIX 26
(from page 76)

CLINICS AND HOSPITALS IN CUBA—LISTED BY PROVINCE

Key: I = International/Foreigner Services and Facilities
    M = Major Hospital

For more information about international clinics and hospitals, contact:

Cubanacan Turismo y Salud Telephone: (537) 204 4811 al 13. Fax: (537) 204 1630 E-mail: medicos@sermed.cha.cyt.cu; webmaster@sermed.cha.cyt.cu

PROVINCE OF CAMAGUEY

Camaguey
Hospital Provincial
Carretera Central, km 4.5
Camaguey
Tel: (32) 28-2012

Santa Lucía
Santa Lucia Clinic (I)
Residencial No14
Playa Santa Lucía, Nuevitas
Phone: (32) 33-6203

PROVINCE OF CIEGO DE AVILA

Cayo Coco
Cayo Coco International Clinic (I, M)
Ave. de los Hoteles (end)
Phone: 302158 (switchboard)
        302159 (switchboard)
24 hours a day

Ciego de Avila
Hospital Maximo Gomez
Ciego de Avila

Tel: (33) 22-2429

Moron
Hospital
Avenida de Libertad
e/ Agramonte y Bonachea
Tel: (335) 50-3530

PROVINCE OF CIENFUEGOS

Cienfuegos
International Clinic (I)
Calle 37 #202 e/ 2 y 4
Phone: (43) 55-1622 , (43) 55-1623
24 hours a day

CITY OF HAVANA

Centro Habana
Hospital Hermanos Almeijeiras (I, M)
Padre Varela, esq San Lazaro
Centro Habana
Tel: (7) 876-1000

Miramar
Clinica International Cira Garcia (I, M)
Calle 20 #410, esq Avenida 41
Miramar
Tel: (7) 204-4300, 204-2811
Fax: (7) 204-2660

Playas del Este
International Clinic Santa Maria del Mar (I, M)
Ave Las Terrazas No 36
Playas del Este
Phone: 961819 (ext 102, 104, 107)
24 hours a day

PROVINCE OF GRANMA

Bayamo
Hospital Carlos Manuel de Cespedes
Carretera Central km 1.5
Tel: (23) 42-5012

Manzanillo
Hospital Celia Sanchez
Circunvalacion y Ave Jesus Menendez
Tel: (23) 54011

PROVINCE OF GUANTANAMO

Guantanamo
Hospital Agostinho Neto
Carretera El Salvador, km 1
Tel: (21) 35-5450

Baracoa
Hospital General Docente
2 k e of town

Clinica Internacional (I)
Hostal Habanera
Maceo #68 esq Frank Pais
Tel: (21) 45273

PROVINCE OF HOLGUIN

Holguin
Hospital Lenin
Avenida Lenin y Garavalde
Tel: (24) 42-5302

Guardalavaca
Clinica Internacional (I)
Hotel Club Amigo Guardalavaca
Tel: (24) 3031

ISLA DE LA JUVENTUD

Clinica International
El Pueblo, Cayo Largo
Tel: (45) 24-8283

Hospital Heroes de Baire
Calle 18 y 41
Tel: (46) 32-2236

Policlinico Provincial de Emergencia
Calle 41, e/32 y 34
Nueva Gerona
Tel: (46) 32-6084

PROVINCE OF LAS TUNAS

Hospital Che Guevara (I)
Avenida Carlos J. Finlay
esq Avenida 2 de Diciembre
Las Tunas
Tel: (31) 45-012

PROVINCE OF MATANZAS

Varadero
International Clinic (I)
Calle 61 y 1ra Ave
Phone: (45) 66-7226
        (45) 61-4755
        (45) 66-8611
24 hours a day

Cardenas
Hospital Jose M. Aristegui
Calle 13Tel: (45) 52-2114

PROVINCE OF PINAR DEL RIO

Pinar del Rio
Hospital Leon Cuevo Rubio
Gerardo Medina
Tel: (82) 75-2229

Hospital Abel Santamaria
Carretera Central
Tel: (82) 76-3113
        75-4443

PROVINCE OF SANCTI SPIRITUS

Trinidad
Trinidad Clinic (I)
Calle Lino Pérez No 103
esq. Anastasio Cárdenas
Phone: (419) 6492
Fax: 6240, 6309
24 hours a day

Hospital
Maceo #6
Tel: (41) 93201

Sancti Spiritus
Hospital Provincial Camilo Cienfuegos
Bartolome Maso
Frente Plaza de la Revolucion
Phone: (41) 24017

PROVINCE OF SANTIAGO DE CUBA

Santiago de Cuba
Santiago de Cuba Clinic (I,M)
Ave. Raúl Puyol Esq.
Calle10 S/N
Phone: (22) 642589, (22) 642589
Fax: 687001
24 hours a day

PROVINCE OF VILLA CLARA

Santa Clara
Policlinico Docente (I)
Serafin Garcia Oeste #167
e/Aleman y Carretera Central
Tel: (422) 20-2244

APPENDIX 27
(from page 78)

WHERE AND HOW TO BUY MEDICAL AND TRAVEL INSURANCE FROM A CUBAN MEDICAL INSURANCE COMPANY

Foreign visitors to Cuba can purchase medical insurance from a Cuban insurance company by contacting **Asistur, S.A.** at the address and telephone numbers listed below. Insurance is underwritten by **La Isla Travel Insurance, S.A.**, in Havana, Cuba. (Address and contact information also provided below.)

Travelers to Cuba can also purchase the insurance through international or domestic travel agencies acting as agents for the insurer. One such agency in Cuba is **Cuba Linda,** telephone (7) 553-686; fax (7) 553-980; website www.cubalinda.com. In the U.S., only OFAC-licensed Travel Service Providers (TSPs) can act as agents for the Cuban insurer, and the TSP will only sell you a policy if you have a Specific or General License to travel to Cuba. Appendix 3 on page 164 lists a few of these TSPs.

Coverage is limited to $25,000 per insured person, per trip for sickness or accident that occurs in Cuba. Up to $7,000 in repatriation or transportation costs is also covered. Duration of the coverage begins the moment the insured person arrives in Cuba and ends the moment the insured person exits Cuba.

There are other special conditions, limitations, and exceptions to the coverage. (I.e., injury caused as a result of war, acts of terrorism, and demonstrations; and expenses for sea or mountain rescues.) Request the full written details of conditions and exceptions of coverage from the agent selling the policy.

ASISTUR, S.A.
Paseo del Prado #254
Old Havana, City of
Havana
Tel: (7) 33-8527;
(7) 35-8339; (7) 33-8920;
(7) 57-1314; (7) 57-1315
Fax: (7) 33-8087
E-mail: guro@asist.sld.cu

LA ISLA, S.A. TRAVEL INSURANCE
Calle 14 No. 301
Esq Calle 3ra
Miramar, Havana
Tel: (7) 247490-93
Fax: (7) 24-7494
E-Mail:
laisla@laisla.getcma.net

APPENDIX 28
(from page 83)

TELEPHONE AREA CODES FOR CITIES IN CUBA

When making long-distance domestic calls within Cuba, dial "0" first, followed by the area code and the local telephone number. Do not dial "0" when making a local call within the same city.

City	Code	City	Code
Agramonte	59	Consolacion Del Sur	8
Aguacate	64	Corralillo	42
Alto Sedro	24	Cortes	84
Antilla	24	Cruzes	433
Artemisa	63	Cueto	24
Baracoa	21	Cumanayagua	43
Banes	24		
Baragua	33		
Batabana	62		
Bauta	680	El Caney	23
Baya Honda	86	El Cobre	22
Bayamo	23	El Cristo	22
Buenaventura	24	Esmeralda	32
		Falcon	42
Cabaiguan	41	Florida	32
Caibarien	42	Fomento	41
Calabazar de Sagua	42	Gaspar	33
Camaguey	322	Granma (prov.)	23
Camajuani	42	Guanajay	686
Campechuela	23	Guane	84
Candelaria	85	Guantanamo	21
Cardenas	5	Guardalavac	24
Casilda	419	Guayabal	31
Cascorro	32	Guines	62
		Guira de Melena	67
Cauto cristo	23	Guyamoro	32
Chambas	33	Havana	7
Cienfuegos	432	Hauko	64
Ciego de Avila	33	Holguin	24
Cayo Largo	45	Jaguague	41
Cayo Coco	33	Jaguey Grande	59
Colon	5	Jamaica	21
		Jara	23

Jatibonico	41
Jibacoa	42
Jobabo	31
Jovellanos	5
Imias	21
Isabela de Sagua	42
La Maya	22
Las Tunas	31
Los Palacios	8
Madruga	62
Majari	24
Manacas	42
Manicaragua	42
Manzanillo	23
Mantua	84
Mariel	63
Marti	5
Matanzas	52
Minas	32
Moa	24
Moron	335
Motembo	42
Niquero	23
Nueva Gerona	46
Nueva Pais	62
Nuevitas	32
Omaja	31
Pinar del Rio	82
Placetas	42
Puerto Manati	31
Puerto Padre	31
Remedios	42
Rodas	43

Sagua la Grande	42
Sagua de Tanamo	24
San Juan y Martinez	8
San Cristobal	85
San German	24
San Jose de Las Lajas	64
San Jose de Marcos	59
Sancti Spiritus	41
San Luis	8
San Nicolas De Bari	62
Santa Clara	422
Santa Cruz Del Norte	692
Santa Cruz Del Sur	32
Santa Fe	7
Santa Isabel De las Lajas	433
Santa Lucia	416
Santiago de De Cuba	226
Santiago de Las Venas	42
Santo Domingo	42
Sibanicu	32
Siboney	22
Sola	32
Tunas de Zaza	41
Trinidad	419
Varadero	45
Vazquez	31
Velasco	33
Vertientes	32
Vinales	8

BLANK PAGE FOR NOTES

ACKNOWLEDGMENTS

Encountering roadblocks, dead-ends, dangerous holes, and wild tigers while trekking the path of a vision is a natural part of the process of reaching that vision. There is no magic wand that can make these obstacles disappear, but there is plenty of magic in certain people one meets while on this path—people who take a moment to temporarily put their own problems aside in order to help another.

In my quest to complete this travel manual, I would like to thank the following people who were extremely generous with their time, showed touching empathy for my needs, and, in their own way, used their unique talents to help my vision become a reality:

Bernardo Navarro at Cuban Art Space, a department of Sandra Levinson's Center for Cuban Studies in New York City; Christopher Kush and Kevin Schultz at Voltaire Books for their instant enthusiasm and quick action to help get this book launched; my co-worker and friend Mark Fisher for his invaluable feedback and for introducing me to Christopher and Kevin; Robert Cobb and Ed Scales for their political savvy and legal insights; my team of selfless editors Patsy Morrow, Sam Hull, Fran Goldston, Chuck Banks, Libbie Meyer, Rebecca Moffitt, Kathleen Moffitt, Sean Moffitt, Lauren Goldston, David Broadlick, and Wesley Young, all of whom worked long hours without pay; the Key West Citizen columnist and editor Ralph Morrow for his input; Kat Joplin for her translation work on German websites; Jack Joplin for his research on U.S. embargo violations case history; Ken Debono at Falcon Books for being so amenable and actually answering the telephone every single time I called; also Editor-in-Chief Roberta Tennant at Falcon Books for her keen eye, speedy work, and excellent recommendations; Genevieve Canizares, Maegan Postiy, Karl Malsheimer, and Alexis Boveda at Office Max in Key West, the best print and document services team in Office Max history, for their expertise and going way beyond the call of duty to help me (how they manage to stay so cheery in the face of such demanding customers I'll never know); librarian director Kris Neihouse and Monroe County historian Tom Hambright at the Key West branch of the Monroe County Public Library System; Lori Kelly, director of the Learning Resource Center at Florida Keys Community College; Bill Moffitt for his technical wizardry with computer software and website design; my boss Sandy Silts at the Westin Key West Resort and Marina, and my other bosses Becca Tifton, Sean McConnell, and Bill Lay at LaTrattoria Restaurant on Duval Street for their flexibility with my work schedule, which allowed me the free time to write this book, and for making work actually enjoyable; songwriter, musician, fellow artist, and visionary Dave Aaron for the inspiring talks and the hundreds of *café con leches* at Harpoon Harry's in Key West; Naja and Arnaud D'Albissin for directing me to Falcon Books; their two amazing kids Alexis and Clementine for inspiring me to use my talents and make the world a better place; Rob O'Neal, columnist and photographer at the Key West Citizen for letting me use his fantastic photographs for this book, and for his invaluable feedback and input stemming from his extensive experience with Cuban affairs (just because he sees—with his own eyes, and through a camera lens—great beauty in Cuba and her people does not make him a communist or a Castro supporter, as some venom-spitting, uncompromising Castro-haters accuse him of being); and David Sloan of Phantom Press for unhesitantly taking the time out of his own hectic book publishing schedule to apply his graphic and design genius to the front and back covers of this book.

So far it's a veritable army that helped in the creation of this book, isn't it?

I am convinced that God sent three people in particular on a special mission to make sure I had whatever I needed after I took a leave of absence from my two jobs and rented out my house so that I wouldn't have to worry about where the money was going to come from to pay the mortgage. These three people are Ron Heck, Patsy Morrow, and Ralph Morrow. For more than a year they gave me a bed to sleep in, use of their showers, a closet to store my clothes, a room in which to write, and unrestricted use of their own homes. Many of my family members and my friends, including Libbie, Wesley, and Chuck, whom I mentioned earlier, also offered their roofs whenever I needed one, and I feel extremely lucky to have so many people in my life who are there for me whenever I need them.

Finally, I would like to thank Angel Garcia in Key West, and all my friends and family in Cuba for their instant trust and for their readiness to help me in any way, not just with the research for this guide, but also with my safety and welfare as I strayed into dangerous territory while casting for details in a country governed by a political party that is hyper-sensitive about its image.

I dedicate this book to my mother, Joanna Bellows-Keys, a lady who died while pursuing her own vision of writing, a vision rife with its own obstacles of being single, working a full-time job, raising five children, and having no formal education beyond eleventh grade. Despite those obstacles, she did a good job instilling integrity and character into her kids. And, even though she had little money to spare, she did a few things—like picking up the flock and living abroad—that forever after helped me become insightful, strong, daring, and adventuresome, qualities that came in handy in the making of this book.

Special love and thanks goes to my step dad Richard Keys, who, for a large part of my youth, was instrumental in helping me develop good habits and in helping my mother get through the tough times.

U.S. Congress   February 5, 2009
U.S. State Department
President Barack Obama
Washington, D.C.

If by any chance the words on this page reach the eyes of any U.S. government officer in high levels of U.S.-Cuba foreign policy—including the President's office, members of Congress, and the State department—the author has a special request for them: Please endeavor to lift the U.S. travel restrictions to Cuba and amend some of the harsh trade embargo laws that punish the Cuban people. While punitive measures against governments that repress their people and violate international law are obviously necessary, it is the innocent people of these repressive governments who always suffer the consequences of crippling sanctions. Page 101 of this manual highlights a few arguments that suggest that U.S. trade embargo laws actually exacerbate the repression in Cuba and prolongs the impotency of the Cuban people.

One possible amendment: Allow U.S. citizens a bare minimum of "trading" privileges with the Cuban government and members of the Cuban Communist Party that would allow payment of embarkation fees, tourist cards, and visas so that U.S citizens can legally enter Cuba, and then allow greater "trade" with non-government, privately owned businesses. More financial freedom for the Cuban people means less dependency on the Cuban government for their needs.

History has shown that change in countries wrestling under the yoke of repressive governments is fostered by opening up the communication lines and allowing for an exchange of ideas and information across the divide—not by erecting walls, isolationism, and abandonment.

Support for continuing the travel restrictions and the U.S. trade embargo against Cuba is no longer unilateral. For the first time ever, polls show that more Cuban Americans are now against the embargo than for it. Each year, the House of Representatives approves a proposal, originally introduced by congressman Jeff Flake (R-Ariz) and congressman William Delahunt (D-Mass), that would strip the U.S.Treasury Department of its authority to enforce the travel restrictions. But the U.S. Senate has always knocked this proposal down, and President George W. Bush has always guaranteed a veto. The author, along with many millions of other U.S. citizens, believes that President Obama is on the right track with his philosophy of dialogue with the Cuban government.

Mike Bellows

ABOUT THE AUTHOR

Michael Bellows lives in Key West, Florida. He was born in Washington, D.C. and grew up on the Lower East Side in New York City and the Mediterranean island of Ibiza, Spain. He has lived and traveled extensively in the United States, Europe, the Caribbean and Central America. With his sister Jo, he owned and operated a travel company and led anthropological and archaeological tours to Mexico. In 1989, during the contra war in Nicaragua (and with his other sister Susie), he volunteered as a driver transporting equipment and supplies to the Managua office of the U.S.-based watchdog group Witness for Peace.

After graduating from Dowling College in Long Island, N.Y. in 1981 with a Bachelor's degree in business, he pursued freelance journalism. His articles have appeared in various newspapers and magazines throughout the U.S. and cover a wide range of subjects including urban homelessness, New Age healers, folk rock musicians, poet Allen Ginsberg, and actor and comedian Dom DeLuise.

His interest in Cuba intensified after cultivating a close friendship with a Cuban man who fled the Caribbean nation on a makeshift raft during the Cuban *balsero* (rafter) crisis in 1994.

Two weeks after moving to Key West in 1996, he bought his first sailboat (a 26-foot, no-frills '69 Seafarer), took crash courses (literally) in sailing from his buddies "on the hook" off Christmas Tree island, and a few months later sailed to Cuba to investigate things for himself.

The 100-mile crossing took him ten days because of delays caused by bad weather, hull leaks, a jammed keel, a ripped sail, and a busted boom. He would like to take this opportunity to thank Tito and Diana of the fishing vessel *Crusader* for the wonderful crab salad on crackers during this ordeal, and also Dry Tortugas park ranger Roy Apuglese for the emergency water ration.

Bellows has since improved his sailing skills considerably, and he has traveled to the forbidden island many times, by boat and by plane. The country has become a second home for him, and many of the people he has met during his explorations, including the relatives of his *balsero* friend in Key West, have turned into a rather large extended family across the Straits. The book you hold in your hands is a result of all those years of research and discovery and would not have been possible without the kindness, generosity, willingness, and trust of all these wonderful Cuban people.

Author at the colonial-era Plaza de La Catedral in Habana Vieja, Havana

Western and Central Cuba

CIUDAD DE
LA HABANA

Havana

Mariel
LA
Artemisa
HABANA
Jo
Minas de
Matahambre
San Cristobal
Güira de
Melena
Güines
Arroyos
de Mantua
**PINAR
DEL RÍO**
Pinar
del Río
Surgidero
de Batabanó
M
La Fe
Guane
Golfo de
Batabanó

Nueva
Gerona

**ISLA DE LA
JUVENTUD**
(special
municipality)
La Fe
Isla de la
Juventud

N

Yucatan Channel

C a r i b b e

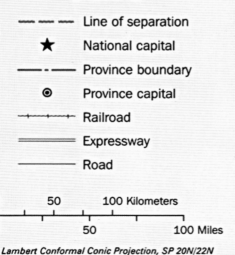

Cuba

— — — — Line of separation

★ National capital

— — · — Province boundary

◉ Province capital

+—+—+ Railroad

═══ Expressway

——— Road

0	50	100 Kilometers

0	50	100 Miles

Lambert Conformal Conic Projection, SP 20N/22N

George Tow

Cay Sal
Bank
(THE BAHAMAS)

BA

ARCHIPIÉLAGO
DE SABANA

Cárdenas

Colón

Isabela de
Sagua

VILLA CLARA

Caibarién

ARCHIPIÉLAGO
DE CAMAGÜEY

Guinchos Cay
(THE BAHAMAS)

CIEGO
DE ÁVILA

Santa
Clara

Placetas

Cay Lobos
(THE BAHAMAS)

CIENFUEGOS

ada de
ajeros

Cienfuegos

Sancti
Spíritus

u/c

Morón

SANCTI
SPÍRITUS

Ciego
de Ávila

Florida

Nuevitas

Camagüey

CAMAGÜEY

LAS TU

Amancio

ARCHIPIÉLAGO
DE LOS JARDINAS
DE LA REINA

n Sea

Santa Cruz
del Sur

Manzanillo

Golfo de
Guacanayabo

Pilón

G

Little
Cayman

Cayman
Islands
(U.K.)

and
rman

Provinces and Municipalities

1. ISLA DE LA JUVENTUD
2. PINAR DEL RIO
3. CITY OF HAVANA
4. HAVANA PROVINCE
5. MATANZAS
6. CIENFUEGOS
7. VILLA CLARA
8. SANCTI SPIRITUS

9. CIEGO DE AVILA
10. CAMAGUEY
11. LAS TUNAS
12. GRANMA
13. HOLGUIN
14. SANTIAGO DE CUBA
15. GUANTANAMO

CONTINUED
NEXT PAGE ➡

JAMAIC

la Mar

Oc
Ri

Spa
To

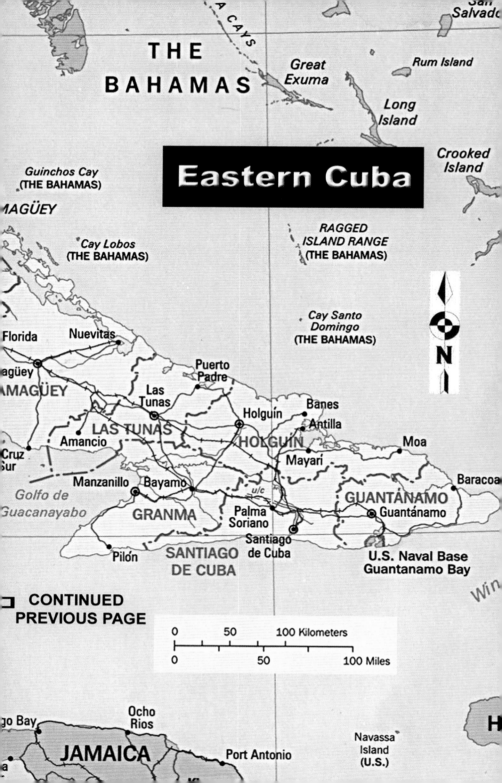